D1559945

Savage Perils

SAVAGE PERILS

Racial Frontiers and Nuclear Apocalypse in American Culture

PATRICK B. SHARP

UNIVERSITY OF OKLAHOMA PRESS : NORMAN

Library of Congress Cataloging-in-Publication Data

Sharp, Patrick B., 1967–
Savage perils : racial frontiers and nuclear apocalypse in American culture / Patrick B. Sharp.
p. cm.
Includes bibliographical references and index.
ISBN 978-0-8061-3822-0 (hardcover : alk. paper)
1. Racism—United States—History. 2. United States—Race relations. 3. National characteristics, American. 4. War and civilization—United States. 5. Nuclear warfare—Social aspects—United States. 6. Frontier thesis. 7. Darwin, Charles, 1809–1882—Influence. 8. Racism in literature. 9. Nuclear warfare in literature. 10. Science fiction—History and criticism. I. Title.
E184.A1S5725 2007
305.800973—dc22

2006026321

The paper in this book meets the guidelines for permanence and durability of the Committee on Production Guidelines for Book Longevity of the Council on Library Resources. ∞

1 2 3 4 5 6 7 8 9 10

For Mom and Dad,
to whom I owe everything.

CONTENTS

Figures

ACKNOWLEDGMENTS

This book came out of the dissertation I wrote in the Department of English at the University of California, Santa Barbara. My dissertation began over lunch with Shirley Lim one day in 1995, when she kindly refused to let me leave the table until I came up with the core of a project. I settled on the representation of the atomic bomb. Little did I know that I would spend the next ten years digging further and further into the past, ranging across a number of different disciplines and areas of specialization as I tried to make sense of the atomic age. Shirley Lim and Charles Bazerman gave me invaluable mentorship, guiding me through my early conference papers and publications while helping me develop my prose style. Shirley and Elliot Butler-Evans trained me in the traditions of multiethnic American literatures, while Charles gave me a thorough grounding in the field of science and technology studies. Mark Rose and Frank McConnell guided my explorations in the field of science fiction. Together, these professors helped save me from writing a boring dissertation on Modernist novels by nurturing and shaping my unorthodox interests into a coherent and wide-ranging project. I am extremely grateful for everything these professors have given me over the years.

The other major influence on my dissertation project came from the science and technology studies community at UCSB. With Charles Bazerman from English and Michael Osborne from history, I was able to organize and participate in a faculty research focus group that was funded by the UCSB Interdisciplinary Humanities Center. Drawing faculty and graduate students from across the campus (and, at times, from across the country), this research focus group engaged in regular and spirited conversations on work from a wide variety of disciplines and perspectives. I would like to thank everyone involved in the research focus group, especially Charles Bazerman and Michael Osborne. Those three years of conversations honed my critical understanding of science and technology and helped me develop an ability to communicate across the language and paradigm gaps that separate the disciplines.

I would like to single out a few individuals from the research focus group and acknowledge their special contributions to this project. First, I must thank Lawrence Badash of history for his guidance in studying the science and history of nuclear weapons. Thanks also to Lawrence for braving the great Santa Barbara flood of 1995 to make our on-campus meeting, where he gave me copies of a number of nuclear-themed novels and helped get me started on the study of nuclear narratives. Thanks to Michael Osborne and Anita Guerini of history for their guidance in the history of biology. Thanks also to Benjamin Zulueta and Zuoyue Wang for their useful comments and help in developing my understanding of the history of Asian Americans with regard to science and the myth of the yellow peril.

While I was at UCSB, my writing group colleagues helped me hone my prose and develop sections of my argument for publication. Special thanks to Laura Holliday, Claire Busse, Roze Hentschell, Kate Sullivan, and Rita Raley for all of their valuable feedback and for fueling me with caffeine when I really needed it. Thanks also to Vincent Willoughby for his discussions of the finer points of science fiction and popular culture. During the heaviest phase of my primary research, George Slusser of the Eaton Science Fiction Collection at the University of California, Riverside provided much logistical support that gave me access to materials I never dreamed I would find. Thanks to George for his guidance and moral support during my long hours in the Eaton collection.

The postdoctoral phase of this project took shape at Georgia Tech's School of Literature, Communication and Culture. Lisa Yaszek of Georgia Tech and Doug Davis of Gordon College provided me with sources, feedback, and support on countless occasions over the past five years. I am thankful for our many conference presentations together and look forward to our continued collaboration in the years to come. Hugh Crawford and Carol Senf of Georgia Tech made a number of useful suggestions with regard to the structure of my argument about Hersey's "Hiroshima" and Darwin's *The Descent of Man*, for which I am grateful. I also owe a large debt of gratitude to Alan Rauch from the Department of English at the University of North Carolina at Charlotte. Alan's guidance in my study of Darwin's life and work led me to realize that Darwin's argument should be at the center of the entire project.

Since coming to the Department of Liberal Studies at California State University, Los Angeles, I have revised the manuscript into its current form. Thanks to my colleagues Alejandra Marchevsky, Jennifer Faust, Micol Seigel, and Rob DeChaine for their advice and support in the final stages of the writing process. I am grateful to my deans, Judith Hamera, Bryant Alexander, and Carl Selkin, for their support of my work. I also need to thank the many students who have engaged with the material covered in this book in several of their classes and taught me new things at every turn. Dean Moody, Margaret Salazar, Traci Salazar, and Yesenia Hernandez pointed me to new sources that helped make this book stronger. My editor at the University of Oklahoma Press, Matthew Bokovoy, has been a source of unwavering encouragement and support over the past eighteen months. His critical appraisals of the project and his feedback on my prose helped make the argument much stronger and more clear. The insightful comments of Allan Winkler and H. Bruce Franklin also helped me take my argument to the next level. Finally, thanks to my wife Sharon Sharp for all of her feedback and support over the past ten years.

Savage Perils

INTRODUCTION

On 29 January 2002, President George W. Bush gave the first post-9/11 State of the Union address. The United States had invaded Afghanistan and struck at the bases of Al Qaeda, the terrorist organization responsible for the attacks. However, Bush saw a much bigger threat to "the civilized world": he asserted that an "axis of evil" was "seeking weapons of mass destruction" and urged that the "war on terror" be expanded beyond the borders of Afghanistan.[1] The "axis of evil" consisted of Iraq, Iran, North Korea "and their terrorist allies."[2] In the days, months, and years that followed, Bush committed the United States to a wide-ranging series of military operations under the banner of the "war on terror," a war that eventually led to the controversial invasion and occupation of Iraq. At the heart of Bush's rhetoric was a basic opposition, a "fight between civilization and terror" that threatened to undermine the "existence of free nations."[3] Time after time, Bush attempted to invoke fear in his audience by warning that technologically backward "terrorists" were close to getting their hands on advanced modern weapons, including that most feared weapon of all, the atomic bomb.

Bush's representation of terrorism bore a striking resemblance to the notion of savagery that once dominated American national discourse. By representing terrorists as the opposite of the "civilized world," Bush tapped into a rich vein of racism that extended back to the dawn of the United States, when the idea of civilization was intimately connected to the idea of race. Beginning in the 1750s, these two ideas were developed by scientists and intellectuals in Europe and America who were attempting to account for the supposed cultural and biological inferiority of people who were not of European descent.[4] The distinction between white civilization and nonwhite savagery became deeply entwined in American colonial discourse and served as a rallying point for white Americans as they pushed the frontier across the continent. By the 1850s, scientists in the United States had developed a theory of human difference known as polygenesis. This theory asserted that different races originated from separate creations and thus constituted separate species. Polygenesis was a product of a society deeply invested in the connection between white superiority and American national identity. The enslavement of African Americans, the war against Mexico, and the repeated atrocities against Native Americans were all justified in part by appealing to the belief in an ongoing racial war between civilization and savagery. If the polygenists were correct, then the nonwhite races were not fully human and did not have a claim to the rights spelled out in the founding documents of the United States. Long after the scientific ideas of the polygenists were rejected, their formulation of race still held currency in the United States. The reason was simple: polygenism was merely one expression of a deeply racist society that was built on the notion of civilized progress replacing savagery.

The work of Charles Darwin in the late nineteenth century reformulated the ideas of race, civilization, and savagery around the theory of evolution. Synthesizing the work of others and crystallizing the ideology of Victorian England, Darwin argued that humanity had progressed along a path from humble animal origins to total mastery of the planet. The key to Darwin's vision of evolution was technology: he argued that humans had been naturally selected for their ability to invent and use technology and he created a vision of human history that became known in later years as man the toolmaker. Darwin extended his argument to account for the perceived struggle between civilization and savagery brought about by European colonial expansion. For Darwin, the victories of civilized Europeans over their savage foes were due to technological superiority and were therefore just another example of natural selection that had been shaping humanity since the beginning. Darwin's ideas influenced American historians such as Theodore Roosevelt and Frederick Jackson Turner, who crafted visions of American history that showed the progression of technologically superior whites over the forces of savagery. By the end of the nineteenth century, warfare was so bound up with the ideas of savagery and race that a common vocabulary had emerged. In the United States, racist language and the specter of savagery dominated discussions of the wars against Native Americans, Mexicans, Filipinos, and the Japanese.[5]

In Britain, a number of authors wrote future-war stories that extrapolated from Darwin's arguments to make dire warnings about falling behind in the arms race of the industrial age. British military officer Sir George Tomkyns Chesney's story "The Battle of Dorking" (1871) dramatized how new technologies could strengthen Britain's enemies to the point where they could subjugate Britain to their will. By connecting fears of technology with fears of a perceived enemy, Chesney hit on a narrative formula that proved immediately popular, especially among military and government officials trying to scare up support for military budgets and aggressive foreign policies. In 1914, H. G. Wells wrote a future-war story called *The World Set Free* that took a critical look at a global arms race between countries armed with a new weapon he called the "atomic bomb." For Wells, the atomic bomb was particularly dangerous in the hands of men ruled by savage impulses: he argued that only a peaceful civilized world could use atomic energy for proper purposes. In the United States, the fear that savages could acquire advanced technology fueled stories about the "yellow peril." Asian immigration, the industrialization of Japan, and the success of the Japanese in the Russo-Japanese War of 1904–1905 led a number of commentators to see Asians as the biggest threat to the future of the United States. Men such as Jack London represented the Japanese as a bizarre mutation because of their ability to master modern technology. Like Darwin, London believed that whites were superior toolmakers, but the Japanese ability to "imitate" white achievements made them an evolutionary threat to white supremacy in London's eyes.[6]

For the first half of the twentieth century, stories about a technologically threatening yellow peril pervaded American culture. These stories fueled racist sentiments that eventually led to the internment of Japanese Americans during World War II. The imprecision and irrationality of racist thinking led to representations of the Japanese that characterized them as savage, technologically advanced, backstabbing, loyal, mindlessly fearless, and cowardly. The old idea that the United States was a white country was explicit in the attacks on Japanese Americans. According to this way of thinking, to be American was to be of European descent and people of other races needed to be monitored and controlled to prevent them from threatening civilized white America. These racist arguments formed the groundwork for the official representation of the atomic bombings of Hiroshima and Nagasaki in August 1945. Using its wartime propaganda machine, the U.S. government attempted to control the meaning of the atomic bomb by vilifying the Japanese and extolling the heroism of the white scientists and soldiers who had developed and deployed this ultimate weapon.

In its postwar future-war stories and civil defense campaigns, the U.S. government asserted that American civilization could survive and win a nuclear war. The publication of John Hersey's "Hiroshima" in August 1946 challenged the official representation of the atomic bomb. Hersey's story countered the racism of the official narrative and evoked sympathy for the Japanese civilians who struggled through the horrible wasteland created by American technological might. Hersey's careful description of radiation sickness and fallout refuted official claims that the atomic bomb was just a very big conventional weapon. Drawing on Hersey's account, science fiction writers challenged the official visions of future atomic war throughout the late 1940s and 1950s. They imagined that nuclear war would mean the collapse of civilization and a return to a brutal struggle for survival. However, many science fiction writers also drew on the imagery of the frontier—and its racist vision of a savagery that threatened to swallow civilization—to romanticize their accounts of life after a nuclear war. With their emphasis on civilized white protagonists who were reborn through their confrontation with savagery, nuclear frontier narratives repeated the white supremacist formulation of American civilization. At the same time, the happy ending many nuclear frontier stories offered made nuclear war actually seem appealing.

In the 1950s, civil defense officials mobilized their campaigns around the imagery of the white suburban family. In their films, pamphlets, and other publications, civil defense officials crafted an image of the white suburban home as the core of American civilization. Though civil rights groups protested the segregationist mentality of civil defense, the propaganda mill put together by U.S. government officials continued to grind out visions of a white America that was triumphant on the nuclear frontier. As the decade progressed, science fiction writers began to grapple more explicitly with the racial dimension of the nuclear frontier. Authors such as Walter Miller Jr. and Pat Frank produced popular novels in which segregation collapsed along with corrupt American civilization after a nuclear war. In order to survive, humans had to live, work, and even intermarry with people of other races. It is unfortunate that these desegregated visions of the nuclear frontier still relied on the racist image of the savage. Though science fiction authors were clearly attempting to support the efforts of civil rights groups, their visions of the future still foundered under the weight of America's racial imagination.

The connections between race, civilization, and technology have taken on a number of forms since the 1850s. In narratives produced in the United States, the image of the savage served as both a threat to white civilization and a noble foil to the corruption of the modern world. What remained stable in these various stories was the equation of whites with American civilization and nonwhites with savagery. In general, savages were seen as incapable of producing or handling modern technology. In some stories, this was seen as a marker of nonwhite inferiority and the white heroes simply struck down the savage foes of white civilization. In some stories, the noble simplicity of nonwhites served as a critique of the corruption inherent in white civilization. When they were adept with technology, nonwhites were portrayed as a threat. At the same time, they were still represented as less adept than the tool-making whites. The nineteenth-century belief in whites as superior toolmakers survived the collapse of the scientific theories that supported it. The Darwinist myth of man the toolmaker remains popular despite the successes of the civil rights movement, the rejection of race as a fundamental biological category, and the pluralization of American history. Clearly, a number of Americans still believe in the racially charged opposition between civilization and savagery.

This history provides the necessary context for understanding President Bush's rhetoric about the "war on terror." Bush did not create the image of the terrorist: in the 1970s, the concept of the terrorist emerged as the modern manifestation of the savage in American political rhetoric. Like savages, terrorists were described as cruel, irrational, dark-skinned primitives bent on destroying the "civilized world." Since the Iran hostage crisis of 1979–1980, the U.S. government has used a parade of nonwhite terrorists and dictators to whip up support for its policies. It has used the images of Ayatollah Khomeini, Muammar Khadafi, Saddam Hussein, Osama Bin Laden, and Kim Jong Il to reinforce the sense that white American civilization is under siege by nonwhite savages. As President Bush's repeated comments underscore, the threat that terrorists will get control of high technology remains the biggest fear in the "war on terror." According to the U.S. government, only increased military expenditures and continuous warfare can contain the terrorist threat to American civilization. President Bush's "war on terror" is only the latest installment in an ongoing fictional saga that has been at the heart of American identity since the beginning of the republic. Understanding this saga is essential if we want to eliminate such racist mythologies from American life.

Part I

Technological Superiority

Darwin's Theory and the Representation of Future War

Chapter 1

The Triumph of Civilization

Race and American Exceptionalism before Darwin

In early 1854, Josiah C. Nott and Joseph R. Glidden published *Types of Mankind*, a book that achieved a popular following and became the leading scientific text on racial differences in the mid-nineteenth-century United States.[1] *Types of Mankind* synthesized two decades of work by men such as Samuel George Morton and Louis Agassiz, the two most widely respected scientists of what became known as the American school of ethnology. Due largely to the work of Morton and Agassiz, science in the United States made great strides in establishing a solid institutional structure while gaining an international reputation. Dedicated to the memory of Morton, who had passed away in 1851, *Types of Mankind* put forward the case that the different races of mankind actually constituted distinct species.[2] Furthermore, the text argued for the supremacy of the "Caucasian races" over the other "inferior" races of mankind, asserting that history had proved the superiority of Caucasian racial characteristics. In the first chapter, Nott claimed that "the higher castes of what are termed Caucasian races, are influenced by several causes in a greater degree than other races. To them have been assigned, in all ages, the largest brains and the most powerful intellect; *theirs* is the mission of extending and perfecting civilization—they are by nature ambitious, daring, domineering, and reckless of danger—impelled by an irresistible instinct, they visit all climes, regardless of difficulties."[3] Nott emphasized "*theirs*" in this passage to show how adamantly he believed the idea that whites stood as the bearers of civilization. His characterization of the "higher castes of . . . Caucasians" followed standard cultural stereotypes for the day: whites (especially Anglo-Saxons) were understood as a tough and daring race whose nature drove them to colonize. From a modern scientific perspective, *Types of Mankind* had little to do with biological reality. Nonetheless, the original printing sold out immediately, despite a heavy $5 price tag, and the book had gone through nine editions by the end of the 1800s.[4]

The success of white supremacist narratives in American science was not surprising, since the United States was at the height of an expansion propelled by the racist ideology of manifest destiny. During the era when Morton and Agassiz produced their most influential work, slavery remained a major institution, "Indian removal" robbed major tracts of land from Native Americans, and the boundaries of the United States and its territories grew to encompass what is now the lower forty-eight states. The racism and expansionism endemic to the United States in the nineteenth century was not new: it had grown steadily over three centuries of European colonization. As European colonists and their descendants began to narrate their experiences in the New World, they gradually established new identities and separated themselves from the world they had left behind. The myth of the frontier embraced both intellectual and popular beliefs about the inherent superiority of European colonists and their descendents, people believed to be divinely and biologically destined to spread civilization during the inevitable march westward across the continent.[5] In the early nineteenth century, the work of the American school of ethnology and the popularization of the frontier myth in literature helped engender a racial nationalism in the United States that survived through the first part of the Cold War and still malingers today.

The themes and imagery of frontier stories began with the earliest European colonists and developed over a long period of time.[6] American frontier narratives wove together several strands of European colonial ideology and American experience. Early European Americans saw themselves as superior to the "savages" they encountered in the New World, and they believed themselves to be superior to the antiquated and corrupt civilizations they had left behind in Europe. The frontier myth imagined that this newly discovered land provided European Americans with the opportunity to both prove and develop their exceptional status: while they defeated and subdued the savagery of the New World, they shed the negative aspects of western Europe. In their rejection of both the old civilization and the newly discovered savagery, Americans saw themselves as progressing toward a new type of civilization. From their first stories, the English Puritan colonists set the tone for the frontier myth by emphasizing their experiences in "Indian wars." Through their accounts of these wars, the Puritans "could emphasize their Englishness by setting their civilization against Indian barbarism; they could [also] suggest their own superiority to the home English by exalting their heroism in battle, the peculiar danger of their circumstances, and the holy zeal for English Christian expansion with which they preached to or shot at the savages."[7] Narratives of frontier conflict became an important way for these early Americans to demonstrate their religious and cultural superiority to both the English and the indigenous peoples of America.

The European idea of the "savage" took special shape in the Americas: it was attached to the Native Americans Christopher Columbus, the Puritans, and other European colonizers encountered. Columbus gave Native Americans the name *los Indios* (Indians) in 1493 and provided the first widely distributed images of Native Americans. The images of the Native Americans Columbus encountered emphasized their nakedness, low level of technological development, and lack of Christianity. Columbus described some of the inhabitants of the Caribbean islands as hostile and depraved cannibals, a characterization that was to be repeated ad nauseum about many different Native American peoples European colonists saw as savage. Columbus also initiated the practice of acknowledging the diversity of Native Americans even as he lumped them all into the essentialist category of "Indians." The development of the printing press allowed the writing of Columbus to be spread throughout Europe, distributing his accounts of savage "Indians" that populated the new colonial frontier.[8] Even though Europeans sometimes used the image of the "noble savage" to describe the peoples of the Americas, the negative rendition of the depraved savage was more common, especially among American colonists.[9]

As did the early inhabitants of other European colonies, the early American colonists saw themselves as superior to the native peoples they encountered because of their religion and culture. English colonists demonstrated a sense of superiority because of their beliefs about the religious and institutional history of the Anglo-Saxons. In England, arguments for Anglo-Saxon superiority went back as far as the 1530s and Henry VIII's attempts to separate the English church from the Roman Catholic church. English clerics and scholars claimed that the Norman conquest of England in 1066 had corrupted the "purer practices" of the established Saxon church. During the Elizabethan period, these arguments were refined and the history of the uncorrupted Anglo-Saxon church was traced back to the early days of Christianity.[10] In the seventeenth century, the political crisis between the English Parliament and the king sparked interest in the political institutions of the pre–Norman conquest period as well. The Anglo-Saxons were seen as a "pure" group of people with a love of individuality and representative government. In this sense, the king was associated with the "post-Conquest tyranny" that corrupted the pure Saxon institutions.[11] This sense of Anglo-Saxon religious and political purity was particularly influential among the colonists in America. During the Revolutionary period, men such as Thomas Jefferson evoked the myth of pure Anglo-Saxon institutions in their rejection of the corrupt government of England. In the newly formed United States, people of English descent shared a general sense of superiority to England itself and believed that they were being true to their Saxon forefathers by moving closer to the older uncorrupted religion and government of the distant English past.[12]

With the rise of the modern concepts of race and civilization, Anglo-Saxon cultural superiority became associated in the United States with the presumed biological superiority of white Americans. In the period of the Revolutionary War, the scientific idea of "race" became increasingly important to distinguish those of European descent from the peoples they attempted to dominate in their colonial expansion. Nicholas Hudson argues that the words "race" and "nation" had the same meaning before the middle of the eighteenth century: both terms referred to groups with a common ancestry.[13] During the early era of European colonialism, European travelers and commentators generally focused their arguments about the inferiority of non-Europeans on cultural habits, especially religion.[14] By the middle of the nineteenth century, the word "race" had become the standard term for biologically distinct groups of humans with a common ancestry. "Nation" had become a subcategory of race, a term that referred to culturally distinct groups that share traits such as a common language, mythology, and political system. The change in these terms was largely due to the influence of natural history and its emphasis on taxonomy.[15]

The Enlightenment and the dawning of the industrial age were characterized by increasing attention to physiological differences. For Europeans and those of European descent who were measuring the relative worth of the peoples of the world, these physiological differences became obvious markers for the inferiority of others. Swedish botanist Carolus Linnaeus, the founder of the modern method of systematically classifying nature, worked, like many scientists of his day, to assist European colonial expansion. As his students traveled the world with the Swedish East India Company, Linnaeus developed a system by which they could break down and classify the various natural specimens they came across. The method Linnaeus outlined in the highly influential 1758 edition of *Systema Naturae* included a four-race breakdown of humanity that was revised and expanded by later scientists (including Thomas Jefferson) as they grappled with the "problem" of human diversity and origins.[16] In this way, race became the key concept for scientists and other intellectuals of the late eighteenth century as they attempted to categorize and evaluate humans according to their physiological differences.

This was also the period when the modern concept of civilization developed. Though the distinction between civilized, barbaric, and savage peoples had been around since the time of the ancient Greeks, the idea was redefined between 1750 and 1850.[17] George W. Stocking Jr. explains that in 1750, men such as "Adam Smith in Edinburgh and Baron Turgot at the Sorbonne" engaged in a series of lectures that attempted "a more general or scientific formulation of the idea of progress in civilization."[18] What was revolutionary here was the inclusion of time: civilization became the product of a sequential linear progression. Civilization came to be understood as "the generic term for both the overall process of human progress and its cumulative achievement in every area of human activity."[19] This notion of civilization and progress dovetailed with the emerging new definition of race to reinforce a sense of European cultural and biological superiority.

Using what is known as the comparative method, natural historians argued that peoples and cultures that were less civilized constituted earlier stages of human development. To study these peoples and cultures was to study how civilized Europeans had once been themselves before they progressed to their lofty position. Merging with the notion of the "Great Chain of Being," these scientists continually categorized and slotted into their place the peoples of the world in a hierarchy that stretched from the lowest form of life to the highest European.[20] In the colonial context of the United States, this consciousness of race and civilization was particularly high: people of European descent saw themselves as builders of a nation through the destruction or enslavement of peoples they saw as inferior. For a country such as the United States, which was purportedly based on egalitarian principles, theories of race provided a necessary justification for excluding nonwhites from full citizenship in this new civilization. If some races were biologically unfit, then it was seen as only natural that they should be eliminated, enslaved, or relegated to inferior social positions as the country progressed.[21] Therefore, the concepts of race and civilization reinforced white Americans' sense of their own superiority and contributed to the idea that to be American was to be from European stock.

After the Revolutionary War, the myth of the frontier played a central role in perpetuating the notion of white superiority in the culture of the United States. In 1784, author and land speculator John Filson made Daniel Boone a famous man. Filson's portrayal of Boone's adventures made the Kentucky backwoodsman "the archetypal hero of the American frontier."[22] Boone was the white man who had mastered the wilderness, whose democratic virtues stood in stark contrast to the failed civilizations of Europe and the degraded savagery of the New World.[23] Boone provided a unique and compelling image for a new nation that was trying to establish an identity separate from that of its erstwhile English masters. Filson's Boone asserted the superiority of the United States over England and Native Americans and made the American system of government seem as though it had sprung from the unique characteristics of the frontier itself.

Novelist James Fenimore Cooper further popularized the image of the frontiersman through his Leatherstocking stories in the 1820s and 1830s.[24] Like Filson's Boone, Cooper's Leatherstocking character—who was called Hawkeye in *The Last of the Mohicans* (1826)—embodied the best aspects of what Cooper felt was the truly American character. Cooper used Hawkeye to highlight the outdated and useless nature of the British empire in the face of the American frontier. Set during the French and Indian Wars in the middle of the eighteenth century, with the American Revolution clearly on the horizon, Cooper's omniscient narrator asserted that "the imbecility of her military leaders abroad, and the fatal want of energy in her councils at home, had lowered the character of Great Britain from the proud elevation on which it had been placed by the talents and enterprise of her former warriors and statesmen. No longer dreaded by her enemies, her servants were fast losing the confidence of self respect."[25] Cooper asserted the popular belief that the antiquated civilization of Great Britain had failed, implying that the Revolutionary War represented a necessary separation from the Old World. Americans, the "servants" of the British empire, could regain their self-respect only by throwing off the yoke of incompetent and lackluster British leadership as they proceeded to conquer the continent. To underscore the degraded character of the British and the exceptional abilities of Americans, the text revealed how George Washington had saved the British army from destruction at the hands of a few French and Indian troops. In this way Cooper represented Anglo Americans as the only competent masters of the New World.

Hawkeye, the white protagonist of the novel, underscored this theme by spending much of the story demonstrating the uselessness of British civilization in the middle of a frontier war zone. Hawkeye mediated between the British and their noble "savage" allies and fought the bloodthirsty and corrupt "savages" who allied themselves with the French. Cooper presented Hawkeye as the white master of the frontier, a man who took the best of British civilization and the best of Indian customs and developed into a tough, self-reliant, fair, honest, and freedom-loving pathfinder for the nascent civilization of America. By contrasting Hawkeye with stereotypes of pampered Englishmen, noble savages, and bloodthirsty Indians, Cooper represented him as the perfect combination of characteristics for the American frontier. Like Filson's Daniel Boone, Hawkeye was put forth as the quintessential American hero.

Although he celebrated the virtues of the Anglo American frontiersman, Cooper also revealed a basic ambivalence about civilization through his representation of Hawkeye's heroic Mohican sidekick Chingachgook. We know from Cooper's earlier novel *The Pioneers* (1823) that the noble Chingachgook was the last Mohican chief, a man who eventually succumbed to alcoholism as his people succumbed to extinction.[26] Even though he used the language of natural royalty to describe Chingachgook in *The Last of the Mohicans*, Cooper had already established the inevitability of his descent into degradation. The tragedy of Chingachgook highlighted Cooper's feeling that civilization exterminates the virtues of the frontier: the noble Chingachgook helped paved the way for progress, but there was no place for him in the civilized world. The essential incompatibility of Chingachgook with American civilization reinforced the idea of savage racial identity. Indeed, Cooper observed several times in his frontier novels that Indians were incapable of participating in the dawning American civilization because of their savage nature, an issue that he foregrounded with his constant references to "race" and "blood."[27] Even though Cooper was sympathetic to Chingachgook, he represented him as a "creature of nature" who relished taking scalps in battle.[28] Instead of presenting Chingachgook and the indigenous peoples of northeastern America as agrarian, Cooper portrayed them as nomadic hunters who had not cultivated the land.[29] Cooper explained the distinction through the civilized white hero Major Duncan Heyward, who remarked, "The tribes are fonder of the chase, than of the arts of men of labour."[30] Through this historically inaccurate description, Cooper reinforced the Euro-American belief that Native Americans had no true claim to the land because they had not used it to build any kind of civilization. In the march of progress, it was the Europeans and their descendants who advanced civilization. Although Cooper did not present civilization as inherently desirable, he presented the march of progress toward civilization as natural and inevitable. As a noble but nomadic hunter, Chingachgook embodied Cooper's ideal of an admirable but archaic culture that succumbed to the hardworking farmers and townspeople of America.

Cooper's frontier stories of the 1820s and 1830s played an important role in the development of a unique and professional American literature and spawned countless imitations.[31] Frontier themes and imagery emerged as a central aspect of American cultural and national identity. The dominant themes of frontier literature were regeneration and progress: white frontiersmen and settlers cast off the degraded old civilization of Europe and renewed themselves as they came into peaceful contact and violent conflict with both Native Americans and the wild frontier landscape.[32] The frontiersmen were heroes who led the way in the triumph of a new American civilization over the savagery of the American wilderness.

The frontier narratives of Cooper and his imitators were clearly in dialogue with contemporary debates about "Indian removal," or the coercion of the remaining Native American peoples east of the

Mississippi River to move to new lands in the west. Groups such as the Cherokees in Georgia had made significant strides in assimilating to European American norms of civilization. They had developed a written language, forged a constitution, and established courts, laws, and schools. Some Cherokees ran successful farms and cotton plantations, even going so far as to acquire slaves to work the land.[33] However, the desire of European Americans for land and the growing belief in permanent and insurmountable racial differences overwhelmed the Native Americans and their political allies. Many proponents of Indian removal appealed to the stereotype of the nomadic savage perpetuated in Cooper's popular frontier fictions. Despite the obvious exceptions like the Cherokee cited by their opponents, men such as President Andrew Jackson continued to assert that Indians were wild savages who needed to be removed to the west for their own protection with the hope that one day they could become civilized.[34] Over strong opposition from sympathetic whites and Native Americans themselves, Indian removal policies were enacted during the 1820s and 1830s that led to the forced removal of tens of thousands of people from their ancestral homes. The government broke several promises regarding food, financial support, and protection along the way. Using bribes, legislation, and brute force, the United States and several state governments devastated Sac and Fox groups in the north and Cherokee, Choctaw, Creek, Chickasaw, and Seminole groups in the south. Several thousand Native Americans died in the process, all in the name of progress and the supposed destiny of the Anglo-Saxons to expand westward across the continent.[35]

Native Americans, of course, were not the only nonwhites to be treated as inferior and incapable of full participation in the growing civilization of the United States. African Americans also bore the brunt of the stigma of the "savage" as white scientists, authors, ministers, and intellectuals proposed explanations for black "inferiority" that was presumed to be inherent. Racial theories popular in the United States before the late nineteenth century focused on the idea that Africans were natural slaves. The most popular theories had little to do with science, emphasizing instead interpretations of the Bible to find a religious justification for treating blacks as either slaves or second-class citizens. One popular argument was based on the biblical story of Ham, the son of Noah, whom God cursed along with his descendents into a life of servitude. Ham had mocked his father when he saw him drunk and naked, and many believed that God had given Ham dark skin color as a part of the curse. Africans, who were believed to be the sons of Ham, were therefore seen as ordained by God to be slaves.[36] In the antebellum south, this "sons of Ham" argument was an important part of a larger justification of slavery as "a beneficent institution" that enacted "part of God's plan to elevate a degraded race by introducing it to civilization and Christianity."[37] The development and dissemination of such nonscientific arguments testified to how important the emerging concepts of race and civilization were becoming in the United States. However, theories of essential biological differences between the races and their relative fitness for civilized life were most thoroughly developed among scientists.

Scientific arguments for racial differences based on the idea of monogenesis, or the belief that all human beings had a common origin, suffused British and American culture. In general, these monogenist arguments were consistent with the traditional biblical account of Adam and Eve in the Garden of Eden and more recent Enlightenment arguments about the unity of mankind. Monogenist arguments emphasized the common features of human anatomy and explained racial variation as the product of environmental factors. Despite the theory's emphasis on common origins, many monogenists supported the idea of white superiority. This was accomplished through appealing to an environmental argument about degeneration: the environment of some areas such as America and Africa, it was argued, had led its human inhabitants to degenerate into degraded races. In this way, many monogenists were able to reconcile prevailing Euro-American beliefs about race and white superiority with the entrenched belief in the unity and common origin of the species.[38]

Despite the widespread acceptance of monogenesis, however, arguments for polygenesis became increasingly common in the nineteenth-century United States. Polygenesis was the belief that the various human races had separate origins. Emphasizing racial differences instead of anatomical similarities, most proponents of polygenesis asserted that the various human races constituted separate species. Polygenists viewed race as an immutable and unchanging aspect of human physiology, a basic difference that could not be overcome by changes in environment. Nonwhites were therefore considered to be completely incapable of improving themselves to the level of white civilization, an argument that had obvious negative social and political consequences for them.[39] Though polygenesis was never widely accepted outside scientific circles, the polygenist formulation of race as an unchanging aspect of biology was widely accepted. Some American scientists maintained well into the twentieth century that social aptitudes and character traits were determined by race.[40]

Polygenist arguments began to appear in print in the United States in the late eighteenth century. Invoking the old notion of the great chain of being, men such as English surgeon Charles White argued that "the Negro" was an intermediate form between the European and the ape. Using an early form of anatomical comparison, White asserted that the various races were created as separate species and remained distinct despite some interbreeding.[41] Polygenist arguments using comparative anatomy gradually became more common in the early nineteenth century and reached new heights with the work of Samuel George Morton in the 1830s.[42] Morton was a physician and anatomy professor from Philadelphia who became world renowned for his quantitative approach to the issue of human races. Though clearly flawed by modern standards, Morton's work to prove that racial differences were immutable and that Anglo-Saxons were superior to all others found acceptance among his peers. Morton's work was based on the assumption that the intelligence of races was related to the average volume of their skulls. More concisely, he believed that the bigger the brain, the smarter the race. With this assumption, Morton engaged in an active campaign to acquire skulls from around the globe, an endeavor that gave him the most admired collection of such skulls in the world at the time. His two major works, *Crania Americana* (1839) and *Crania Aegyptiaca* (1844), engaged in a comparative quantitative analysis of the skulls he had collected. Filling the cranial cavities with mustard seed (and later with lead shot), Morton attempted to measure the size of the brains the skulls once held. Not surprisingly, Morton's conclusions reinforced the standard arguments about race. Morton concluded that the bigger brains of whites had always made them superior, the smaller brains of "Negroes" had always made them servants, and the inferior brains of Native Americans made them incapable of being civilized.[43]

Morton's reasoning was flawed from the start: later scientists demonstrated that brain size is proportional to body size. It has no relation to intelligence.[44] Stephen J. Gould showed how Morton's supposedly objective work was also skewed methodologically in favor of his racial assumptions. Reviewing the raw data published by Morton, Gould found that he had distorted racial identifications, sample groupings, measurements, and tabulations to demonstrate white superiority. The fact that Morton published all of his raw data, however, led Gould to conclude that his distortions were unconscious; why would he publish raw data that contradicted his final calculations and conclusions? Gould highlights the fact that Morton's work bears the hallmark of a scientist working unconsciously to match his findings to a preconceived ideological commitment. Morton had tried to match his research to the hierarchy of race that was accepted by most educated white Americans of the period. Morton had not tested an open question; he simply justified an a priori conviction.[45] Morton did not ask *if* blacks and Native Americans were inferior to whites, he merely measured *how* and *to what extent* blacks and Native Americans were inferior to whites. The fact that Morton's peers did not rise up en masse to condemn his distortions of his published data suggests that they shared his ideological commitment to the hierarchy of race. The continued praise for Morton long after his death showed the depth of this ideological commitment within Euro-American society.

American polygenists won many converts, and Morton's work provided the "hard evidence" for their increasingly bold and popular arguments. Morton's greatest convert was Swiss naturalist Louis Agassiz. Long before his trip to the United States in late 1846, Agassiz had earned an international reputation as an outstanding scientist. Once in the United States, he immediately toured major scientific institutions and met with notable scientists of the northeast. In Philadelphia, Agassiz met Morton and was impressed by his skull collection. The two became close friends and Morton's work and views made a major impact on Agassiz's science. Agassiz also gave a number of lectures that gained him a popular following as well as some new professional prospects. Eager to finance science in order to fuel the growing industrial transformation of the northeast, a number of businessmen donated money to establish a new scientific school at Harvard University. Impressed by the great European naturalist, the new school and its supporters made Agassiz an offer he could not refuse. Agassiz would help build the nascent scientific institutions of Boston, and Harvard would gain immediate credibility for its new school by adding a scholar of such distinction. In late 1847, Agassiz accepted the post of professor of zoology and geology at Harvard's Lawrence Scientific School and solidified his move to the United States by sending for his assistants and his library from Europe.[46]

Before coming to the United States, Agassiz had already proposed a theory that was close to the polygenist argument. Despite the fact that Agassiz believed in many different "centers of creation" (and not just the one discussed in the Bible), he still argued that all humanity came from a common origin. This changed after his trip to Philadelphia in 1846, where Agassiz had his first close contact with African Americans at his hotel. From that time forward, Agassiz became an increasingly vocal proponent of the idea that the various races had separate origins and were actually separate species.[47] When Nott and Glidden published *Types of Mankind* in 1854, Agassiz detailed his own ideas in an introductory essay, "Sketch of the Natural Provinces of the Animal World and Their Relation to the Different Types of Man," that outlined Agassiz's theory about the "centers of creation" that order the natural world. Agassiz divided the world into major geographic regions based on the distribution of distinct flora and fauna and argued that each region had been created with its current population of plants and animals (see Figure 1). Agassiz observed that the regions of distinct plants

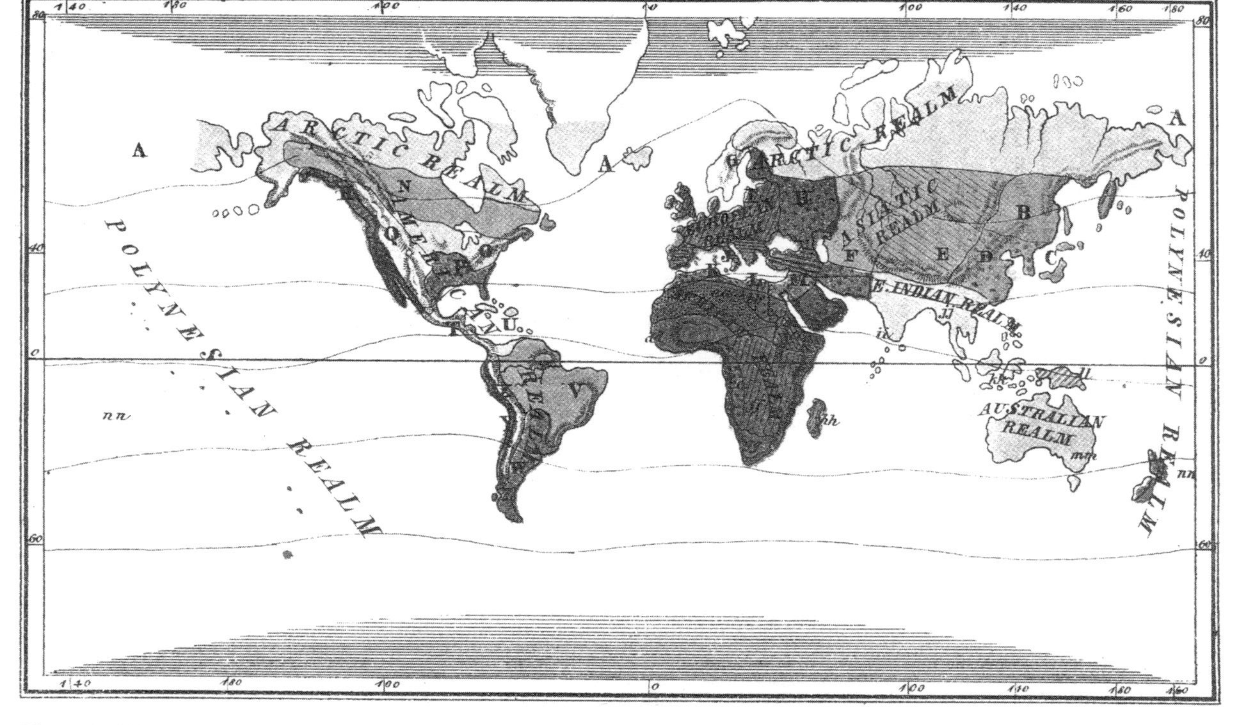

Figure 1. This map accompanied Agassiz's article "Sketch of the Natural Provinces of the Animal World," which outlined the various "centers of creation" and appeared at the beginning of Nott and Gliddon's *Types of Mankind* (1854). The map shows what Agassiz believed were the various "zoological realms" that corresponded with the centers of creation and the "species" of humanity.

and animals also corresponded to the geographic distribution of the different races of mankind. He concluded that "I must, in presence of these facts, insist at least upon the probability of such an independence of origin of all nations; or, at least, of the independent origin of a primitive stock for each."[48] With these words, Agassiz asserted that each race or "primitive stock" was created independently of the others. As did his fellow polygenists, Agassiz also accepted the argument that races subdivided into different nations.

Having concluded that the various races came from separate creations, Agassiz turned to the question of whether they should also be classified as separate species. Appealing to examples from "well known" animals, Agassiz maintained that "the differences existing between the races of men are of the same kind as the difference observed between the different families, genera, and species of monkeys or other animals; and . . . these different species of animals differ in the same degree one from the other as the races of men—nay, the differences between distinct races are often greater than those distinguishing species of animals one from the other."[49] Agassiz drove a biological wedge between Caucasians and other races farther than naturalists who simply had asserted that each race is a separate species (see Figures 2 and 3). He believed that his conclusions "in no way conflict with the idea of the unity of mankind, which is as close as that of the members of any well-marked type of animals."[50] For Agassiz, "the general plan which unites all organized beings into one great organic conception" provided the unity for the separate species of the human genus.[51] By appealing to a divine plan, Agassiz implied that the differences between the various races were unchanging and ordained by God. Despite the supposed "unity of mankind," Agassiz clearly believed that the inferiority of nonwhite races was part of God's natural order.

Agassiz clarified his belief in God's racial order using the example of the "European zoological realm," which, he claimed, "is circumscribed within exactly the same limits as the so-called white race of man, including, as it does, the inhabitants of south-western Asia, and of north Africa, with the lower parts of the valley of the Nile."[52] Agassiz made some suspect claims about the racial status of a number of

Figure 2. This tableau of fauna from "Sketch of the Natural Provinces of the Animal World" (1854) shows what Agassiz believed were the different comparable species in the European and American "zoological realms." Notice how the drawings of the head and skull of the American (Indian) are exaggeratedly small compared to that of the European. This was consistent with the polygenist belief that Europeans had larger brains that gave them superior intelligence.

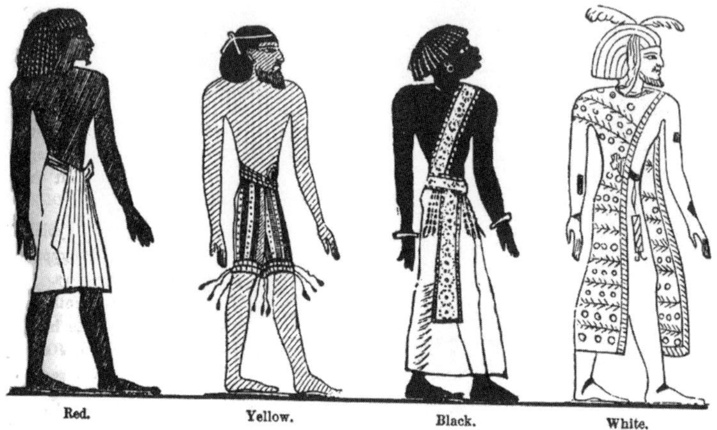

Figure 3. Nott and Gliddon interpreted drawings from ancient Egyptian monuments as evidence for the permanence of racial divisions. The caption for this image from *Types of Mankind* (1854) read "The ancient Egyptian division of mankind into four species—fifteenth century B.C." This reflected the polygenist belief that the various races were actually separate species and that these species came from separate centers of creation.

peoples, but his logic became more explicit when he asserted that it was "very striking, that the different sub-divisions of this race, even to the limits of distinct nationalities, cover precisely the same ground as the special faunae or zoological provinces of this most important part of the world, which in all ages has been the seat of the most advanced civilization."[53] By drawing the boundaries of the "European zoological realm" as he did, Agassiz claimed such ancient civilizations as Persia and Egypt for the white race. This categorization completed the claim that whites were the true bearers of civilization and those of African descent (as distinct from those of *north* African descent) were incapable of civilization. Despite interracial realities brought about by several centuries of intermarriage, migration, and conquest in southern Europe, the Mediterranean, and northern Africa, Agassiz believed in the permanence of racial types. This belief led him to draw relatively solid lines of demarcation for the "aboriginal . . . distribution of man" and claim anything he saw as an important civilization for the white race.[54]

In the first few chapters of *Types of Mankind*, Nott pushed the connection between whites and civilization even further to draw out distinctions between the races. Repeating earlier arguments made by Morton and Agassiz, Nott asserted that the bigger brains of Caucasians had led them to be natural colonizers, spreading around the globe "extending and perfecting civilization" while the inferior races remained close to their centers of creation.[55] In describing the characteristics of Caucasians, Nott simply resorted to a stereotypical listing—"ambitious, daring, domineering"—and associated these characteristics with "an irresistible instinct" to spread out across the globe.[56] Nott offered no scientific proof to back up his claims about Caucasian character traits; instead, he simply assumed that they were true and attributed them to biology. Biological inevitability gave title to Caucasians, driven by their "instinct," to conquer "inferior" races. Furthermore, Nott's racism led him to assume that the "inferior types of mankind" would eventually pass away during the onslaught of the "superior" Caucasians.[57] Nott identified racial determinism as the driving force behind the history of civilization: "Looking back over the world's history, it will be seen that human progress has arisen mainly from the war of races. All the great impulses which have been given to it from time to time have been the results of conquests and colonizations."[58] Nott mobilized polygenist science to justify the enslavement of African Americans and the decimation of Native Americans that was part of his political and cultural environment. Nott's argument simply implied that this was progress, a natural process where superior races exterminated those he deemed inferior. So much for the unity of mankind.

While many rejected the polygenist argument that the different races were distinct species, the polygenist assertions of innate, measurable, and immutable differences in intelligence between the races were widely accepted.[59] The American school of ethnology had created an entire worldview of human progress that was consistent with the frontier myth of Cooper and his followers. According to this worldview, superior whites violently destroyed inferior savages in the natural, divinely ordained, and inevitable advance of civilization. The intellectual support of distinguished scientists confirmed the racial worldview of nineteenth-century European Americans, adding a gloss of scholarly rigor to the belief that race war preordained history and natural law. As a movement within the science and literature of American culture, racial nationalism became increasingly attractive to the purveyors of national identity. From the 1830s to the 1850s, racial nationalism was evoked to justify slavery, Indian removal, and the conquest and expropriation of northern Mexico to expand the right and title of Anglo-Saxons to land that reached to the Pacific Ocean.[60] Anglo-Saxons and other branches of the white race saw themselves as the only leaders in the expansion of civilization. They argued that freedom was wasted on other races, since the presumed mental and physical degradation of nonwhites revealed that only whites could truly love liberty. Darwin's *The Origin of Species* was only five years away when Nott and Gliddon published *Types of Mankind.* Darwin's evolutionary perspective would eventually destroy many of the arguments of the American school of ethnology, but his emphasis on conflict and racial hierarchy gave new life to American exceptionalism. Under the flag of Darwinian evolution, racial warfare on the frontier became an even more salient feature of Victorian culture and society at the turn of the century.

CHAPTER 2

MAN THE TOOLMAKER

RACE, TECHNOLOGY, AND COLONIALISM IN DARWIN'S *THE DESCENT OF MAN*

The influence of Charles Darwin on modern Euro-American culture is difficult to overstate. Despite the controversial aspects of the theory of evolution and seemingly endless battles over science education (especially in the United States), many of the most popular stories that we tell ourselves are Darwinist. As Gillian Beer notes, Darwinist ideas have become so ingrained in modern Euro-American culture that "we pay Darwin the homage of our assumptions. Precisely because we live in a culture dominated by evolutionary ideas, it is difficult for us to recognise their imaginative power in our daily readings of the world."[1] We are constantly repeating Darwin's ideas without being fully conscious of where they come from; they have become part of the fabric of our thoughts. Aspects of human behavior such as selfishness, competition, and conflict are now seen as "natural"—and more specifically, as driven by biological imperatives and the laws of life—largely due to Darwin's work. In some ways Darwin's ideas were radical and inventive, providing a powerful new perspective on the natural world. For the most part, however, Darwin consolidated older claims about race, progress, and the order of the natural world into a streamlined and modified narrative of human history. Like most of his monogenist and polygenist contemporaries, Darwin did not question the superiority of Europeans and their descendents; instead, he attempted to account for this assumed superiority by applying his novel theory of natural selection to human development.

The initial negative response to Darwin's *On the Origin of Species by Means of Natural Selection* (1859) was predictable because it seemed to many like an anarchistic rejection of established institutions and ideas. However, the response to *The Descent of Man; and Selection in Relation to Sex* (1871) was largely positive.[2] It presented a compelling "adventure of the English evolving, clambering up from the apes, struggling to conquer savagery, multiplying and dispersing around the globe."[3] Darwin's story of human progress centered on technology, with man the toolmaker asserting his authority over the rest of the natural world. Despite Darwin's relatively liberal position on many issues, his work played a major role in establishing Anglo-Saxon superiority as a scientifically proven "fact." His narrative of human progress asserted that Europeans were superior tool users and the most evolved branch of the human species. Darwin's vision of racial progress provided a worldview not only for future scientists but also for historians and fiction writers trying to account for the importance of race and technology in the modern world.

Most of Darwin's ideas were neither unique nor original. Even the concept of "natural selection" was developed independently by Alfred Russel Wallace, who shared credit for the idea when it was presented to the Linnean Society in 1858.[4] However, Darwin's corpus of work provided the nineteenth century's most sustained and influential articulation of evolutionary ideas: it synthesized an incredible amount of data, philosophy, and social belief into a relatively coherent theory and settled long-standing disputes in natural history, a field that was rife with idiomatic and contradictory ideas. Darwin's work established a broad paradigm that served as a model and foundation for future work in a number of different scientific fields.[5] The tension in the concept of natural selection between heredity and environment, Darwin's updated spin on the classic "nature versus nurture" debate, mapped the terrain that modern biologists and anthropologists still fight over.[6] More important, Darwin developed a model of human nature that became central to Euro-American culture.

At first, Darwin avoided publicly extrapolating his ideas about evolution to humans for fear that it would increase the backlash he was anticipating against his work.[7] In *The Origin of Species*, which was published in November 1859, Darwin focused on the "lower animals" exclusively.[8] His only reference to humans was his understatement near the end of the conclusion that asserted that "light will be thrown on the origin of man and his history."[9] Darwin used the knowledge people had gained from selectively breeding animals as the foundation for his argument and called the changes brought about by selective breeding "variation under domestication." He moved on to discuss "variation under nature," or the process by which animals change over time without the guiding influence of humans. Darwin reasoned that if humans can change animals over time through selective breeding, then nature must be able to do the same. In the place of popular ideas about divine intervention, he proposed his (and Wallace's) new idea of "natural selection" to explain how animals changed (or evolved) in a state of nature. Darwin argued that nature chose certain characteristics as favorable and that these favorable characteristics gave the animals that possessed them a competitive advantage in the struggle for survival. Over time, the accumulation of these characteristics within certain populations would eventually lead to the generation of a new species. Thus, Darwin's idea of animal evolution was gradual and dynamic; species changed and diverged over time to become better adapted to their ever-changing environments.

As Darwin feared, the publication of *The Origin of Species* caused a huge backlash among the scientific community and in the general public. In fact, this was a significant aspect of its revolutionary impact: Darwin ignited a broad public debate about a field of science that had previously been interesting to only an insular community of scientists and scholars.[10] In 1859, the evolution of life became an everyday topic of discussion among aristocrats, clerics, and commoners who had never before taken an interest in natural history. Darwin's book far outstripped its expected sales; the demand was so high that Darwin immediately began work amending it for a second edition.[11] A number of conservatives wrote reviews attacking *Origin*; scientists such as Richard Owen and clerics such as Samuel Wilberforce, the bishop of Oxford, weighed in against what they viewed as Darwin's unsound and atheistic argument. However, Darwin had a number of highly respected and influential scientists on his side, such as anatomist Thomas Henry Huxley and botanist Joseph Hooker. Huxley led the charge in support of *Origin* by writing and arranging positive reviews and earned the nickname "Darwin's Bulldog" for his dogged defense of his friend and ally. The war of ideas that ensued raged throughout Victorian society and Charles Darwin quickly became a household name.[12]

Despite Darwin's careful avoidance of the topic, many reactions to *The Origin of Species* focused on the implications of evolution for human ancestry. In the popular press and in pulpits, people speculated about the relationship between Darwin's argument and the origins of humanity, usually as a method of discrediting *Origin*.[13] The highest levels of the scientific community began to address the subject publicly only after Owen broached it in an attack on Huxley in March 1861. In an article entitled "The Gorilla and the Negro," Owen charged that Huxley was an "advocate of man's origin from a transmuted ape."[14] Huxley took this as an opportunity to put forth the case that humans had evolved from a lower primate. He had been lecturing on similarities between humans and apes for years, but Owen now gave him an opening to expand this discussion and explicitly address all of its implications.[15] Huxley was rapidly expanding his power and influence in England's scientific institutions using Darwin's ideas as a cudgel to smite the opposition. Atheists, political radicals, and some in the popular press had been arguing that man had bestial origins for decades. In Huxley, they now found a legitimate well-respected man of science to champion their cause.[16] Huxley gave public lectures to working-class men on the ape origins of humanity that were so popular that people had to be turned away. He also worked to publish pro-Darwinist scientific essays and pamphlets on the topic.[17] Much to

Darwin's delight, Huxley finally published his major treatise on human evolution, *Evidence as to Man's Place in Nature*, in early 1863. Geologist Charles Lyell, a relatively recent convert to the idea of human evolution, also published his *Geological Evidences of the Antiquity of Man* in 1863 despite his lingering doubts about the importance of natural selection.[18] These works and many others had a great influence on Darwin and prepared the way for his entry into the fray.[19]

A number of important scientific discoveries lent credence to both Darwin's evolutionary arguments and the speculations of his followers about "lowly" human origins. Several archaeological digs such as the one begun at Brixham Cave in 1858 unearthed primitive tools from "savage" men that pushed back the antiquity of the human race; similar digs uncovered fossil bones of Neanderthals.[20] Travelers from Africa reported discoveries of new primate species, and the first "gorilla" specimens toured England in the 1850s: in 1855 a "traveling menagerie" exhibited a live young female gorilla, and in 1861 Paul du Chaillu toured with his collection of gorilla heads.[21] The public furor over *Origin* waned as the debate moved to the terrain of human origins and, by extension, human nature. By the time Darwin published *The Descent of Man* in early 1871, the argument that man had descended from an ape-like ancestor was simply old hat.[22] Where Darwin's work had seemed like radical heresy a dozen years before, the public received his new two-volume tome as a major pronouncement on a familiar subject by the great man of evolutionary science. There were still many negative reviews and legions of detractors, but evolution was becoming accepted as orthodox science. The sales of Darwin's new 900-page book were as enormous as the book itself, and it soon became the talk of England.[23]

Darwin waded into the ring with his sights set on settling a number of troublesome debates in natural history about human origins. One particular dispute that Darwin wanted to settle in *The Descent of Man* was that between the growing number of evolutionists and the older monogenists and polygenists. Monogenists, who emphasized religious orthodoxy and human degeneration, remained vocal critics of evolutionary science.[24] However, their arguments were inconsistent with industrial-age notions of progress. Darwin and his followers put forward ideas about human development that matched a belief in human progress and the steady advance of civilization. Polygenists emphasized the separate origins of the races. Darwin and his followers focused on a common ancestry for all humanity (and, indeed, all organic life) but retained a notion of racial difference that was still consistent in some ways with the polygenist formulation of race.[25]

Race was an important aspect of *The Descent of Man*. In the introduction, Darwin made explicit the priorities of his argument: "The sole object of this work is to consider, firstly, whether man, like every other species, is descended from some pre-existing form; secondly, the manner of his development; and thirdly, the value of the differences between the so-called races of man."[26] For Darwin, the question of race was inseparable from the concept of human evolution. Like the monogenists and polygenists before him, Darwin felt the need to answer the question of race: What was the importance of racial differences for understanding human origins and development? With the phrase "so-called races," Darwin hinted that he disagreed with the emphasis placed on race by scientists such as Harvard's Louis Agassiz, the great "theorist of polygeny" who was one of Darwin's most fervent detractors.[27] Darwin had fretted about the status of "savages" since his trip on the *Beagle* in the 1830s, but he rejected the idea that they constituted a separate species.[28] In Chapter VII of *Descent*, entitled "On the Races of Man," Darwin argued that "those naturalists . . . who admit the principle of evolution, and this is now admitted by the majority of rising men, will feel no doubt that all the races of man are descended from a single primitive stock; whether or not they may think fit to designate the races as distinct species, for the sake of expressing their amount of difference."[29] Darwin took issue with the polygenists, arguing that the "principle of evolution" disproved their claim that different races originated from different sources. However, he still retained the notion of clearly demarcated racial differences that appealed to polygenists.[30]

Though Darwin accepted the idea of pronounced racial differences, his argument focused on the similarities of the various races. Early in

Chapter VII, Darwin listed physical differences that might lead scientists to conclude that different races should be categorized as different species. Darwin acknowledged the striking differences between races in "the texture of the hair, the relative proportions of all parts of the body, the capacity of the lungs, [and] the form and capacity of the skull" along with the "color of the skin and hair."[31] However, Darwin rejected the relative significance of these differences and argued instead that the evidence was overwhelming that the various races should be classified as branches of the same species. Darwin pointed to miscegenation as one compelling fact: despite polygenist claims to the contrary, interfertility was impossible between distinct species. Darwin stated that "the races of man are not sufficiently distinct to inhabit the same country without fusion; and the absence of fusion affords the usual and best test of specific distinctness."[32] According to Darwin, if the various *races* were actually separate *species*, they would not be able to produce fertile children with one another. The fact that there were so many documented racial mixtures in the world undermined the polygenesis argument and pointed toward an evolutionary unity of mankind. Darwin emphasized the "resemblance between the several races of man in bodily structure and mental faculties," traits that could not have been "independently acquired" and that must have been "inherited from progenitors who had these same characters."[33] Darwin surmised that the various races were best termed "sub-species" while admitting that the term "race" would likely remain in use "from long habit."[34] Ultimately, Darwin concluded that "when the principle of evolution is generally accepted, as it surely will be before long, the dispute between the monogenists and the polygenists will die a silent and unobserved death."[35] Darwin's vision was realized, and his articulation of evolution—in its general form, if not in all its particulars—had become the paradigm in the biological and social sciences by the end of the century. Though his work did not provide an overnight settlement to this decades-long debate, Darwin's argument that all races were closely connected biologically and shared a common ancestry eventually transformed the field of natural history to the point where the dispute between monogenists and polygenists became meaningless.[36]

Darwin's relatively liberal conception of race manifested itself in his politics. Darwin was a great abolitionist and never missed an opportunity to lambaste the "great crime" of slavery.[37] He also used his money and political influence to promote progressive causes that he felt would help "savages" instead of eliminating them. For Darwin, this was a morally evolved way to treat other races. He asserted in his discussion of "Moral Sense" in *The Descent of Man* that the evolution of compassion was a key component of morality: "But as man gradually advanced in intellectual power . . . [and as] his sympathies became more tender and widely diffused, extending to men of all races, to the imbecile, maimed, and other useless members of society, and finally to the lower animals,— so would the standard of his morality rise higher and higher."[38] Darwin made clear his belief that compassion is a sign of an evolved moral sensibility. Therefore, being kind to "men of all races" instead of destroying or enslaving them was a central part of Darwin's identity as a "civilized" Englishman. This was especially important for Darwin because of his belief that civilized Europeans shared a common ancestry with men of other races and therefore had a moral responsibility to treat their brothers well.[39]

Darwin had confronted the colonial dilemma of how to treat indigenous peoples during his voyage on HMS *Beagle*. Traveling through Argentina in 1833, Darwin visited General Manuel de Rosas to secure safe passage to pursue his scientific explorations inland. General Rosas was in the process of waging a war of extermination against "wandering tribes of horse Indians" under orders from "the government at Buenos Ayres."[40] Darwin felt ambivalent about the situation: he sympathized with the besieged white landowners and recognized how the war would benefit the economy but he deplored the wanton destruction of the Indians.[41] Like a good Unitarian abolitionist, he felt that both slavery and genocide were morally contemptible and corrupting institutions.[42] Darwin described General Rosas as a stern disciplinarian whose men were a mixed-race "villainous, banditti-like army."[43] Though impressed by General Rosas, Darwin clearly felt that he and his men were poor representatives of Christian civilization. Darwin's account of General Rosas contrasted starkly with his description of Captain Robert FitzRoy of the *Beagle*. Where General Rosas engaged in "exterminating" Indians, Captain FitzRoy funded an attempt to civilize native Fuegians. Though the attempt was unsuccessful, Darwin lauded Captain FitzRoy's "noble hope" and "generous sacrifices" on behalf of the Fuegians.[44] Later in life, Darwin supported Christian missions, such as Captain FitzRoy's, that aimed to civilize the Fuegians.[45] Darwin was a believer in progress, the forward march of civilization, and the unending improvement of knowledge and morality.[46] For him, funding such a mission was a way of supporting the improvement of Fuegian "savages" rather than simply exterminating them as General Rosas tried to do.

Darwin also became outraged at the atrocities committed by E. J. Eyre, the governor of Jamaica, in 1866. Eyre had unleashed a campaign of violence to suppress a peasant uprising that had become a heated topic of discussion in England's intellectual circles that year. Darwin joined his friends Wallace, Lyell, Huxley, and Herbert Spencer on the Jamaica Committee to Bring Eyre to Justice and donated money to the cause.[47] Darwin's belief that other races could be improved stood in marked contrast to his polygenist adversaries: for polygenists, race was a primordial and unchanging aspect of human physiology. His belief in evolution and the possibility of progress for all races set him apart from men such as American polygenist Josiah Nott, who believed that it was "false philanthropy" to treat "inferior types of mankind" as if they were capable of changing their nature and contributing to civilization.[48]

That being said, Darwin's work also embodied the arrogance and contradictions of Victorian ideology with regard to race. While Darwin was relatively liberal and believed that all races could improve themselves, he did not believe that all races had equal physiological endowments. His argument in *The Descent of Man* made clear that he believed in the same hierarchy of races as his monogenist and polygenist antagonists, with whites at the top and nonwhites at the bottom. In the second chapter of *Descent*, Darwin meditated on the importance of craniometry, a nineteenth-century science that assumed that the average brain size for each race was linked to its relative intelligence.

Despite Darwin's skepticism about the relation between brain size and intelligence, he found that craniometry's racist implications made it more believable:

> No one, I presume, doubts that the large proportion which the size of man's brain bears to his body, compared to the same proportion in the gorilla or orang, is closely connected with his higher mental powers. . . . On the other hand, no one supposes that the intellect of any two animals or of any two men can be accurately gauged by the cubic contents of their skulls. It is certain that there may be extraordinary mental activity with an extremely small absolute mass of nervous matter: thus the wonderfully diversified instincts, mental powers, and affections of ants are notorious, yet their cerebral ganglia are not so large as the quarter of a small pin's head. . . .
>
> The belief that there exists in man some close relation between the size of the brain and the development of the intellectual faculties is supported by the comparison of the skulls of savage and civilized races, of ancient and modern people, and by the analogy of the whole vertebrate series. Dr. J. Barnard Davis has proved, by many careful measurements, that the mean internal capacity of the skull in Europeans is 92.3 cubic inches; in Americans 87.5; in Asiatics 87.1; and in Australians only 81.9 cubic inches.[49]

Darwin began this passage by accepting the argument that brain size relates to "higher mental powers" but then expressed skepticism about the quantifiable nature of such arguments.[50] Darwin then changed course (again) and actually lent credence to the quantifiable nature of intelligence by citing the work of Davis favorably. Victorian ideology with regard to race led Darwin and others of his day to accept the studies of men such as Davis; their belief in nonwhite inferiority made any study that supported the standard racial hierarchy seem more plausible. The skull data that Darwin cited in *The Descent of Man* simply repeated the standard racial hierarchy for the Victorian period, with the superior whites on top, Native Americans and Asians in the middle, and Native Australians at the bottom. Darwin accepted that the "savage races"—Native Americans, Asians, and Native Australians—were biologically inferior in their "intellectual faculties" to the "civilized" race of Europeans. Misguided theory, sloppy methodology, and the Victorian ideology of race combined to make European intellectual superiority seem like a quantifiable fact for Darwin and his contemporaries.[51] From a modern perspective, Darwin's attitude in this regard can only be classified as racist.

Darwin associated this hierarchy of race and intelligence with the evolution of society. Drawing on "the comparative method," Darwin followed the example of earlier nineteenth-century thinkers and endorsed the view that human history follows a standard "developmental sequence . . . through a series of stages which are often loosely referred to as savagery, barbarism, and civilization."[52] In this model, the supposedly lower races represented the savage stage of universal development, while Europeans and their colonial descendents represented the highest civilized stage. In the absence of historical or physical evidence, Darwin and his followers included examples from "savage" races to fill in details about this single path of evolutionary development.[53] Throughout *The Descent of Man*, Darwin recounted endless anecdotes about savages as a way to explore how Europeans used to be before their rapid ascent to civilization. He even devoted a section of one chapter to a disquisition about how the "civilized nations were once barbarous": "The evidence that all civilized nations are the descendants of barbarians, consists, on the one side, of clear traces of their former low condition in still-existing customs, beliefs, language, etc.; and on the other side, of proofs that savages are independently able to raise themselves a few steps in the scale of civilization."[54] Darwin argued that "savages" could actually evolve without the help of whites, a relatively liberal position for the day that contradicted the claims of polygenists. However, he implied that they could come only a few steps up the scale of civilization on their own, a scale where Europeans occupied the top position. Savages, whom he assumed were less evolved biologically than "civilized" Europeans, served in his argument as a sort of living relic to be studied for their scientific value. For Darwin, savages illustrated the way whites used to be before their rapid physiological and social development led to their ascension up the "scale of civilization." Darwin was careful not to use the term "savage" to apply to the ancestors of "civilized nations" like Great Britain; instead he used the term barbarous, a term free from the connotations of racial inferiority. If savages could move up the scale of civilization a bit, Darwin implied, then surely barbarous Europeans could have moved up the scale to their current lofty position.

By the time Darwin began writing about evolution, most scientists saw technology as an obvious and quantifiable way to measure the relative position of a group of people in the scale of civilization. Technology was very important for industrial-age Europeans and Americans, and it became closely associated with race in their arguments about the inferiority of other peoples.[55] Darwin synthesized prevailing perceptions of racial superiority, technological sophistication, and the stages of civilization in *The Descent of Man* and provided a complete narrative about the interface of human biology with technology that naturalized this method of evaluating races.[56] In *Descent*, the human brain and the human hand evolved in concert with technology. Darwin asserted that it was this increasing ability to both invent and manipulate technology that made humans such exceptional animals. He claimed that "man in the rudest state in which he now exists is the most dominant animal that has ever appeared on this earth. . . . He manifestly owes this immense superiority to his intellectual faculties . . . and to his corporeal structure. The supreme importance of these characters has been proved by the final arbitrament of the battle for life."[57] Darwin related the intellectual faculties and the corporeal structure to technology. Superior tool use became associated with superior humans, especially at the level of the group. According to Darwin, "in the rudest state of society, the individuals who were the most sagacious, who invented and used the best weapons or traps, and who were best able to defend themselves, would rear the greatest number of offspring. The tribes, which included the largest number of men thus endowed, would increase in number and supplant other tribes."[58] In Darwin's estimation, intellectual faculties were singled out by natural selection because they directly related to the development and use of tools. Those who were smart enough to invent and use tools well would thrive and reproduce more, and those who were not so smart would falter and reproduce less. Darwin also pointed to the group dynamics of tool use as a measure of superiority. In essence, groups that invented and used tools well would be more successful and survive in greater numbers than rival groups.[59] This concept of human nature, which became known as man the toolmaker, formed the foundation for Darwin's naturalization of Euro-American colonialism later in the text.[60]

According to Darwin, the natural selection of humans on the basis of technological mastery had a marked effect on human physiology. First and foremost, Darwin associated the hand with technology and intellect, arguing that "man could not have attained his present dominant position in the world without the use of his hands, which are so admirably adapted to act in obedience to his will."[61] Darwin argued that because of the necessity of using the hands to manipulate tools, over time humans "have become more and more erect or bipedal. They would thus have been better able to defend themselves with stones or clubs, to attack their prey, or otherwise to obtain food. The best built individuals would in the long run have succeeded best, and have survived in larger numbers."[62] Over time, better posture and manual dexterity would be naturally selected for because of technology. Those better able to grip and use a tool because of a more dexterous hand or a more upright posture would be more likely to survive. Darwin then expanded this argument to the human brain, saying that "as the various mental faculties gradually developed themselves the brain would almost certainly become larger."[63] Those with stronger spines and a more upright posture would be privileged by natural selection because of their ability to support a heavier cranium. Darwin created a narrative where human evolution was driven by the invention and use of technology: natural selection had led humans to have increasingly larger brains, dexterous hands, and erect postures because this enabled better mastery of technology.

In hindsight it is easy to see the ideological nature of Darwin's argument. Based on the evidence from the fossil record, present-day scientists working on human origins argue that "millions of years of evolution separated bipedal posture, tool use, and expansion of the brain."[64] Of course, Darwin did not have access to today's extensive fossil record when he argued that these developments in human evolution were simultaneous and mutually reinforcing. What he did have was the mindset of a man whose family had become rich from investing in the infrastructure of the industrial age.[65] Darwin believed in the industrial-age myth of progress, and like so many of his contemporaries, he placed technology at the center of this progress; like his fellow scientists, he accepted technology as a yardstick for measuring the relative progress of societies. Michael Adas has shown that Darwin and other Europeans in the nineteenth century "came to view science and especially technology as the most objective and unassailable measures of their own civilization's past achievement and present worth" and began to use machines as the "measure of men."[66] The narrative of *The Descent of Man* can be read as an extrapolation from the industrial-age present into the distant past, where Darwin traced *how* human physiology was intimately tied up with technology instead of asking *if* this was the case. Darwin's argument provided a scientific explanation and justification for how Great Britain had risen to the status of global power while also showing how Victorian society had become dependent upon modern conveniences. The confluence of Darwin's argument with Euro-American ideology accounted for much of its popularity and staying power.

What is most troubling about Darwin's man-the-toolmaker narrative is the way it reinforced racial ideology. Immediately after his argument about increasing brain size, Darwin launched into a discussion of the skull capacities of the various races (quoted earlier). The implication was clear: "savage races" have smaller brains than whites and therefore are inferior toolmakers with inferior intellects. This information about the "inferior" brains of the "savage races" became a direct biological justification for colonialism. By Darwin's day, the British had a long history of colonizing the lands of Native Americans, Asians, Africans, and Native Australians. Nineteenth-century European commentators attributed British success primarily to superior intelligence and technology. Darwin accepted this argument and gave it a gloss of biological inevitability in *The Descent of Man*.

Darwin once wrote in a notebook that "when two races of men meet, they act precisely like two species of animals—they fight, eat each other, bring diseases to each other, etc., but then comes the more deadly struggle, namely which have the best fitted organization, or instinct (i.e. intellect in man) to gain the day."[67] Darwin expanded this idea in *The Descent of Man* and applied his theory of natural selection to human conflict and warfare. For Darwin, conflict and warfare was an inevitable outcome of the laws of nature. He explained colonial warfare in racial terms; the members of the superior civilized race had the most fitted organization, intellect, and technology, which allowed them to conquer inferior "savage races." While Darwin condemned genocidal warfare, he claimed that "all that we know about savages, or may infer from their traditions and from old monuments . . . show that from the remotest times successful tribes have supplanted other tribes. . . . At the present day civilized nations are everywhere supplanting barbarous nations, excepting where the climate opposes a deadly barrier; and they succeed mainly, though not exclusively, through their arts, which are the products of the intellect. It is, therefore, highly probable that with mankind the intellectual faculties have been mainly and gradually perfected through natural selection."[68] For Darwin, the "arts" included all products of the human intellect, especially technology. By claiming that among savages, "tribes have supplanted other tribes," Darwin asserted that it was natural for humans to colonize and destroy one another. The implication was clear: civilized (white) nations have supplanted barbarous and savage (nonwhite) nations because of their physiological superiority, as manifested in their invention and use of technology. The British were able to conquer spear-wielding "savages" because of their bigger brains and superior tools, and while this was sometimes regrettable, it was simply a form of "natural selection." Thus, Darwin's evolutionary narrative reinforced a number of particulars of Euro-American ideology and made the expansion of the European and American empires seem like the latest development in the inevitable and natural process of the replacement of inferior humans with superior ones. In this regard, Darwin's argument was nearly identical to that of polygenists such as

Nott who believed that it was the destiny of the white race to exterminate all of the other races of the world.[69]

One important difference between Darwin and men like Nott was that Darwin did not believe that racial progress was inevitable and that civilization was inherently good. From the historical examples of Greece and Rome it was clear to Darwin that barbarians could overwhelm advanced civilizations. These civilizations had led their citizens into decadent behavior, according to many commentators, and the same could happen with modern industrial civilization. Indeed, many worried that the technology of modern civilization had insulated civilized humans from the effects of natural selection.[70] This led to the fear that civilized humans were becoming weaker than previous generations, a fear that fueled the eugenics movement and the call from men such as President Theodore Roosevelt for Americans to live "the strenuous life" to maintain the vitality of the nation and the race.

While Darwin speculated about the implications of his arguments for modern society, he passed away before the full flowering of the various forms of social Darwinism that dominated so much of the late nineteenth and early twentieth century. When he died in 1882, Darwin's status and popularity was such that he was buried in Westminster Abbey among the greatest men of modern British history.[71]

Since that time, we have continued to honor Charles Darwin by making his vision of man the toolmaker so widely accepted and repeated that it remains one of the primary aspects of the modern Euro-American worldview. Darwin was an admirable man of great scientific skill, deep thought, and compassion. He was a liberal on the issue of race who believed that nonwhites were closely related to Europeans. At the same time, his work reflected the arrogant assumption of European superiority that was so common among nineteenth-century intellectuals. Like other liberals of his day, he abhorred slavery and the cruel treatment of other races; he even believed that other races could be helped to evolve and improve over time.

However, he did not believe other races were the intellectual or biological equals of Europeans. In *The Descent of Man*, Darwin provided a very convincing narrative of human history and human progress that made European political and social hegemony seem natural and inevitable. European history was the history of civilization driven forward by technology, and it was only natural for Europeans to "supplant barbarous nations" as they expanded their empires around the globe. This narrative of progress assumed that human evolution had only one path and that Europeans had moved the farthest along this path. Darwin's narrative had the effect of making the colonial expansion of technologically "superior" Europeans seem like a natural aspect of human progress. Darwin's man-the-toolmaker argument proved to have a deep influence on the biological sciences and (to a lesser extent) the social sciences. It also provided an important formulation of human nature for historians and fiction writers. Darwin's ideas were reshaped and rearticulated according to new discoveries, disciplinary interests, and changes in ideology, but the narrative that he articulated in *The Descent of Man* still lies at the heart of many Euro-American formulations of human nature.

Chapter 3

The Darwinist Frontier

Roosevelt, Turner, and the Evolution of the West

In his 1900 forward to *The Winning of the West*, historian Theodore Roosevelt—at the time the governor of New York—claimed that the recent Spanish-American War finished "the work begun over a century before by the backwoodsman" by driving "the Spaniard outright from the western world."[1] Roosevelt described the history of the United States in explicitly Darwinist terms, arguing that the backwoodsmen had "won great triumphs for civilization no less than for their own people; yet they won them unwittingly, for they were merely doing as countless other strong young races had done in the long contest carried on for so many thousands of years between the fit and the unfit."[2] Roosevelt was a racial nationalist who believed that war was the way races and nations showed their strength; he asserted that in the Spanish-American War, the United States had shown "no falling off in the vigor and prowess shown by our fighting men."[3] Roosevelt criticized those who opposed war, asserting that "the general opposition to expansion" was the equivalent of opposing "national growth and national greatness."[4] Roosevelt had fought in the Spanish-American War and gained notoriety for his heroic leadership in the decisive Battle of San Juan

Hill.[5] Clearly, he counted himself among the fit Americans who had won "great triumphs for civilization" by defeating the Spanish. In one sense, Roosevelt's description of the war allowed him to trumpet his own heroism and attack his enemies at a crucial point in his political career. However, his writing and public speeches also showed the heartfelt sincerity of Roosevelt's argument: he believed that science had uncovered the basic laws of nature and had shown that violence was the primary path to greatness and virility. With the decadence of overcivilization a constant threat, Roosevelt believed that Anglo-Saxon individuals and nations had to engage in what he called the "strenuous life" of battle and conquest to remain at the top of the hierarchy.[6]

Roosevelt's *The Winning of the West* recounted a history of the United States that reconciled Darwin's narrative of man the toolmaker with previous arguments about American exceptionalism and the supremacy of the white race. Like so many before him, Roosevelt focused on the frontier as the site where European Americans had distinguished themselves from their European predecessors. He represented racial purity, genocidal warfare, and colonial expansion as keys not only to American successes of the past but also to the progress and health of the nation in the present and the future. Roosevelt's reading of American history was widely influential because his military and political exploits brought him into the public eye and increased public interest in his writings. While his influence on later historians was moderate, his influence on popular culture and national identity in the United States was enormous and continues to this day.[7]

Roosevelt grew up in a United States that was defined by conflict and expansion. The Civil War divided the nation from 1861 to 1865, a conflict that reorganized the nation in a number of basic ways and left approximately 600,000 dead. African American slaves were freed in 1865, but the legacy of racism continued unabated into the Reconstruction era and far beyond.[8] The northern system of industrialism won out over the southern agrarian slave economy, and the United States careened headlong toward becoming a major economic and military world power. Giants of American industry such as Andrew Carnegie (iron and steel production) and John D. Rockefeller (oil production) began their major business ventures during the Civil War and had built them into legendary monopolies by the end of the century. Between 1860 and 1900 an immense rail transit system had developed that connected the east and west, a development that allowed eastern producers easier access to the markets of Asia.[9] Steam and electrical power replaced the biological power of humans and horses, industrial production increased exponentially, and the population of the country's urban centers exploded.[10] With widespread industrial development came economic depression, labor riots, and increased class stratification.[11]

In the west, the territories the United States had acquired before the Civil War were rapidly being "settled" by whites, a euphemism that meant the (usually violent) removal or eradication of Native Americans. Many veterans of the Civil War were mobilized to the west for a series of Indian wars against the Sioux, Cheyenne, Comanche, Kiowa, Apache, Crow, and Blackfeet nations, among others. These conflicts led to such infamous events as the Sand Creek massacre in 1864, the Battle of Little Big Horn in 1876, and the Wounded Knee massacre in 1890.[12] When the results of the 1890 census were published in 1891, the frontier was declared closed; "only four territories—Utah, Oklahoma, Arizona, and New Mexico—were awaiting statehood."[13] For many contemporary commentators, the loss of the frontier was directly related to the rise of urban squalor, labor unrest, and social disintegration. The decline of Jefferson's model of the virtuous agrarian democracy and the ascendance of industrialization led to a strong sense of anxiety that was exacerbated by the findings of the 1890 census. Without the safety valve of the frontier to relieve the pressures of urban poverty and immigration, many interpreted the increasing social unrest of the 1880s and 1890s as a sign that the civilized United States was falling into the same trap as its European predecessors. Fears about the loss of the continental frontier eventually fueled calls for colonial expansion overseas.[14]

The seemingly endless conflict and violence of the late nineteenth century shaped the young Roosevelt, and for a generation of Americans he became the embodiment of the new United States that arose at the turn of the century. Roosevelt was born to an aristocratic New

York family on 27 October 1858, and his early childhood was marked by a consciousness of the Civil War. His parents were divided like the nation: his father was a Yankee to the core, while his mother was a southern belle who supported the confederacy. Young Theodore became an ardent patriot on the Union side. From an early age Roosevelt was drawn to the heroism and violence of warfare, and he idolized the wounded veterans who marched with President Lincoln's funeral procession outside his grandfather's mansion in April 1865.[15]

As a youth, Roosevelt was afflicted with asthma and was forced to spend much of his time indoors as an invalid. One of his doctors diagnosed Roosevelt's condition as a product of "overcivilization," which reflected the common belief of the time that the rich and pampered classes were particularly prone to physical ailments. Insulated from nature by their wealth and technologies, people like the Roosevelts were believed to have become relatively soft and decadent.[16] Roosevelt's poor health prevented his parents from sending him to boarding school and he was tutored at home instead.[17] Not surprisingly, the overcivilized young invalid became fascinated with animals and the outdoors.[18] He became an avid reader who expressed a strong interest in natural history from an early age, even going so far as to collect animal specimens for what he called the Roosevelt Museum of Natural History.[19] His father had helped found the American Museum of Natural History, and he encouraged young Theodore in this direction.[20] The elder Roosevelt arranged for his son to take lessons in taxidermy from a man who had worked with Audubon and even used his connections to get his son special access to the unpacking of a famous collection of mounted animals at the museum.[21] Young Roosevelt devoured the writings of Darwin and Huxley and later in life cited them as interesting and enthralling authors whose work statesmen "ought to read."[22] Darwin's idea that the struggle to survive was a productive force in nature provided the key for Roosevelt's nascent philosophy of the strenuous life. As Roosevelt grew older he became a physically disciplined and energetic man of adventure who saw his continual confrontations with nature and his pursuit of martial competition as the remedy for overcivilization.[23] His successful struggle to overcome his asthma and his study of Darwinian evolution provided the core of the philosophy of the strenuous life that he preached for all Americans throughout his later years.

Young Roosevelt continued his studies in natural history at Harvard, where he used the newly created system of electives to take undergraduate courses in botany, zoology, comparative anatomy, and geology.[24] Darwinian arguments were common in these courses, including the implications of Darwin's ideas for the study of history and social stratification.[25] After his freshman year, he published his first work, *The Summer Birds of the Adirondacks* (1877), which was also his first foray into the career he desired as a natural historian.[26] While he eventually abandoned his aspirations of becoming a professional scientist, his writings on history, politics, and human nature were clearly informed by his scientific mindset. He accepted Darwin's arguments implicitly and saw the laws of nature at work in everything from warfare between nations to motherhood.

Nowhere was Roosevelt's Darwinism clearer than in his writing about the frontier, especially *The Winning of the West*. Roosevelt's fascination for the frontier was sparked by reading the works of men such as James Fenimore Cooper as a young man.[27] As an adult he spent time as a cowboy and deputy sheriff on ranches he owned in the Dakotas, an experience that contributed to his lack of sympathy for Native Americans and his glorification of the frontier spirit. Roosevelt published the first volume of *The Winning of the West* in 1889.[28] The first chapter, "The Spread of the English-Speaking Peoples," combined familiar arguments for Anglo-Saxon superiority with Darwin's narrative of progress. Roosevelt's account emphasized violence and what he saw as the superior form of colonization practiced by the English and their American descendents. Roosevelt traced the origins of the English to the ancient "Germans" who held off the Roman onslaught and eventually "went forth from their marshy forests conquering and to conquer."[29] Roosevelt asserted that when the German conquests waned, "their brethren who dwelt along the coasts of the Baltic and the North Atlantic"—a clear reference to the Vikings—took up the sword until all of Europe "in turn bowed to the warlike prowess of the stalwart sons of Odin."[30] The use of terms such as "warlike prowess" and "stalwart sons" showed Roosevelt's admiration for what he saw as the traits of a superior race. Roosevelt's Darwinism led him to value battle as the true test of an individual and a people. He argued that by conquering Europe, the early "kings of Teutonic or Scandinavian blood" showed their fitness.[31] However, he was critical of how they handled their occupation of most of their newly conquered lands.

The problem Roosevelt cited with the German and Nordic conquests was that "the victorious invaders merely intruded themselves among the original and far more numerous owners of the land, ruled over them, and were absorbed by them."[32] Roosevelt implied that this had the effect of thinning their blood: by mixing it with the blood of inferiors, they allowed their superior stock to be swamped by inferior stock. At the same time, the infusion of German and Nordic blood strengthened the stock of those they conquered. The result of this, according to Roosevelt, was that "the mixed races of the south—the Latin nations as they are sometimes called—strengthened by the infusion of northern blood, sprang anew into vigorous life, and became for the time being the leaders of the European world."[33] Such passages demonstrated how Roosevelt used scientific conceptions of race to "explain" European history. He asserted that the hegemony of countries such as France, Spain, and Italy in the Middle Ages and the Renaissance was due to biology: the influx of "northern" blood, the blood of the mighty (and closely related) Teutonic and Nordic races, was what led to the military prowess of southern Europeans. Roosevelt was not concerned here with art or culture; instead, he felt that history was made by violence and aggression, the mastery of strong races over weak races.[34] Superior biology led to military, political, and cultural dominance, and Roosevelt implied that without the addition of German and Nordic blood, the "Latin" nations of Europe would have remained weak and backward.

Roosevelt claimed that the rise of the British empire was also due to biology. Roosevelt asserted that the French and Spanish were "mixed races" of dubious ancestry who had been conquered several times, whereas "the English race, on the contrary, has a perfectly continuous history."[35] The Germanic conquest of England was unique, because instead of allowing themselves to be swamped by inferior races, "the sea-rovers who won England to a great extent actually displaced the native Britons."[36] In Roosevelt's history, the Germans who conquered the European continent had been "absorbed by the subject-races," whereas the Germans who invaded England "slew or drove off or assimilated the original inhabitants."[37] This made the Germanic blood of England purer than that of France and Spain and allowed the English to eventually rise and dominate over their continental rivals. Roosevelt also associated England's ascension to global hegemony with technology: he cited the superiority of English ships in the seventeenth century as the factor that made the difference in England's war with Spain.[38] Like a good Darwinist, Roosevelt associated superior tool use with race; the superior English branch of the Germanic stock produced superior weapons.[39] He argued that those with the purer Germanic and Nordic blood eventually won out over the mixed and diluted blood of their Latin rivals, an argument that explicitly championed the value of genocide and extermination over peaceful cohabitation. Roosevelt clearly believed in the violent aspects of Darwin's theory and showed repeatedly in his public speeches and political positions that he thought war was the only true test of men, nations, and races.

Roosevelt claimed that all of this European history was "not foreign to American history."[40] For Roosevelt, the conquest of America was the greatest and most important instance of "race expansion" the world had ever seen: "It was the crowning and greatest achievement of a series of mighty movements, and it must be taken in connection with them. Its true significance will be lost unless we grasp, however roughly, the past race-history of the nations who took part therein."[41] Roosevelt's race history of America included colonization by England, France, and Spain. For Roosevelt, however, the most important and dominant race that colonized America came from England. Roosevelt considered the United States to be an Anglo-Saxon nation, and he read American history through the lens of this racial ideology. For the future president, the United States was a white nation whose history was explained by racial characteristics. For Roosevelt, the conquest of Native Americans was not only justified but was also a mark of the greatness of the nation.

The key to the success of English colonization for Roosevelt was violence and the ability to maintain racial purity: "It is of vital importance to remember that the English and Spanish conquests in America differed from each other very much as did the original conquests which gave rise to the English and the Spanish nations. The English had exterminated or assimilated the Celts of Britain, and they substantially repeated the process with the Indians of America; although of course in America there was very little, instead of very much, assimilation. The Germanic strain is dominant in the blood of the average Englishman, exactly as the English strain is dominant in the blood of the average American."[42] Here Roosevelt reiterated his racist and Darwinist belief that genocide was a superior way to handle indigenous peoples. While Darwin ultimately believed that the conquered "savages" should be raised up and helped by their conquerors, Roosevelt championed the value of extermination because it had allowed the "Germanic" and "English" strains of blood to remain stronger in those he considered to be average Americans. According to Roosevelt, this contrasted with the Spanish conquests in America, because the Spanish—whom he had already characterized as a mixed race—"simply sat down in the midst of a much more numerous aboriginal population."[43] Roosevelt implied that this led to the thinning of the already-diluted Germanic and Nordic blood of the Spaniards and therefore to the weakening of their racial stock. In Roosevelt's view, this was a lethal mistake: his belief in biological determinism and the inherent traits of specific races led him to condemn the Spanish conquest as a failure. He showed the folly of that conquest by discussing Spain's eventual defeat by the British and the defeat of the Mexican descendents of Spaniards by the relatively pure-blooded Americans. For Roosevelt, the importance of mercilessly seeking conquest and maintaining relatively pure blood was obvious: superior races showed their superiority through conquest, and to allow their blood to become mixed with the blood of inferior races was a way to ensure eventual defeat. Thus, Roosevelt viewed his later participation in the Spanish-American War as the completion of this process of the superior Anglo-Saxons driving the supposedly inferior Spaniards from the Americas once and for all.

Roosevelt did not stop with simply asserting the superiority of the purer Germanic blood of the English and Americans over the mixed blood of their rivals: he also argued for the superiority of the Americans over their English antecedents. Roosevelt represented the English as suffering from overcivilization while he represented the Americans as tough and superior because of their constant battles to survive on the frontier. Roosevelt made this argument in *The Winning of the West* as he discussed the expansion of the United States after the Revolutionary War. According to Roosevelt, "The Americans when they became a nation continued even more successfully the work which they had begun as citizens of the several English colonies."[44] While England had defeated Spain in the global contest for supremacy, "it was under the banner of the American Republic, not under that of the British Monarchy, that the English-speaking people first won vast stretches of land from the descendents of the Spanish conquerors."[45] This was an important distinction for Roosevelt. While he argued that the average American had mostly English blood, he saw Americans as superior colonizers who had distinguished themselves from their colonial forebears. The unique context of the American frontier had brought about changes that distinguished Americans from the English in blood as well as deeds. When discussing American blood, Roosevelt listed infusions from other northern European sources brought by Dutch, German, Irish, and Scandinavian immigrants (in that order of importance). While he contended that these were the same strains that originally combined in England, he implied that the new combination was unique from the strain the English provided.[46] He also downplayed infusions of other blood that were not from northern Europe, dismissing the introduction of African and Indian blood as localized and minimal.[47] The image of Americans that emerged from Roosevelt's history was that of a racially homogenous and dominating people who had made their mark through violence.

The violence of the frontier is an important key for understanding Roosevelt's image of the United States. Roosevelt's history is marked by what Richard Slotkin calls "regeneration through violence."[48] As Roosevelt represented it, Americans overcame the dreaded overcivilization of their English forebears by returning to "an earlier historical 'stage'" in the harsh environment of the frontier; this return regenerated Americans morally, politically, and physically as they struggled to survive under harsh conditions.[49] The Darwinism that informed Roosevelt's argument assumed that social evolution follows one path that progresses from savagery to barbarism to civilization. Roosevelt exhorted his civilized countrymen to maintain some of the virtues of the barbarian—such as violence—in order to regenerate both biologically and socially. Roosevelt argued that by participating in the strenuous life and continuing violent colonial expansion, his fellow Americans could ward off overcivilization and maintain the great traditions of the frontiersmen and the pioneers.[50]

Nostalgic appeals to frontier virtues were becoming increasingly common in a United States that was suffering from widespread social unrest. Appealing to the frontier entailed an implicit critique of contemporary civilization and the problems of urban life. In the context of the end of the Indian wars and a growing nostalgia for frontier life, it is not surprising that Roosevelt's history of the west and subsequent calls for the strenuous life struck a chord with so many Americans. The popular appeal of the frontier was matched by its scholarly appeal among professionals in the field of history. A growing number of historians began to turn their attention to the frontier as a central component of American history and identity in the 1890s. A young contemporary of Roosevelt's named Frederick Jackson Turner did the most to legitimize and institutionalize the study of the frontier in American universities. Turner received his Ph.D. from Johns Hopkins University, which was considered the best program in the nation at the time. The faculty and graduate students there were devoted to professionalizing history as a discipline and sought to incorporate current social theories and more rigorous methodologies into their work.[51] Turner had studied the work of Darwin and his followers as an undergraduate at the University of

Wisconsin and a graduate student at Johns Hopkins. Turner was interested in putting history on a more scientific footing and had incorporated Darwinian arguments into his writing.[52] Turner was also directly influenced by Roosevelt's work: while a graduate student, he reviewed the first two volumes of *The Winning of the West* and praised them as "scientific" and objective. While Turner privately rejected Roosevelt's emphasis on violence and individual heroism, he agreed with Roosevelt's emphasis on the importance of the western United States as the key to understanding American history.[53] Where Roosevelt popularized a Darwinian vision of the American west with a wide audience, Turner's approach made popular imagery and beliefs about the American west central aspects of a respected academic theory.[54]

Turner presented his famous paper on "The Significance of the Frontier in American History" at the annual meeting of the American Historical Association in 1893. This speech eventually became seen as "the most famous address ever delivered by an American historian" because it provided a foundation for the academic study of the American west.[55] Most professional historians still saw the history of the United States primarily through the lens of either European history or the north-south conflict over slavery.[56] In 1893, Turner was an ambitious young professor at the University of Wisconsin trying to promote his field of specialization.[57] His paper argued against the prevailing beliefs that American history was primarily "the development of Germanic germs" or that "the western advance " was "incidental to the slavery struggle."[58] Instead, Turner argued that "American history has been in a large degree the history of the colonization of the Great West."[59] The "germ theory" was a version of Anglo-Saxonism promoted by institutional historians such as Herbert Baxter Adams, a professor Turner had studied under at Johns Hopkins, who argued that American institutions could be explained as developing from their medieval Germanic predecessors.[60] While not discounting the importance of European influences, Turner argued that "too exclusive attention has been paid by institutional students to the Germanic origins, too little to the American factors."[61] For Turner, American history was unique. He felt that American society had evolved like an organism and that the physical environment played a crucial role in the development of American institutions and character.[62] Turner's argument synthesized and integrated much of the anxiety about the vanishing frontier and the growth of industrialism common to the 1880s and 1890s.[63] In Turner's view, the closing of the frontier announced by the 1890 census marked a turning point, and his 1893 essay was suffused with a sense of loss.

The popular imagery and mythology of the frontier was well established in American culture, but Turner was the first to propose a "social science" definition and hypothesis for what it was and how it functioned. Turner defined the frontier as "the meeting point between savagery and civilization."[64] This one phrase showed that Turner accepted the Eurocentric unilinear narrative of social evolution put forward by Darwin and repeated by Roosevelt. This narrative associated the colonizers of European descent with civilization and Native Americans with savagery and the harsh wilderness of the American landscape. Turner quoted Italian economist Achille Loria in asserting that America might even be the perfect case study in social evolution: "Loria . . . has urged the study of colonial life as an aid in understanding the stages of European development. . . . 'America,' he says, 'has the key to the historical enigma which Europe has sought for centuries in vain, and the land which has no history reveals luminously the course of universal history.' There is much truth in this. The United States lies like a huge page in the history of society. Line by line as we read this continental page from West to East we find the record of social evolution."[65] This vision of social evolution went through many stages that Turner laid out in a hierarchical fashion. The upward trajectory of his argument went from the "savagery" of the Indian to the successive phases of traders, ranchers, farmers, and industrial factories. Turner saw this social evolution as both universal and unique. It was universal because American history was an ideal example of the evolutionary progress that had taken place in Europe and other "civilized" parts of the world. It was unique because the physical environment provided by the frontier allowed Americans to evolve into something quite different from their European ancestors.

Turner argued that the nature of the United States was exceptional.[66] For Turner, the struggle with the frontier environment had a powerful effect on Americans, and this struggle made Americans special. According to Turner, "The frontier is the line of most rapid and effective Americanization. The wilderness masters the colonist. It finds him a European in dress, industries, tools, modes of travel, and thought. It takes him from the railroad car and puts him in the birch canoe. It strips off the garments of civilization and arrays him in the hunting shirt and the moccasin. . . . In short, at the frontier the environment is at first too strong for the man. He must accept the conditions which it furnishes, or perish. . . . Little by little he transforms the wilderness, but the outcome is not the old Europe, not simply the development of Germanic germs. . . . The fact is, that here is a new product that is American."[67] In effect, Turner argued that the frontier was at the heart of American identity and institutions. On the frontier, the colonist had to give up the aspects of comfortable civilized European life in order to survive the struggle with savagery. Turner's colonist was the embodiment of this Americanization process. Turner's colonist ventured out into the wilderness and became neither civilized nor savage but rather something uniquely American. This image of the ideal American was adaptive, as the colonist retained only the aspects of civilization that were necessary while learning modes of living from Native Americans in order to survive. Turner's colonist became a mixture of civilization and savagery, embodying the conflict of the frontier itself. By taking on what Roosevelt called the virtues of both the "barbarian" and the civilized man, Turner's frontiersmen and colonists became superior to savages and Europeans in their inevitable march across the continent.[68]

Technology was central to Turner's notions of civilization. "Industries, tools, [and] modes of travel" such as the railroad car were markers of European civilization, whereas the birch canoe of Native Americans was a marker of savagery. In Turner's argument, civilized technology was one of the "disintegrating forces of civilization" that "entered the wilderness."[69] Using the example of the gun, Turner asserted that technology led "primitive Indian life" to pass away.

Turner says that because white traders sold guns to the Indians, they not only stopped living a "primitive" life but also slowed the advance of civilization through their increased military power.[70] Roosevelt had made a similar point in *The Winning of the West*. Roosevelt argued that "when the whites first landed, the superiority and, above all, the novelty of their arms gave them a very great advantage. But the Indians soon became accustomed to the new-comers' weapons and style of warfare. By the time the English had consolidated the Atlantic colonies under their rule, the Indians had become what they have remained ever since, the most formidable savage foes ever encountered by colonists of European stock."[71] Both Turner and Roosevelt employed Darwin's idea of man the toolmaker, emphasizing the role of technology in their arguments about the conflict between the "civilized" Europeans and their "savage foes." Both admired Native Americans for what they saw as their adaptability, especially with regard to technology. While Roosevelt felt that they were technologically inferior, he cited their ability to adapt as the key in their becoming the greatest "savage foes" of all. For Turner, their ability to adapt and use guns made them a major obstacle in the westward migration. While both authors clearly considered Native Americans to be an inferior race, both also saw them as powerful foes and argued that their adaptive character was an important factor in the struggle of whites to survive. Roosevelt and Turner claimed that in order to overcome the challenge presented by these greatest of savage foes, Europeans had to adapt, evolve, and become better than they were before. Through this process of improving, they stopped being Europeans and became Americans. Thus, both Roosevelt and Turner saw racial warfare as a central component in the evolution of European Americans.

Where Cooper's frontier novels of the 1820s and 1830s expressed a sense of loss at the supposed vanishing of Native Americans, Roosevelt and Turner showed no such sympathy. Instead, both Roosevelt and Turner focused on the loss of the white frontiersmen and settlers and their self-reliant lifestyle. Both Roosevelt and Turner had mixed feelings about what they viewed as the social evolution of America. Roosevelt thought that this kind of progress was good but worried that overcivilization might make Americans slothful and decadent like the British. Though Roosevelt was nostalgic for the days of the Wild West, he saw industrialization and modern warfare as positive developments that served the cause of civilization. While he was active in establishing nature preserves and promoting what we would now call environmentalist causes, Roosevelt believed that the American character could continue to develop and progress as long as Americans chose the strenuous life of conflict and toil instead of resting on their laurels. Turner was concerned that the closing of the frontier announced in the census of 1890 had dire consequences for the United States.[72] He worried that the values and characteristics of rural America and the farmer would be replaced by the heartless chaos of industrialization and urban America.[73] Turner saw the frontier as what made America unique; with the frontier gone and the farmer rapidly vanishing in the face of industrialization, he worried that America would now face the social problems that had long plagued Europe.[74]

Turner's essay was widely influential among professional historians and politicians. Roosevelt and Woodrow Wilson—both historians who would later become presidents and fierce political rivals—loved Turner's 1893 essay and became strong advocates of its argument.[75] By the end of the decade, Turner's essay had redefined the study of American history.[76] Turner and his followers went on to train generations of American historians, and to this day his ideas hold great power in the field. Despite their many differences, Turner and Roosevelt reshaped the vision of American history, casting it in the image of Darwin's narrative of human evolution. Together they popularized and institutionalized the Darwinist vision of colonization and racial progress as the central aspect of American identity and history. Idealizing this period of frontier conflict was in part a product of nostalgia: both writers, like many others of their day, felt that America had lost something essential with the closing of the frontier. This nostalgia came to be a hallmark of later frontier narratives that ranged from dimestore cowboy novels to science fiction space operas. The frontier provided authors with a space to criticize the various aspects of industrialization and overcivilization that they saw plaguing the modern world. At the same time, these new frontier narratives naturalized the sentiment that America was successfully colonized by superior Anglo-Saxons. Roosevelt and Turner made the idealized characteristics of ancient Saxons and American frontiersmen seem as though they were manifestations of superior biology. As northern Europeans colonized the Americas, Roosevelt and Turner argued that these characteristics were brought forth and sharpened by the struggle with the wilderness.

CHAPTER 4

DARWIN'S BULLDOGS

EVOLUTION AND THE FUTURE-WAR STORY IN BRITAIN

In 1871, the year Darwin published *The Descent of Man*, another revolutionary text emerged in England that played a major role in shaping the understanding of how humans relate to technology. This text was Sir George Tomkyns Chesney's "The Battle of Dorking: Reminiscences of a Volunteer," a short story that provided the model for what I. F. Clarke refers to as "the tale of the next great war."[1] Chesney's story was published anonymously in the May 1871 issue of *Blackwood's Magazine* just a few months after Darwin's *The Descent of Man* had made such a big sensation.[2] Chesney was probably not familiar with the specific arguments of Darwin's latest work when he was writing his story because he had conceived of "The Battle of Dorking" before *Descent* was published.[3] However, like many other educated men in Great Britain at the time, he was very influenced by the Darwinist accounts of progress, civilization, and conflict that dominated the 1860s.[4] He participated in the Victorian obsession with technology and its impact on warfare, especially colonial conflicts (he was, after all, "a distinguished officer in the Royal Engineers" who worked in the India Office).[5] The American Civil War and the Franco-Prussian War of 1870 revealed the great impact that industrialization was having on warfare: mass-produced weapons and more efficient killing machines like the machine gun made their mark in these wars, as did the ability to organize and transport troops using telegraphs, railroads, and steamships. Reflecting on and extrapolating from these developments, future-war stories such as "The Battle of Dorking" were driven by the fear of being left behind in the race for bigger and better war machines.[6] This fear of technological inferiority was intimately connected to the fear that overcivilization and apathy had made modern nations vulnerable in the ongoing struggle to survive. Drawing on these fears, stories such as "The Battle of Dorking" provided terrible warnings about what might happen if nations such as Great Britain did not remain well armed and vigilant against enemy attack.

"The Battle of Dorking" had a major impact on Europe and the United States, and it served as the template for the future-war story until the outbreak of World War I. Chesney was shocked by the Franco-Prussian War of 1870: the Prussians, who were commonly referred to as Germans, had overwhelmed the highly regarded French military through superior organization, especially in their use of technologies such as telegraphs, railroads, ironclad ships, and breech-loading cannons. Chesney's story encapsulated the fear that Germany might now turn its sights on an England that had failed to modernize its military.[7] Germany's integration of new technologies into its military structure made traditional geographical barriers like the English Channel largely meaningless. The Germans had shown their ability to attack at a moment's notice in the war with the French. The British were fully aware that the Germans could telegraph for troops to board trains that would hurry them to ironclad ships. These ships could then steam the troops into the English Channel with amazing speed, which was precisely what happened in "The Battle of Dorking." Chesney's story detailed this scenario of the not-too-distant future to warn his readers of what could happen if the British did not radically reorganize and update their military to account for these new technologies.[8] England had built its empire in large part on the strength of its navy and had traditionally seen the fleet and the channel as impossible hurdles for would-be invaders. By the time Chesney wrote "The Battle of Dorking," that confidence had significantly eroded. New technologies had made a quick strike across the channel a realistic possibility, and the British were terrified by the prospect of their new vulnerability.[9]

One of Chesney's major innovations was to present the story through the perspective of a middle-class "everyman" narrator, an anonymous member of the Volunteers who had seen the battle first-hand.[10] The Volunteers, who had been created in 1859 to shore up "home defence," consisted mainly of artillery batteries, engineers, and infantry "organized into brigades."[11] As Clarke observes, the use of a Volunteer as the narrator served two important functions: it transformed "the old-style military tract into a vivid narrative" and it provided a critique of the "well-intentioned" but poorly trained Volunteers.[12] This allowed Chesney to show both the heroism of the British and the folly of their system of national defense. The story was narrated from the future, as the old Volunteer told his grandchildren how a war fifty years earlier had led to a series of humiliations at the hands of the Germans. The appeal to national pride was a major aspect of the narrative, and Chesney confronted his readers at the outset with the image of a Great Britain cowed before her conquerors. The great British colonizers had become the colonized, whipped by the Germans into a weak and economically destitute nation. The Volunteer repeatedly lamented what could have been if only the people of Great Britain had heeded the threat that a unified German army posed.

Chesney hammered away at the fears of his British readers through a detailed accounting of how Britain's organizational inefficiency and technological incompetence led to its defeat. The Volunteer spent hours stuck on trains, scrambling for supplies, and complaining about the breakdown in communication between the leaders and the troops. The valor of the troops was ultimately not enough to overcome their lack of organization. The lesson of the Volunteer's story was explicit: the British military needed to be radically reorganized to counter the new German threat. Its failure to reorganize had led to its ignominious defeat. This transparently political lesson made "The Battle of Dorking" read at points like military propaganda and led to harsh criticism from several quarters for months after its initial publication.[13] At the same time, its popularity and notoriety were a clear testament to Chesney's effectiveness in making his points.

One aspect of "The Battle of Dorking" that was singled out for criticism was Chesney's use of a science fiction technique: the mighty British fleet defending the channel was sunk by mysterious new "fatal engines" invented by the Germans, paving the way for the German invasion.[14] While condemned as a weakness in the story, this scene provided another dimension to the theme of German technological superiority. Chesney's "fatal engines" were not as much a flaw as they were an acknowledgement of the importance of new inventions for national defense. The "fatal engines" showed how the British could not keep pace with the Germans in the race for new inventions. The fear of falling behind in an arms race—in which scientists in the laboratories race to provide powerful new weapons for the battlefield—came to dominate military planning and national defense debates. Europeans and Americans still worry that dangerous technologies such as chemical, biological, and nuclear weapons will fall into the hands of our perceived enemies. Chesney's "fatal engines" were merely an early version of technology-centered national security concerns.[15]

After recounting the German victory at Dorking, Chesney put the nationalist thumbscrews to his British readers with his account of the occupation by the German army. Time and again, the gentleman Volunteer evoked middle-class ideals of home, leisure, and family in his narration of the German atrocities. After his retreat from the front lines, the Volunteer awoke wounded and weakened in the home of Travers, his dead friend and comrade in arms. He found Travers's home occupied by a "rough, boorish" pack of Germans feasting on provisions they had taken from the cellar: "occasionally grunting out an observation between the mouthfuls," the Germans insulted the British army, sat with their "very dirty legs on the table," and smoked the "best cigars" of the dead man of the house.[16] Chesney used stereotypes of Germans to underscore both the humiliation of defeat and the necessity of updating the British military. If the British did not reorganize their military right away, Chesney argued, they could end up with dirty Huns as their unwelcome house guests. The Germans thoroughly defiled idealized middle-class British life, not only killing Travers's young son but also menacing his defenseless wife. The behavior of the Germans stigmatized them as the enemy and naturalized the middle-class values they defiled. Grunting during their meals and putting their feet on the dining-room table marked them not simply as enemies but as rude uncultured lower-class Germans. The menacing of Travers's wife served as an additional affront to the Victorian ideal of chastity: Chesney warned that if the British did not update their military, they might not be able to protect the virtue of British women. The demonization of the enemy through narrative was certainly not new in 1871, but it became a central aspect of future-war stories that followed the Chesney model. Whether the enemies were from another nation, another race, or another species, they were drawn as grotesque caricatures designed to play on the fears of the intended audience.

Before 1871, future-war stories were largely confined to pamphlets and satire, focusing on political situations rather than detailing the effects of technological advances on military campaigns.[17] Chesney's story was innovative in a number of ways and was pitched to the right audience at the right time. *Blackwood's Magazine* was a widely read and highly influential middle-class monthly, and the response to Chesney's story was so enormous that its influence quickly extended beyond the magazine's usual middle-class readership.[18] The publication of "The Battle of Dorking" caused an uproar, and by July 1871 over 80,000 copies of a six-penny pamphlet edition had been sold.[19] The reaction was so great that even Prime Minister W. E. Gladstone felt compelled to participate in the months-long debate the story sparked. Gladstone was irritated by the story's "alarmism" and warned his constituents about unnecessarily spending huge amounts of money on defense.[20] With the publicity generated by Gladstone's attack, William Blackwood felt that he could now market the story to "a new class of people" and prepared to release a "people's edition."[21] Reprinted many times in England, translated into several different languages, and marketed in numerous foreign countries (including

Germany, France, and the United States), "The Battle of Dorking" successfully popularized Chesney's new style of future-war story with a wide and diverse audience.[22] The Franco-Prussian War of 1870 had changed the power system in Europe and increased anxieties about war and technology.[23] "The Battle of Dorking" capitalized upon and heightened these anxieties, spawning a host of imitators in the process. Writers throughout the English-speaking world began to produce similar stories with the enemies and plot situations changed to accommodate the nationality and political position of the author. The future-war story quickly became an important part of the modern narrative landscape in the late nineteenth century.

The publication of Darwin's *The Descent of Man* and Chesney's "The Battle of Dorking" within a few months of one another speaks to both the urgency and the shape of the converging fears about race, nationalism, war, and technology in the Victorian period. The industrial age had spawned a horde of new machines and revolutionary ideas that made the foundations of Euro-American civilization seem like shifting sand. Darwin's narrative looked to the past and provided an ideologically palatable argument about European (and Anglo-Saxon) supremacy. While still threatening to some, Darwin's ideas assured many that the "civilized race" rose to preeminence through solid morality, superior intellect, and masterful toolmaking. Colonialism was an ugly business, but Darwin made it seem like a natural and inevitable process of sorting the strong from the weak. Chesney's story provided a warning about the future: if the British did not continue to be vigilant and develop their military capabilities, they would eventually lose the struggle for survival with the other nations of Europe.[24] Evolution had favored Britain thus far, but nobody was invincible. The colonizers could easily become the colonized and the strong could easily become the weak if it did not maintain technological superiority. These two narratives of the past and the future came to form an important nexus in the Euro-American worldview of the late nineteenth century.

For the remainder of what Clarke calls the "first phase" of future-war stories, from 1871 to 1890, British authors tended to follow the

Chesney model of writing short stories for specific purposes.[25] This began to change with improvements in mass literacy and mass media and the simultaneous increase in nationalist sentiment in Europe. In the 1890s there was a surge in the number of periodicals that printed science fiction, and future-war stories following the Chesney model became increasingly prevalent.[26] With the expansion of both the literate audience and the periodical press, longer future-war stories became both possible and profitable in Great Britain in the 1890s. Longer stories could be published serially in a periodical and then reprinted as a book. Future-war stories became increasingly diverse and experimental, though still centering largely on the themes of nationalism and technology.[27] This was the milieu and the moment that produced one of the great writers of modern fiction: Herbert George Wells.

Wells came from a strict working-class English background, and through a mixture of luck, ingenuity, and hard work managed to make himself one of the most prolific and widely respected authors of his era.[28] After escaping a soul-draining apprenticeship with a draper, Wells worked his way into a position at a school and managed to win an award that paid for his further education at the Normal School of Science and Royal School of Mines.[29] The dean of the normal school was none other than "Darwin's Bulldog," naturalist Thomas Henry Huxley, who by the time of Wells's attendance in 1884 was the great man of English science. Wells saw this as a turning point in his life, and he spent his first year at the normal school in Huxley's course on elementary biology. The young Wells could feel the presence of Darwin in the air at the normal school: Wells commented that in the hall where he listened to Huxley's lectures, "Charles Darwin had been wont at times to come through those very curtains from the gallery behind and sit and listen until his friend and ally had done. In my time Darwin had been dead for only a year or so (he died in 1882). These two were very great men."[30] Wells called his first year of study with Huxley "beyond all question, the most educational year of my life."[31] He had been initiated into the Darwinian brotherhood and, inspired by his thorough grounding in evolutionary science from the finest mind of his day, he began to develop ideas that merged his working-class socialist beliefs with Darwinian theory. He also began to write, and for several years after leaving the normal school he struggled to make a living through teaching, journalism, and fiction. This was made more difficult by bouts of ill health and an infamously complicated personal life.[32] Finally, he achieved a stunning success with his publication of *The Time Machine* in 1895. Like all of his early fiction, *The Time Machine* was published serially in popular magazines before being published as a book. This first great "scientific romance" caught the imagination of England and put both his literary reputation and his finances on a solid footing that lasted for the rest of his life.[33]

The combination of evolutionary science and Wells's socialist sensibility was clearly evident from this first novel. *The Time Machine* told the story of the distant future when humans had diverged into two separate species engaged with one another in a struggle for survival.[34] These two species were clearly associated with contemporary Victorian class divisions, and Wells's story provided a Darwinian warning about the dangers of allowing unequal social conditions to remain in place for too long.[35] Wells continued to publish on similar themes with his Darwinian updates of the Frankenstein myth in *The Island of Dr. Moreau* (1896) and *The Invisible Man* (1897). Both of these novels provided detailed explorations of evolution, scientific responsibility, and social marginalization. Wells finally turned to an all-out exploration of future war in 1897 when he published *The War of the Worlds* serially in *Pearson's Magazine* (in England) and *Cosmopolitan* (in the United States).[36] This story was a scientific romance that Clarke calls "the most remarkable fantasy of imaginary warfare that has so far appeared in the history of the genre."[37] It was immediately influential in England and the United States, and within the year similar stories by other authors began to appear in which Martians attacked such cities as New York and Boston.[38]

As in Chesney's "The Battle of Dorking," the narrator of *War of the Worlds* was an unnamed middle-class gentleman who witnessed a not-so-distant future invasion of England. However, the invading race was a dramatic departure from Chesney's Germans. Wells's invaders come from another planet rather than from another country. With death rays, poison-gas cannons, and towering war machines, the Martians easily routed the overmatched British army. The Martians' ability to traverse worlds with their superior technology made the "fatal engines" of Chesney's Germans seem primitive by comparison. Martian superiority placed the nationalism of previous future-war stories in perspective: in the narrator's words, "I felt . . . a sense of dethronement, a persuasion that I was no longer a master, but an animal among the animals, under the Martian heel."[39] The invasion shattered human hubris about being the center of the universe, and the importance of nationalism dissipated.[40] When the Martians were defeated by disease at the conclusion of the narrative, a "commonweal of mankind" arose to replace the petty bickering of national politics.[41] Wells's use of another *species* as the invader created a vision of human solidarity that transcended nationality and race.

At the heart of Wells's attack on nationalism was his extended critique of colonialism.[42] The genesis of the story came from his brother Frank while they were discussing the British "discovery" and massacre of the Tasmanians; Frank thought that it would be interesting to tell a story about men falling from the sky to attack the British, thus putting the British in the position of the Tasmanians.[43] At several points in the novel, Wells attacked the moral justification for subjugating "inferior races."[44] Technological superiority did not provide a Darwinian justification for colonization; in fact, the microbes that brought down the Martians—a parallel to the myriad diseases that plagued British colonials—provided the evolutionary proof that the Martians did not belong on Earth. Wells turned the Darwinian justification for colonization and the global English empire on its head. In the place of national empires and racial divisions, Wells promoted a vision of the globe in which nations were obsolete and all humans were joined by common interest instead of conquest. Wells repeated this narrative in different forms for the remainder of his life.

Wells appealed to middle-class British ideals of domesticity to dramatize the horror of the enemy invasion. However, he used this narrative technique to undermine rather than inflame nationalist sentiment. Where the Germans in "The Battle of Dorking" simply defiled an English home, Wells's Martians completely pulverized a home by crashing a cylinder (their interplanetary vehicle) on top of it.[45] The narrator, trapped in the ruins of an adjacent home, then got an up-close look at the horror of Martian dining. Where Chesney's Germans simply demonstrated poor table manners, Wells's Martians fed off human blood through intravenous transfusions.[46] Using the long mechanical tentacles of one of their machines, the Martians probed the ruins of the home to try to find the narrator, who narrowly escaped becoming a main course in one of the Martians' vampiric feasts.[47] In this way, Wells used middle-class British ideals of domesticity to foreground the sheer horror of the alien invasion: they did not want to take our homes and eat our food, they wanted to flatten our homes and use us as food.

Wells also used his representation of the Martians' bodies to deconstruct the use of cultural and racial stereotypes so common in earlier future-war stories. Like Chesney's ugly-jawed, ill-mannered Germans, the Martians evoked fear and revulsion.[48] In his initial description of the Martians, the narrator focused on their strangeness and foreshadowed their hostile intentions: "Those who have never seen a living Martian can scarcely imagine the strange horror of its appearance. The peculiar V-shaped mouth with its pointed upper lip, the absence of brow ridges, the absence of a chin beneath the wedgelike lower lip, the incessant quivering of this mouth, the Gorgon groups of tentacles . . . above all, the extraordinary intensity of the immense eyes—were at once vital, intense, inhuman, crippled and monstrous. There was something fungoid in the oily brown skin, something in the clumsy deliberation of the tedious movements unspeakably nasty. Even at this first encounter, this first glimpse, I was overcome with disgust and dread."[49] The emphasis on bodily difference—"fungoid . . . oily brown skin," strange "movements," missing "brow ridges"—evoked craniometry and the science of classifying races according to superficial physiological characteristics. Wells's description distanced the Martians from the white middle-class readers of late-nineteenth-century Great Britain and associated them with other "strange" brown-skinned races like the Tasmanians. In this case, however, the colonial tide had turned: it was the British who were the technologically inferior race that was doomed to be conquered and colonized by brown-skinned invaders.

In descriptions of the Martians in the second half of the novel, however, Wells's narrator subtly subverted the initial strangeness of the invaders through a rigorous scientific analysis. This mode of writing must have come easily to a man who had studied under a brilliant comparative anatomist like T. H. Huxley. Using fictional autopsy data, the narrator folded a more in-depth understanding of Martian physiology into his observations. As Frank McConnell noted, the picture of the Martians that emerged was that *they* were *us*: the Martians were modern humans after eons of evolution.[50] Because of their dependence upon technology, the Martians had evolved into "merely heads" who lacked the internal organs of humans that caused so much of the "organic fluctuations of mood and emotion."[51] The Martians were "intellects vast and cool and unsympathetic" who fed by injecting the blood of humans directly into their veins.[52] Ultimately, it was this physical frailty that doomed the Martians: they had no defense against the microbes that live in human blood. Besides their gigantic heads, the only other major aspect of the Martian anatomy was their sixteen "whip-like tentacles" that served as hands.[53] These hands allowed them to manipulate the various machines they used to dominate the British. In essence, the Martians were a distillation of Darwin's man-the-toolmaker argument: through the process of natural selection, all that was left of the Martians' original human-like anatomy was the head and the hands, the parts of the body that Darwin singled out because of their usefulness for inventing and manipulating technology. The technology itself had come to replace the rest of the body; the Martians put on a new body-machine for each task they performed.[54] Their evolutionary trajectory was an extrapolation of Darwin's narrative of human progress and a nightmare vision of machine-driven Victorian society gone horribly wrong.

Wells's representation of the Martians achieved several ends. First, they provided a dire warning of what would happen to humans if we allowed ourselves to become overcivilized. The Martians were products of overcivilization taken to an extreme, and Wells made clear that if humans depended upon modern technology and the comforts of civilization too much we would reach an evolutionary dead end.[55] Second, and more subtly, Wells made human racial and national distinctions appear superficial: even such a strange species as the Martians had a family resemblance to the white middle-class narrator. The narrator's descriptions of the Martians reinforced some problematic notions of biological determinism. However, in the context of the Martian invasion, the evolutionary differences in the human population seemed trivial at best. The narrator learned that androcentrism, narrow evolutionary models, and superficial physiological distinctions not only missed the larger evolutionary picture but also threatened the future of the human species itself. Wells hated the argument that evolution was an inevitable trajectory upward and that progress was somehow built into the process of evolutionary change.[56]

Wells had sympathies with eugenics arguments and worried about the long-term implications of science and technology on the health of the species.[57] However, he was not a technophobe; his ambivalence about technology and progress was deeply rooted in his ambivalence about human nature. Like his American contemporary Theodore Roosevelt, Wells believed that humans have some amount of control over our evolutionary destiny. Roosevelt argued that people and nations must retain some of the virtues of the barbarian and pursue the strenuous life of violence and conquest to ward off overcivilization and evolve along productive lines.[58] Wells went in the opposite direction from Roosevelt to argue that humans were not yet civilized enough: the real danger for Wells was that humans still retained too much of their barbarian nature and needed to overcome their violent tendencies to evolve along more productive lines. As Peter Kemp argues, Wells "became obsessively concerned with the possibility that man may also turn out to be a terminating ape—destroying his own species, unless he can adapt his animal nature to rapidly changing circumstances."[59] While convinced that science could serve as both a guide and salvation, Wells worried that humanity's animal nature might not be able to cope with the power provided by its own intellect.

This worry manifested itself in a series of future-war stories where new technologies caused the collapse of traditional geographical barriers and the destruction of civilization. In these stories, Wells dramatized the struggle of man the toolmaker to overcome his "animal nature." "The Land Ironclads," a short story that first appeared in 1903, explored the potential impact of armored tanks on the existing system of trench warfare. Wells imagined the impact of flying machines on war in his 1908 *The War in the Air*. Finally, on the eve of World War I, Wells completed a story that coined the term "atomic bomb" and provided the first narrative of a nuclear apocalypse. Entitled *The World Set Free*, the story was published serially in *English Review* beginning in 1913 and released as a book in 1914. This story established the scenario in which civilization is destroyed by an exchange of atomic bombs dropped from airplanes. Wells coupled the geography-spanning capabilities of the airplane with the destructive power of atomic bombs in a way that anticipated the dilemmas of the Cold War.[60] It also established the narrative structure that continues to be used to imagine an all-out nuclear war.

While *The World Set Free* was dedicated to chemist Frederick Soddy's *The Interpretation of Radium*, the book began with an evolutionary narrative of human progress that could have come straight from the pages of Darwin's *The Descent of Man*.[61] The entire book was written in the form of a future history; an omniscient voice narrated future events as if they had happened in the past. The narrative voice announced in the opening lines that "the history of mankind is the history of the attainment of external power. Man is the tool-using, fire-making animal. From the outset of his terrestrial career we find him supplementing the natural strength and bodily weapons of a beast by the heat of burning and the rough implement of stone. So he passed beyond the ape."[62] This beginning explicitly evoked Darwin's formulation of man the toolmaker and the idea that human progress could be measured in terms of technology. The connection between human nature and "the attainment of external power" extended Darwin's argument to include such developments as the harnessing of electrical power and the internal combustion engine. Wells asserted that it was this "supplementing of the natural strength" with fire and tools that lifted humans to their lofty position in the animal kingdom above the apes. Wells continued with this narrative of human evolution for several pages, walking the reader through several discoveries and the scientific spirit that led to them.[63] Though Wells rejected the idea that progress was inevitable and was built into human biology, he accepted Darwin's formulation of one line of progress for all humanity. Wells measured what counted as progress—or, later in the text, as regress—using a universal scale of savagery, barbarism, and civilization that was calibrated using Euro-American norms.

The central problem of Wells's future world was the inability of human political and educational institutions to keep pace with the rapid progress of science. Wells condemned government throughout the text, saying that it came from "the rude compromises of relatively barbaric times."[64] While "science and intellectual movement" had progressed immensely in the world of Wells's story, the "world of the lawyer-politician" was hopelessly archaic: "Social organization was still in the barbaric stage."[65] Wells linked this barbarism directly to humanity's animal origins and its struggle to overcome that animal nature. In an early passage Wells commented that "the history of man is not simply the conquest of external power; it is first the conquest of those distrusts and fiercenesses, that self-concentration and intensity of animalism, that tie his hands from taking his inheritance. The ape in us still resents association."[66] The world of Wells's novel displayed an increasing imbalance: scientific progress greatly accelerated while social progress stagnated. The lack of social progress combined with the power of new technologies to form a dangerous mixture. Wells asserted that in order for humanity to save itself, new institutions were needed to control its animal nature by encouraging cooperation rather than extending conflict. However, the barbaric institutions of the past had to be razed before humanity could establish a scientifically based (and fully civilized) social order.

In *The World Set Free*, the rise of "the Age of Energy" brought about the end of what Wells called the "history of the Warring States."[67] Driven by civilized characters Wells called "seekers," one invention after another created the possibility for an incredible improvement in the life of all humanity. The spirit of "the seekers"—those eccentric and curious men who sought after knowledge—provided both the will and the vision necessary for progress.[68] The harnessing of atomic power was the ultimate development that transformed the world of Wells's novel. Coal power, steam power, and electrical power all changed the world, but for Wells the harnessing of the atom promised to set the world free. He made this clear early in the text through a speech by a professor named Rufus. Lecturing on "Radium and Radio-activity" in Edinburgh, Professor Rufus provided the reader with a basic overview of chemistry and radioactive decay (as it was understood at the time Wells was writing).[69] Rufus then put this science within a firmly Darwinian framework, saying that "we stand to-day towards radio-activity exactly as our ancestor stood towards fire before he had learnt to make it. . . . At the climax of that civilization which had its beginning in the hammered flint and the fire-stick of the savage . . . we discover suddenly the possibility of an entirely new civilization."[70] Rufus informed his audience that once humanity mastered this new "fire" of radioactivity, "that perpetual struggle for existence, that perpetual struggle to live on the bare surplus of Nature's energies will cease to be the lot of Man. Man will step from the pinnacle of this civilisation to the beginning of the next."[71] Here Wells spelled out his belief that radioactivity held the key to unlimited energy and that atomic energy had the potential to end the violent and uncomfortable aspects of the Darwinian struggle to survive once and for all. The mastery of radioactivity became the key for the mastery of nature as a whole. Unfortunately, the failure of humanity to tame its own animal nature initially thwarted the promise of this new science. While civilized seekers like Rufus understood the larger importance of radioactivity, the petty and barbaric men who controlled social institutions continued to frustrate the progress of humanity.

The selfish nature endemic in Wells's future world took hold of atomic science. The invention of the first several engines driven by atomic energy led to a series of squabbles over patents, widespread unemployment, and social chaos.[72] The economic systems of the world collapsed and the political systems were unable to cope with the subsequent unrest. Inevitably, Wells's future society spiraled into an all-out war. The quintessential barbaric institution that failed to adapt to the new atomic science was the military. As Wells put it, "No first-class intelligence had been sought to specialize in and work out the problems of warfare with the new appliances and under modern conditions."[73] Through the narration of an everyman soldier named Frederick Barnet, Wells pointed out the complete inadequacy of military leaders and their strategies. Wells reserved especially harsh criticism for trench warfare, which he represented as incredibly stupid in the face of modern technologies such as the "atomic aeroplane" and "motor-guns."[74] When the last war came, Barnet saw firsthand the complete collapse of the military and civilization as a whole. The reason given for this collapse was that "all through the nineteenth and twentieth centuries the amount of energy that men were able to command was continually increasing. Applied to warfare that meant that the power to inflict a blow, the power to destroy, was continually increasing. There was no increase whatever in the ability to escape. Every sort of passive defence, armour, fortifications, and so forth, was being outmastered by this tremendous increase on the destructive side."[75] For Wells, this increasing ability to destroy was particularly dangerous in the hands of a barbaric social institution such as the military and was epitomized by atomic bombs, the ultimate military application of atomic energy. Even though military men had the weapons, they did not understand their strategic importance or even how to use them well. Wells represented the mere fact that such weapons were invented as a sign of the military's barbarism. In "The Last War," Wells commented that "these atomic bombs which science burst upon the world . . . were strange even to the men who used them."[76] The massive devastation caused by these new weapons made war impossible.[77] Unfortunately, in Wells's future world, small-minded military leaders did not figure this out until it was too late.

The military embodied barbarism for Wells because of its devotion to conflict rather than cooperation. Wells labeled the aspect of human nature devoted to physical conflict as "Man the warrior" and characterized it as an animal aspect of human nature that needed to be overcome if humanity was to progress to the next "pinnacle of civilisation."[78] In "The Last War," Wells personified the barbaric nature of the warrior in two characters. The first was a French marshal named Dubois who was the leader of the allies (which included France, England, and "the Slavs") against the "Central European Powers." Marshal Dubois spent his time looking grave and ignoring the suggestions of younger men while ordering pieces around a board in the war room in Paris. When his enemies launched an atomic bomb attack on Paris, Dubois was wiped out along with the heart of his archaic institution. Dubois embodied the outdated military methods that failed to account for new technologies.[79]

The second character associated with the warrior was an unnamed "brutish young aviator" who was "in charge of the French special scientific corps."[80] When he heard about the atomic bombing of Paris, the aviator laughed and ordered an immediate retaliation. Wells's description of the aviator highlighted his barbaric (and even savage) nature:

> He had in his hands the black complement to all those other gifts science was urging upon unregenerate mankind, the gift of destruction, and he was an adventurous rather than a sympathetic type. . . .
>
> He was a dark young man with something negroid about his gleaming face. He smiled like one who is favoured and anticipates great pleasures. There was an exotic richness, a chuckling flavour, about the voice in which he gave his orders, and he pointed his remarks with the long finger of a hand that was hairy and exceptionally big.[81]

Wells's physical description of the aviator's "negroid face" evoked race as a marker of his brutish nature. As did Darwin, Wells linked nonwhite races with a lack of civilization. The aviator's hairy hand and pleasure in destruction demonstrated that he was lower down the evolutionary ladder than the civilized white men such as Wells's seekers. Wells implied that progress was impossible with the "gift of destruction" in the hands of men like this. In fact, survival itself became problematic when barbaric people without sympathy held the ability to use these new atomic bombs. The aviator embodied the darkest part of what Wells saw as humanity's animal nature: the drive for conflict and destruction. With the atomic bomb in their hands, the aviator and the military destroyed entire cities and brought about the collapse of world order.

Before showing the aviator's attack on the Central European Powers, Wells gave his description of the atomic attack on Paris from the point of view of a witness on the ground, a young French secretary. Wells's omniscient narrator described what she saw as the atomic bombs fell on the allied headquarters:

> She crouched together against the masonry and looked up. She saw three black shapes swooping down through the torn clouds, and from a point a little below two of them there had already started curling tails of red. . . .
>
> She felt torn out of the world. There was nothing else in the world but a crimson-purple glare and sound, deafening, all-embracing, continuing sound. Every other light had gone out about her, and against this glare hung slanting walls, pirouetting pillars, projecting fragments of cornices, and a disorderly flight of huge angular sheets of glass.[82]

This description of a flash of light—in this case a "crimson-purple glare"—is now a very familiar metonym for a nuclear explosion. As a sudden disruption of the everyday world, the destructive flash of light served as an ominous doppelganger to the light of enlightenment: the light of the atomic bomb brought with it death and disorder, not progress. The violence of the sudden atomic explosion was so great that it turned buildings into fragments and the noise of the cataclysm left the secretary deaf. In the few minutes before she was swept away by the redirected Seine River, the secretary looked around to find "a ruinous world, a world of heaped broken things."[83] In Wells's narrative, as well as in later nuclear apocalypse narratives, the fragmented cityscape was a symbol of the collapse of the existing social order. For Wells, this destruction was an inevitable result of having the "gifts [of] science" in the hands of brutal men such as the "negroid" French aviator.[84] Ironically, the annihilation brought by the atomic bomb crippled the barbaric institutions that started the war in the first place. In essence, these institutions destroyed themselves, making possible the social progress that came later in the novel. Once the "luminous, radio-active vapour" cleared from the cities and humanity learned the lessons of this final war, a new civilization arose with a more wholesome distribution of population and culture.[85] Wells destroyed Paris and London, centers of the old barbaric social order, out of tragic necessity.

Wells also singled out nationalism as a product of animal human nature that needed to be swept away in the name of progress. Where most future-war stories like Chesney's "The Battle of Dorking" served to inflame nationalist sentiments, Wells saw these sentiments as obsolete in the new world of technologies that had "abolished distance."[86] Telegraphs, "aeroplanes," and atomic bombs had made traditional geographic boundaries and living patterns obsolete. With the power to destroy increasing and the power to defend diminishing, Wells asserted that the only way to ensure human progress was "to have but one government for mankind."[87] In the aftermath of the last war, Wells said that "the only possibilities of the case were either the relapse of mankind to the agricultural barbarism from which it had emerged so painfully or the acceptance of achieved science as the basis of a new social order. The old tendencies of human nature, suspicion, jealousy, particularism and belligerency, were incompatible with the monstrous destructive power of the new appliances the inhuman logic of science had produced. The equilibrium could be restored only by civilization destroying itself down to a level at which modern apparatus could no longer be produced, or by human nature adapting itself and its institutions to the new conditions."[88] Wells mobilized the Darwinist notion of universal social evolution to represent humanity's options. Wells contended that with the old barbaric institutions crippled, human nature had an opportunity to evolve and "adapt" itself to a new higher civilization or fall backward down the path of human evolution. When the world leaders in the text realized this, they accepted the lesson that nations were no longer feasible. In the interest of survival, they formed a unified world government based on the principles of scientific knowledge and common sense. In the utopia that arose, "science . . . is the new king of the world."[89]

The World Set Free was written on the eve of World War I, when tensions between the nations of Europe were reaching a fevered pitch. In one sense, Wells seemed to be imagining that the upcoming war would only be "the prelude to civilization rather than its end."[90] With the collapse of the old order in the novel, the world was set free to build a new global order. The modern state established in the second half of Wells's novel was premised on a mature and civilized approach to atomic technologies: peaceful applications benefited all humans equally and military applications were eliminated altogether. Wells's solution to the problem of human survival in a global atomic age was simple: human nature needed to adapt to account for new technologies and nations had to cease to exist. Wells believed that instead of continually trying to assert the global dominance of local beliefs and desires—as European nations and the United States did during their colonial expansions—a global consciousness needed to emerge to peacefully mitigate and supersede local considerations. However, Wells's model of a global government with "science as the basis of a new social order" was simply another form of European colonization.[91] As a system of knowledge that had arisen and been developed in Europe and its former colonies, the science that Wells glorified was not global in its assumptions and priorities.[92] In Wells's ideal civilization, a few enlightened men made the decisions and English was adopted as the new global language.[93] The scientific conquest of nature was never questioned but rather was glorified as the only logical possibility for the evolution of humanity. While Wells thought of it as progress, it was the progress of a Euro-American Darwinist ideology at the expense of the desires of everyone else. In the paternalistic future of Wells's novel, European conceptions of progress were forced on the peoples of the entire globe for their own good.

Still, it is difficult to overstate both the impact and prescience of *The World Set Free*. Wells anticipated the central problems of the Cold War thirty-two years before the nuclear age began. The preachy and pedestrian tone and the farfetched science of the novel initially muted its impact with a general audience.[94] Still, it went on to be very influential on the nascent world of science fiction in the 1920s and 1930s. The text also had a big influence on one very important reader who gave *The World Set Free* a primary role in developing the actual technologies it predicted. Well-known physicist and Manhattan Project scientist Leo Szilard credited his reading of *The World Set Free* with awakening him to the dangers that atomic science posed to the world. Szilard read the book in German while he was at the Institute of Theoretical Physics in Berlin in 1932.[95] He became particularly alarmed by the fissioning of the atom for the first time in 1938 by a pair of German scientists.[96] Concerned that Hitler would gain possession of an atomic bomb—the term that Wells had coined in *The World Set Free*—Szilard approached Albert Einstein to draft a letter to President Roosevelt. This letter warned the president about the dangers to the world if the Nazis developed an atomic bomb and encouraged him to support Allied scientists in exploring the possibility of creating such a bomb.[97] This 1939 letter was instrumental in the genesis of the Manhattan Project.[98]

Beyond its role in the realization of the atomic bomb, *The World Set Free* provided a narrative framework and set of concerns that would be repeated with increasing frequency for decades. Wells's narrative fused concerns about the atomic bomb with Darwin's vision of human nature; the new atomic technology provided the occasion for larger meditations upon progress and the relative benefits of science. Man the toolmaker now had the ultimate tool within his grasp: with it, he had the power to both destroy the existing world and create a new one. Wells's ambivalence about technology was inseparable from his ambivalence about human nature. In his novel, humanity both destroyed and created, showing his worst fears and greatest hopes about our future. At the same time, Wells uncritically repeated Darwin's assumptions about what constituted progress. Those who were deemed barbaric were vilified and occasionally associated with nonwhite races. Wells's vision of the future was a narrow one, where those he despised were wiped out and those who survived saw the truth of his own ideology. In this way, his text also became a template for future authors. Over the next several decades, nuclear apocalypse narratives provided authors with a convenient way to punish or destroy the aspects of society they saw as undesirable or degraded. At the same time, the blank slate created by the apocalypse allowed authors to recreate the world as they believed it should be. Although the ideologies and agendas changed from author to author, this narrative framework remained extremely compelling for modern audiences, especially in the United States.

Part II

Survival of the Whitest

American Future-War Stories and the Representation of World War II

Chapter 5

Conquering New Frontiers

Burroughs, London, and the Race Wars of the Future

In the United States of the late nineteenth century, the field we now call cultural anthropology began the long process of moving away from racism, biological determinism, and evolutionary explanations for cultural phenomena. Franz Boas was the driving force behind this move. After settling in the United States in the late 1880s, Boas developed his anti-evolutionary methodology through his studies of the Inuit and other Native American peoples.[1] Unlike the Puritans and countless other European immigrants, Boas did not see the cultural and racial differences of Native Americans as signs of their inferiority. He developed an extensive critique of cultural evolutionism and the comparative method that he refined for the rest of his life.[2] In a 1920 article in *American Anthropologist*, Boas summarized his argument that all cultures do not follow the same evolutionary path described by Darwin and other evolutionists. According to Boas,

> The evolutionary point of view presupposes that the course of historical changes in the cultural life of mankind follows definite laws which are applicable everywhere, and which bring it about that cultural development is, in its main lines, the same among all races and all peoples. . . .

> As soon as we admit that the hypothesis of a uniform evolution has to be proved before it can be accepted, the whole structure loses its foundation. . . . On the other hand, it may be recognized that the hypothesis implies the thought that our modern Western European civilization represents the highest cultural development toward which all other more primitive cultural types tend, and that, therefore, retrospectively, we construct an orthogenetic development towards our own modern civilization. It is clear that if we admit that there may be different ultimate and co-existing types of civilization, the hypothesis of one single general line of development cannot be maintained.[3]

Boas pointed out that cultures do not all "progress" in the same direction or in the same manner and that evolutionary arguments like those of Darwin and his followers were based on a Eurocentric assumption of cultural superiority. In place of cultural evolutionism, Boas advocated an anthropology based on empirical observation and the analysis of specific cultures. He believed that cultures were relative to their environments and that one culture was not superior or inferior to another.

Boas also proved that physical characteristics associated with race were heavily influenced by environment. Boas came from a German Jewish family and had experienced discrimination firsthand. He was strongly opposed to racism, especially its impact on anthropology and social theory. In the 1900s, he befriended W. E. B. Du Bois and worked with the National Association for the Advancement of Colored People (NAACP) to fight the belief that African Americans were inherently inferior and incapable of full participation in civilization. In public speeches and articles, Boas stressed that traits and characteristics attributed to the biology of race were in fact products of cultural environment.[4]

Beginning in 1909, Boas began a study that measured the heads of immigrants on Ellis Island. He expanded the study to include measurements of the children of these immigrants born in the United States. After compiling an enormous amount of data, Boas concluded that the environment of the United States led the children to have different-sized heads from those of their parents. In effect, Boas proved empirically that head shape—one of the prized markers of racial difference among anthropologists—was actually variable and therefore an unreliable measure of permanent human differences. This was an important step in moving the field of anthropology toward the modern understanding that race cannot be quantified: physical characteristics thought to be markers of racial difference are widely variable within and across human groups. Race is not a permanent and unchanging aspect of human physiology. Race is simply a powerful social myth about human difference.[5] By the 1930s, the methods and approaches of Boas and his followers had come to dominate the field of cultural anthropology, supplanting the racial Darwinism of their predecessors.[6]

Unfortunately, most white authors, scholars, and policymakers in the United States maintained a strong sense of racial determinism during the early twentieth century, despite the work of Boas and his allies.[7] Even the field of physical anthropology held on to the polygenist formulation of race until the 1950s.[8] The travelogue was one major vehicle for reinforcing racial determinism and Darwinist notions of social evolution. It had become a popular staple of scientific writing during the successive waves of European colonial expansion. In the nineteenth century, texts such as Darwin's *The Voyage of the Beagle* (1839) had presented a scientific point of view on the "savage" peoples and cultures of the world to a Euro-American audience. With the narration of scientific explorers such as Darwin, readers were treated to adventures along new frontiers that were also educational. Extensive descriptions of the flora, fauna, and societies of the frontier provided readers an armchair experience of exploration while teaching them about the latest scientific theories and discoveries.

While Boas was fomenting a revolution in the study of human cultures, magazines such as *National Geographic* used the travelogue to perpetuate the popular notion that societies evolved along only one path. In the 1890s and 1900s, the National Geographic Society began to use the travelogue as a part of its mission to support scientific research and popularize scientific knowledge. Gentlemanly amateurs ran the National Geographic Society in the early years, and they were out of touch with advances in the study of nonwestern cultures made by professionals such as Boas. The society and its magazine tried to maintain the traditional notion of natural history that encompassed the diverging fields of anthropology, biology, geography, and geology. At a time when magazines were an important part of white middle-class American life, *National Geographic* became one of the most popular monthlies in the country. Using accessible prose, adventurous narratives, and gripping pictures of "primitive" life, it straddled the line between the scientific and the popular. The acquisition of a number of new territories after the 1898 war with Spain sparked an upsurge of interest in nonwestern cultures, and publications such as *National Geographic* stepped in to feed its American audience a steady diet of stories and images that reinforced the notion that the United States was culturally superior to the backward peoples of the world.[9]

The popularity of the travelogue also led to the popularity of "imaginary voyage" stories in Euro-American culture. One of the earliest and most popular of these was Jonathan Swift's *Gulliver's Travels* (1726), a fictional travelogue that lampooned scientific institutions and told of mysterious lands with strange new races. Jules Verne, the great French novelist, made a career in the late nineteenth century out of his series of fictional "extraordinary voyage" stories that extolled the virtues of scientific progress and exploration. Verne's novels such as *A Journey to the Centre of the Earth* (1863) and *From the Earth to the Moon* (1865) were popular throughout Europe and the United States and helped establish the travelogue as one of the primary modes of science fiction writing.[10] The science fiction travelogue became commonplace in American pulp magazines of the 1910s, a development that was not surprising given the nostalgia for frontier life and the popularity of *National Geographic* in the 1900s. The science fiction travelogue presented readers with exotic new frontiers and exciting adventures that extolled the virtues of civilized heroes in the face of savagery.

Edgar Rice Burroughs was the most well known and influential author of science fiction travelogues during the 1910s and 1920s. His John Carter stories focused on the adventures of a white hero who traveled to the new frontier of Mars. In these stories (and in his more popular Tarzan stories), Burroughs combined the travelogue with its colonial cousin, the captivity narrative. Beginning with the Puritans in the late seventeenth century, captivity narratives told the story of white Christians who were captured by "savages." Forced to confront the moral and physical horrors of captivity, the protagonists in the stories were transformed and revitalized by their struggle to overcome savagery.[11] Captivity narratives presented conflict as the primary mode of frontier life, with the savages serving as the embodiment of depravity that had to be overcome and destroyed. Burroughs published his first John Carter story, "Under the Moons of Mars," in the February 1912 issue of *All Story* magazine; the story was published serially over several months and was released as a book in 1917 under the title *A Princess of Mars*. Later that year, Burroughs published his first Tarzan story in the same magazine.[12] The success of these stories led to numerous sequels over the years, making Burroughs and his characters household names.

The frontier nature of the John Carter stories became clear in the opening chapter of *A Princess of Mars*. Burroughs described Carter as a heavily decorated Indian fighter and Confederate veteran of the Civil War. After the war, Carter went to Arizona with a fellow veteran and Indian fighter named Powell in search of gold. After finding a rich vein, Powell fell victim to a band of Apaches as he made his way back to civilization to file the claim. Burroughs drew on a number of stereotypes and slurs in his descriptions of the Apaches, calling them everything from "red warriors" to "savages" and "red rascals."[13] He asserted that the Apaches "wished to capture Powell alive for the fiendish pleasure of the torture," repeating the common belief that savages took joy in the pain of others.[14] After retrieving Powell's dead body from the Apache camp, Carter fled into a cave filled with a mysterious mist that knocked him out and transported him to Mars. Once on Mars, Carter immediately came into contact with six-limbed green Martians. At this point in the narrative, Burroughs switched into the combination of travelogue, captivity narrative, and violent action that characterized most of his writing. As in earlier frontier stories in the vein of James Fenimore Cooper's *The Last of the Mohicans* (1826), the white hero John Carter had to take on the virtues of both savagery and civilization in order to survive the violence of frontier life. Like that of Cooper's Hawkeye character, Carter's experience on the frontier was defined by his violent conflict with "savages," whether they were the Apaches of Earth or the green men of Mars.

Burroughs's travelogue description of Mars was a racial Darwinist projection of Earth's future. The resources of Mars had become scarce because the planet was farther along in its evolution. This had triggered a struggle for survival that had led the civilized Martians to become much more rugged and practical. The savage nature of Martian life was epitomized by the fact that all the people there were naked, including John Carter. Savage and naked green Martians known as the Tharks took Carter prisoner, and he quickly learned their customs and gained their respect because the weakness of gravity on Mars gave him exceptional strength. Burroughs described the society of the green Martians in elaborate detail and characterized them as "a nomadic race without high intellectual development."[15] The green Martians fulfilled the stereotype of the savage in every particular: they gained social status through violence, took amusement from the torture of others, and refused to engage in cultivating the land. They also lacked a written language, had no appreciation of art, and showed few signs of technological development. What few advanced technologies they had—like guns that fired radium bullets—were handcrafted by Thark artisans and were not manufactured through any kind of industrial process. The savagery of the green Martians was highlighted by the fact that they inhabited the ruined cities of an ancient and highly advanced race. When Carter finally saw a mural depicting members of the ancient race, he realized that they were exactly like the white race of Earth: "These were of people like myself. . . . The scenes depicted for the most part, a fair-skinned, fair-haired people at play."[16] Burroughs's image of this ancient race showed that Mars had followed the same evolutionary path as that of Earth. Burroughs represented the whites as the most civilized race, and like the humans in Darwinist frontier narratives, these white Martians had to give up some of their civilization in order to survive under harsh new conditions.

In *A Princess of Mars*, the green Martians represented the descendents of the white Martians who had gone completely savage in the struggle for survival. The red Martians represented those who had taken the higher road of trying to maintain civilization, and they retained the physical likeness of their ancestors. Carter met his first red Martian when the savage Tharks took a princess named Dejah Thoris prisoner. Carter immediately felt attracted to her civilized nature. Of course, as in all captivity narratives, the princess was threatened with rape and torture by the leader of the Tharks. Aided by the one noble Thark, Tars Tarkas, Carter repeatedly saved the princess and taught the Tharks the meaning of friendship. However, even this friendship was limited by Burroughs's insistence that race drives behavior. As was the character Chingachgook in *The Last of the Mohicans*, Tars Tarkas is presented as a noble exception to the depravity of his race. Despite his noble characteristics, Tars Tarkas took pleasure in battle and the suffering of others. The "friendship" that he learned from Carter was based on violence: they had fought side by side so many times that they had come to trust each other. Compared to the red Martians, Tars Tarkas was still a depraved monster who could not appreciate art, write his language, or understand complicated technology. Tars Tarkas was simply the savage sidekick, the noble chief who helped the white hero get the girl and protect the interests of civilization. The red Martians were the caretakers of the planet who used their advanced technology to promote agriculture and replenish the Martian atmosphere. Burroughs made clear that the red Martians of the city of Helium maintained the "higher" sensibilities of the ancient white Martians: they felt love and sympathy for others, appreciated art, and embodied physical beauty (especially in their women). At the same time, they were not as cultured as the ancient white Martians, who, Burroughs implied, were overcivilized. Because of the ferocity of their struggle to survive against the green Martians, the red Martians had developed a "practical civilization" that was constantly revitalizing itself through conflict with the savages.[17] The red Martian society of Helium was the American ideal: it was in a permanent state of frontier struggle, nobly advancing science and culture without becoming overcivilized.

Throughout the eleven John Carter novels, the protagonist expressed a strong affinity for the rugged and adventurous frontier life of Mars. When he returned to Earth, Carter longed to return to Mars and the "practical civilization" of the red Martians. This nostalgic desire to return to the frontier became increasingly common in the twentieth century; as in the nineteenth century, the frontier served as an imagined space from which one could criticize and escape from modern urban life. Burroughs used the Martian landscape to extend the idealized vision of the American frontier into the future. Driven by racial conflict over scarce resources, white men like Carter could once again distinguish themselves through heroic deeds against a savage enemy. This brand of racial Darwinism dominated frontier narratives of the early twentieth century. In these narratives, white heroes engaged in racial conflicts that either killed or dominated other "less advanced" races. Indeed, narratives of racial conflict permeated American culture as a whole during this period. In the 1900s, the United States had a president who wholeheartedly championed explanations for human behavior that were grounded in racist evolutionary science. Under the influence of President Theodore Roosevelt and Frederick Jackson Turner, the field of American history became dominated by the Darwinist narrative of man the toolmaker and the worldview that U.S. history demonstrated universal evolutionary principles in action. Even worse, Southern Democrat Woodrow Wilson won the election for president in 1912. Despite his successful appeal to African Americans for their votes, Wilson began the widespread segregation of federal institutions in Washington, D.C., and "implemented a plan to systematically phase out African Americans from most federal and civil positions."[18]

Wilson's racist policies were mirrored in the first commercially successful feature film, D. W. Griffith's masterpiece of white supremacy, *The Birth of a Nation* (1915). The film, which represented itself as an "historical facsimile" of true events, dramatized how the Ku Klux Klan supposedly saved the south from the chaos of "negro" rule after the Civil War. The film used pro-Klan quotes from Wilson's *A History of the American People* (1902) to add to its illusion of legitimacy.[19] Unfortunately, Griffith's film was a technical masterpiece that became one of the most celebrated and influential films in history. The film presented a vision of racial conflict that was consistent with the arguments of racial Darwinists like Roosevelt and Burroughs. It also subscribed to a worldview identical to that of racial radicals, who were a major force in southern politics from 1889 to 1915. For Griffith and racial radicals, nonwhites were untrustworthy savages who should not be allowed to move freely about the United States. Instead, they believed, nonwhites needed to be rigorously policed and kept in their place.[20] *The Birth of a Nation* portrayed black men as the main threat to American civilization: a number of scenes showed black men behaving like lust-crazed beasts as they attacked white women. At one point, the men of a few white families prepared to kill their wives and daughters instead of allowing them to fall into the hands of a wild mob of "negro soldiers." The cavalry of the Ku Klux Klan rode in to save the families from the soldiers and in doing so preserved the sanctity of white womanhood and their "Aryan birthright" as the rulers of America. The "birth of a nation" in the film was actually the reunion of the whites of the north and south. Divided by the Civil War (which was fought in the first part of the film), the white men from the north and south joined together in their struggle against the injustices perpetuated by blacks. Grossly distorting history and portraying blacks as subhuman villains, the film promoted white racial solidarity and the violent suppression of African Americans as the foundation for a new nationalism.

During the 1910s, the once-defunct Ku Klux Klan saw a major increase in membership and organization. The revitalized Klan played a leading role in the growing wave of lynchings that swept across the country. *The Birth of a Nation*'s heroic representation of the Klan garnered widespread sympathy and support for their terrorist activities. The film also served as a Klan rallying point. Hooded horsemen in Klan regalia rode through towns to publicize and celebrate its opening; 25,000 Klansmen rode through the center of Atlanta for *The Birth of a Nation*'s premiere in that city in 1915.[21] Wilson's moves to segregate the government and tighten the hold of Jim Crow policies demonstrated that virulent white supremacy had support at the highest levels of government. With "historical" films like *The Birth of a Nation* trumpeting the president's support of the Ku Klux Klan, the United States seemed to be growing more hostile toward nonwhites with each passing year.

A number of future-war stories at the turn of the century took up the notion that white America needed to protect itself against nonwhite hordes with violence. Beginning in 1880, a number of future-war stories in the mode of Chesney's "The Battle of Dorking" started to appear in the United States. These stories frequently warned of a "black peril" or a "yellow peril"; in these stories, the descendents of Africans or Asians rose up in support of an invasion of the United States from their ancestral homeland.[22] Fueled by fear and hatred of racial "others," these future-war stories dramatized the heroism of civilized whites in the face of savagery. Darwinist ideas about race and progress had an enormous impact on the shape of these stories, just as these ideas had shaped American historiography. At the turn of the century, Jack London emerged as a leading voice in the call for vigilance against racial others, especially the Asians that he openly despised.

London was the most popular author from the period in American literature known as American Realism or Naturalism. As a young man, he had read the works of Darwin, T. H. Huxley, and Herbert Spencer and these early influences had left a clear imprint on his writing.[23] Along with writers like Stephen Crane, Frank Norris, and Henry James, London was strongly influenced by Darwin's arguments about natural selection, sexual selection, and the animality of human nature.[24] Making a name for himself with his dog stories such as *The Call of the Wild* (1903) and *White Fang* (1906), London was a fiction writer, reporter, and social commentator who gained a wide audience. As did earlier American authors and his contemporaries in the field of history, he located much of his writing on the frontier.[25] London's frontier writing and commentaries on race expressed a Darwinism that was similar to that of Roosevelt; in his worldview, violent conflict was paramount in establishing the superiority of individuals and groups.

London traveled extensively along various frontiers writing essays, news articles, and short stories based on his experiences. After the publication of *The Call of the Wild* cemented his literary reputation, London traveled to Japan and Korea in 1904 as a correspondent for William Randolph Hearst's *San Francisco Examiner* to cover the

Russo-Japanese War. London became alarmed by what he saw as he traveled with the Japanese army, noting its efficiency as it defeated the Russians. London was a firm believer in evolutionary arguments about race, yet in his correspondence and articles from the Russo-Japanese War, London often praised the characteristics of the Chinese and Japanese.[26] As Andrew J. Furer shows, however, this praise was a sign of an "anxious xenophobia" by which London seemed to be sizing up a people he saw as an enemy.[27] While London was able to travel only with the Japanese army, his sympathies were clearly with the Russians. Though he referred to the Russians as "Slavs" and therefore did not consider them a part of his own Anglo-Saxon race, London lamented their defeat.[28] In the Russians, London saw what might happen to his own Anglo-Saxon race if it did not heed the threat posed by the Japanese military. In one telling article written in Manchuria following a Japanese victory, London developed this theme through his description of some Russian soldiers being held prisoner:

> There was a man, a white man, with blue eyes, looking at me. He was dirty and unkempt. He had been through a fierce battle. But his eyes were bluer than mine and his skin was as white.
>
> And there were other white men in there with him—many white men. I caught myself gasping. A choking sensation was in my throat. These men were my kind. I found myself suddenly and sharply aware that I was an alien amongst these brown men who peered through the window with me. And I felt myself strangely at one with those other men behind the window—felt that my place was there inside with them in their captivity, rather than outside in freedom amongst aliens.[29]

London used standard markers of race—skin color and eye color—to make a connection between the defeated Russians, himself, and his assumed audience of white readers. While London considered his own Anglo-Saxon race to be distinct from the "Slavic" Russians, he considered the Russians to be white and of his own kind when compared to the Japanese. London was haunted by the images of the white Russians suffering under the heel of the victorious Japanese. While he did not explicitly spell out what this might mean for white America in this article, London commented in a letter later that month that "in the past I have preached the Economic Yellow Peril; henceforth I shall preach the Militant Yellow Peril."[30]

In September of 1904, London published the first of several writings on this supposed threat. Entitled simply "The Yellow Peril" and published in Hearst's *San Francisco Examiner*, London did his best to awaken white America to what he saw as the serious danger that the modernized Japanese military posed to the United States. The notion of a "yellow peril" had existed since at least the 1840s and was largely the product of the emerging news media's sensationalized treatment of older cultural stereotypes. Mixed into this fear of an Asian threat was the cultural memory of Mongol campaigns in Europe in the thirteenth century, the first extensively documented contact between Asians and Europeans.[31] Waves of immigrants from China and Japan to the western United States in the late nineteenth century were met by anti-Asian campaigns led by white workers' unions. However, most of the yellow peril arguments were based on economics, not military security.[32] London's comment that he was shifting his focus from "the Economic Yellow Peril" to the "Militant Yellow Peril" indicated that he was an advocate of both arguments. Whether focused on economics or military issues, all "yellow peril" arguments were grounded in the belief that there were inherent and immutable differences between the races.

In "The Yellow Peril," London described his experiences traveling through Korea and China with the Japanese army and used them as a basis for a larger argument about racial characteristics. London began the essay by assailing Koreans, who he saw as "the perfect type of inefficiency—of utter worthlessness."[33] London asserted that "war is to-day the final arbiter in the affairs of men, and it is as yet the final test of the worthwhileness of peoples. Tested thus, the Korean fails."[34] This view of warfare was characteristic of the violent Darwinism popular in the 1900s that President Roosevelt championed. London believed that "superior" races would conquer "inferior" races in what Darwin referred to as "the final arbitrament of the battle for life."[35] For London and Roosevelt, race was a primary evolutionary category that divided humanity into groups and drove them into conflict with one another. In this view, warfare was not simply a manifestation of cultural or political differences between nations but a part of the larger biological struggle between distinct racial groups for survival. London understood warfare as natural and inevitable and held that those who win at war are superior. Therefore, when London witnessed the flight of the Koreans into the hills in the face of the advancing Japanese army, he did not interpret it as an effective survival strategy that allowed the Koreans to live (and reproduce) another day. Instead, he interpreted this flight as a marker of the Koreans' cowardice and "worthlessness."

London argued that compared to the Koreans, both the Chinese and the Japanese were far more "worthwhile" and fit. In fact, it seemed to be their fitness for survival (as London conceived of it) that worried him. The Koreans obviously did not pose a threat to the white world; they ran and hid in the face of a military force. However, to London, the fearlessness and industriousness of the Chinese and the military discipline of the Japanese was quite a different story. For London, these traits made both the Chinese and the Japanese capable of entering the modern industrial world on a level almost equal to that of the whites. London focused on technology as the key for human success in the struggle to survive. London argued that although China had both the population and natural resources to become a modern world power, "originality and enterprise have been suppressed in the Chinese for scores of generations" by their "governing scholars."[36] London feared that Japan, which had a small population and limited natural resources, would take over and organize China. Referring to the Japanese as "brown" and the Chinese as "yellow," London asserted that "the menace to the Western world lies, not in the little brown man, but in the four hundred millions of yellow men should the little brown man undertake their management."[37] London predicted that the "scientific and modern" Japanese would organize the Chinese so that they would engage in an expansionist "race adventure" of the same type as the one the Anglo-Saxons had made.[38]

In 1906, London wrote a future-war story based on this scenario entitled "The Unparalleled Invasion." The story, which was published in the July 1910 issue of *McClure's Magazine*, incorporated several phrases and passages from his "Yellow Peril" essay with only minor modifications.[39] These repeated passages formed the foundation for London's racial Darwinist argument. London argued in "The Unparalleled Invasion" that the attempts of western nations to arouse China and bring it into the industrial age had failed because "the fabrics of their minds were woven from totally different stuffs."[40] In London's future-war scenario, the Japanese succeeded where white westerners had failed because the Japanese and Chinese "were brothers. Long ago one had borrowed the other's written language, and, untold generations before that, they had diverged from the common Mongol stock. There had been changes, differentiations brought about by diverse conditions and infusions of other blood; but down at the bottom of their beings, twisted into the fibers of them, was a heritage in common, a sameness in kind that time had not obliterated."[41] This passage, which was nearly identical to one in "The Yellow Peril," articulated London's belief that race determined human thought patterns and behavior. The racial character of the mind, according to London, made the Japanese able to communicate with the Chinese in a way that whites never could. Evoking blood and evolutionary heritage, London cast cultural differences as biologically determined differences that could never be overcome. By making cultural barriers into insurmountable biological barriers, London attempted to justify his belief that conflict was inevitable in the struggle of races to survive and expand.

In "The Yellow Peril" and "The Unparalleled Invasion," London represented Japan's openness to what he characterized as white science and technology as the primary threat to the United States. London accepted the argument that Europeans and their descendents were adept modern toolmakers and that all other races were less evolved because of their limited technological ability. He made this clear in "The Yellow Peril" when he talked about the Japanese being "equipped with the finest machines and systems of destruction the Caucasian mind has devised."[42] London implied that modern technology was solely the product of "the Caucasian mind" and assumed that before contact with whites the Japanese had no technologies of note. London also called the Japanese "an apt imitator of Western material progress," implying that they were incapable of any significant invention and innovation on their own.[43] London accepted Darwin's association of imitation with lower intelligence and a less evolved mind.[44] He ignored the long history of science in cultures around the world, like the Chinese science that produced a number of insights and inventions that were later adapted by European cultures (for example, that essential military technology, gunpowder).[45]

London's assertion that Japan learned from "the West" seemed to contradict his belief that essential racial differences prevented the exchange of ideas. London dismissed this contradiction with another reference to biology: "Now the Japanese race was the freak and paradox among Eastern people. In some strange way Japan was receptive to all the West had to offer. Japan swiftly assimilated the Western ideas, and digested them, and so capably applied them that she suddenly burst forth, full-panoplied, a world-power. There is no explaining this peculiar openness of Japan to the alien culture of the West. As well might be explained any biological sport in the animal kingdom."[46] London attributed the Japanese ability to learn from "the West" to a random biological mutation. The inadequacy of this explanation in the face of contradictory evidence demonstrated how deeply London was committed to the man-the-toolmaker mythology and racial explanations for behavior.

In "The Unparalleled Invasion," Japan helped China mimic western science and technology in a way that enabled it to exploit its abundance of natural resources, such as iron, coal, and the Chinese obsession with hard work.[47] Japan also helped China to build elaborate systems of canals, factories, telegraphs, and railroads. China became a military threat through its organized management and use of technology and moved to challenge the dominance of the white nations of the world. London claimed that despite its mastery of "Western" technologies, the real threat China posed to the world—its ultimate weapon, if you will—was "the fecundity of her loins."[48] Aided by their new modern infrastructure, the Chinese in "The Unparalleled Invasion" began to outbreed the rest of the world. London's use of breeding-driven expansion played on contemporary American fears about

Asian immigration. In London's hands, immigration became a military weapon that was fueled by China's mastery of technology. With its growing population, China organized mass immigrations to other countries to begin its unique form of conquest. Rather than using military might, the Chinese simply flooded their neighbors with bodies. In London's words, "The process was simple. First came the Chinese immigration (or, rather, it was already there, having come there slowly and insidiously during the previous years). Next came the clash at arms and the brushing away of all opposition by a monster army of militia-soldiers, followed by their families and household baggage. And finally came their settling down as colonists in the conquered territory."[49] London drew on the dominant version of the yellow peril from nineteenth-century America, where Chinese immigration was seen as a threat to Anglo-Saxon jobs and culture. London represented China as an overwhelming mass of primitive flesh, not a highly civilized and technologically sophisticated modern nation. The argument of London's future-war story was consistent with the rampant anti-Asian bigotry of his time. London's use of immigration was particularly contemptible, as the haphazard and decentralized process it actually was became a highly organized tactic in China's strategy for world mastery in his story. In effect, this story was fanning the flames of race hatred that already had led to numerous anti-Asian immigration laws and countless acts of anti-Asian violence in the United States.

When he tabulated the population of China versus the populations of the "white-skinned" world in "The Unparalleled Invasion," London counted European nations such as England, Germany, France, and Italy among the "white-skinned." However, he also included Canada, New Zealand, Australia, South Africa, and the United States in this list.[50] For most twenty-first-century readers, this list of "white-skinned" nations seems absurd: the people in power in these nations were white, but their entire populations certainly were not. This conflation of nation and race, where nations were seen as subsets of racial groups instead of as political and cultural entities, was common for Darwinists such as London. Just like Roosevelt and Turner before him, London saw the expansion of the United States—and, in this case, of China—in racial terms. When the white nations of the world joined together to fight the Chinese in his story, London described the war as "ultramodern war, twentieth century war, the war of the scientist and the laboratory."[51] In order to stop the methodical advance of the Chinese, an American scientist named Jacobus Laningdale approached the president with the idea of dropping plagues in glass vials from airplanes. The white allies adopted this plan for biological warfare and eventually succeeded in exterminating the entire Chinese population.[52] Thus, the Chinese were obliterated from the earth by a new type of war, "the war of Jacobus Laningdale."[53] As the hero of this modern war, the scientist Laningdale preserved Caucasian world dominance by destroying the yellow peril. This conclusion to the war preserved London's conception of the natural order: the Caucasian scientist became the ultimate Darwinian toolmaker, inventing a new weapon that destroyed the uninventive Mongols. As a result of this mastery of invention, the whites were able to continue their colonial expansion around the globe. The resolution of London's race war was genocide, which he clearly represented as a desirable and natural result of racial conflict.

The story concluded with the settling of the new frontier that had opened up with the elimination of the Chinese. The settlement, of course, was modeled on "the democratic American program."[54] With large stretches of land depopulated by a powerful new weapon, those who survived were able to explore and settle the new frontier that emerged. London's story celebrated this new frontier, and his evolutionary struggle between races for world mastery ended in the same genocidal mode as the earlier Anglo-Saxon colonization of the United States. London elevated scientists and inventors to the status of evolutionary heroes and champions of their race.

Despite the efforts of anthropologists such as Boas to contest racial Darwinism, racial intolerance remained deeply entrenched in the United States of the early twentieth century. Segregationist and exclusionist policies based on racist assumptions flourished, and stories about racial conflict became increasingly popular. While the United States continued to expand its colonial influence, popular stories like those published in *National Geographic* continued to present racial hierarchies and cultural evolutionism as natural facts. Authors such as Burroughs and London created white heroes who distinguished themselves as champions of civilization against racially inferior savages. Their heroes of the future were racial heroes whose mastery of technology made them masters of the frontier. In the years leading up to World War II, a growing number of European Americans saw themselves as embattled masters of evolution ready to wage war against the black and yellow peril.

CHAPTER 6

THE YELLOW PERIL

SCIENCE FICTION AND THE RESPONSE TO THE PACIFIC WAR

At the beginning of World War II, Lieutenant General John L. DeWitt argued that the United States should treat people of Japanese ancestry with suspicion because of their race. As the head of the Western Defense Command, DeWitt was in charge of the security of the West Coast. DeWitt wrote to Secretary of War Henry L. Stimson in early 1942 that "in the war in which we are now engaged racial affinities are not severed by migration. The Japanese race is an enemy race and while many second and third generation Japanese born on United States soil . . . have become 'Americanized,' the racial strains are undiluted. . . . It, therefore, follows that along the vital Pacific Coast over 112,000 potential enemies, of Japanese extraction, are at large today."[1] DeWitt believed strongly that race determined behavior and accepted the stereotype that Asians were untrustworthy. DeWitt's racism, which was shared by a large number of Americans, formed the basis for his orders to intern all Japanese Americans living near the West Coast of the United States. A year later, when DeWitt was asked about his relatively favorable treatment of German Americans and Italian Americans during testimony before Congress, he replied,

"You needn't worry about the Italians at all except in certain cases. Also, the same for the Germans except in individual cases. But we must worry about the Japanese all the time until he is wiped off the map."[2] DeWitt was talking about the internment of Japanese Americans, but the ambiguity of his choice of words seemed to imply a genocidal solution for the entire war. In this way, DeWitt echoed the genocidal approach proposed by men like Jack London earlier in the century. With the man in charge of the defense of the western United States openly making unapologetically racist arguments, it was no surprise that a racial double standard emerged in the handling of issues of national security during World War II.[3]

Even though the United States was already a heavily segregated country in the 1940s, Japanese Americans were marked for incarceration because of long-standing fears about their loyalty. London had supported the notion that Asians posed a direct military threat to the United States in his essays and short fiction at the beginning of the twentieth century. London's skill and reputation as a writer gained his stories notoriety, and "The Unparalleled Invasion" is still heralded as an early science fiction classic. However, London was not the first to write such stories: as early as 1879, stories about Asian invasions of the western world began to appear in print. As H. Bruce Franklin has shown, most of these future-war stories had plots where Asian immigrants rose as a "fifth column" in support of the invaders.[4] The fictional premise that Asian Americans were part of a master invasion plan fueled the drive for Japanese American internment. While Italian Americans and German Americans were seen as "individuals," Japanese Americans were lumped together as a racial group and deemed a threat to national security.

Novels such as Roy Norton's *The Vanishing Fleets* helped popularize the narrative of a future race war where Asians invade the United States. *The Vanishing Fleets* was first published serially in newspapers across the United States in 1907 and published in book form in 1908.[5] In the opening of Norton's story, racial differences similar to those London articulated precipitated a war: "For some years there had been mooted questions between Japan and the great American Republic, due in the first instance to troubles of a purely racial character. The Pacific coast, which for many decades had been compelled by its geographical situation to face an economic invasion from the Orient, wanted none of the small men from across the water. . . . [California] had been overruled by the people at large, until the whole country, awakening from its lethargic state, became educated in questions of immigration, to learn too late that the Californians had just cause for grievance."[6] Norton clearly stated the text's anti-Asian position; the immigration of Asians to the United States was considered a "just cause for grievance." The tone of the passage condescendingly assumed that any "educated" American would oppose the immigration of Asians and evoked economics as a secondary cause of what Norton characterized as a racial conflict. Norton underscored the racial character of the problem by having Japan awaken her new ally, China. These two Mongol countries set out to make demands from the United States, and Japan instigated hostilities by attacking Hawaii and the Philippines in the ensuing "racial war."[7]

Norton used the familiar concept of man the toolmaker in *The Vanishing Fleets* by having scientific advances decide the fate of the war. The inevitable Japanese invasion in the story showed the danger that would ensue if new technology fell into the hands of "enemy" races: Japan had developed a modern navy and learned to use it with superior efficiency. However, two American scientists—"Old Bill" Roberts and his daughter Norma—secretly developed a weapon called the "radioplane" that used radioactivity to control gravity. The vaunted Japanese navy, which "equaled in size and probably excelled in fighting efficiency that of the United States," quickly succumbed to this new weapon.[8] Japan surrendered, China never entered the war, and the United States established a new global dominance that even Great Britain and Germany accepted. Norton's heroic white scientists saved America with their ingenuity. They also provided the means to extend the growing empire of the United States around the world.

Giesy's *All for His Country* told an even more virulent anti-Asian story than *The Vanishing Fleets*. Giesy's text was originally published as a serial in *Cavalier Weekly* in 1914 and released as a book in 1915.[9]

Early in the story, Japan coordinated a surprise attack on Hawaii. It then moved quickly to take over California, an action made easier by the numerous Japanese immigrants in the state. When the Japanese military attacked San Francisco, Japanese immigrants all across California rose up to help their brothers. Giesy said that "for years they had been waiting and preparing. In many communities they actually outnumbered the whites, and they all rose at once. Laboring in the fields as pickers of fruit and hops, as gardeners, as railroad navvies, as servants in houses and hotels, they were in reality men sent over to work and wait for a purpose, men who had carried arms and knew how to use them, and did not fear to die for Nippon."[10] This representation of Japanese immigrants played on European American fears about the Asian "others" in their midst. Emphasizing the supposed lack of desire among Japanese immigrants to assimilate, the novel provided a fictional justification for hating them that went far beyond economics. Giesy added military reasons to the popular economic reasons for opposing immigration from Asia by representing Japanese immigrants as well-trained soldiers waiting for their chance to strike. In the scenes that depicted this armed uprising, Japanese immigrants continually performed acts of treachery and cowardice; they were mindless drones driven by their willingness to "die for Nippon." Giesy's novel was dominated by simple-minded stereotypes and it encouraged hatred toward all people of Japanese ancestry as the foundation of racial nationalism. Within the world of the novel, Japanese and American were mutually exclusive terms: only European Americans were true Americans. Immigrant Asian workers searching for a better life were transformed into evil, cunning, and cowardly soldiers by the small-minded bigot holding the pen.

In January 1907, Hearst had published a ridiculous story in the *San Francisco Examiner* claiming that "Japanese immigrants were actually Japanese soldiers in disguise."[11] The image of Japanese immigrants as undercover soldiers was given some plausibility by the emergence of Japan as a major military power, a status it earned with its victory in the Russo-Japanese War of 1904–1905. However, turning Asian immigrants into gun-toting militant hordes was a fictional distortion of the first order that provided a justification for violently oppressing them and excluding them from entering the country. There was no evidence for such claims: they were simply fabrications by racists trying to whip up public animosity against Asians. Giesy went even further in *All for His Country*, evoking the violation of white women to spur his audience along. As the Japanese fleet moved to attack the East Coast, it was confronted by the American fleet. In a scene reminiscent of Chesney's "The Battle of Dorking," the Japanese used a mysterious new "aërial bomb" to make short work of the American ships.[12] With the East Coast completely undefended and the West Coast under Japanese control, Japan issued a list of demands for peace. Predictably, the demands read more like a list of European American fears about Asians than realistic terms of surrender. In addition to certain (quite believable) land concessions, the Japanese demanded that the United States grant full U.S. citizenship and property rights to all Japanese citizens. Furthermore, Japan demanded that Congress recognize "Japanese claims to descent from Aryan rather than Mongol stock, which should establish them as Caucasian people, and [recognize] the full rights of intermarriage between themselves and all persons of both sexes in the United States."[13] This last provision inflamed the ire of President Gilson (a lame allusion to the name of the sitting president, Woodrow Wilson), who raged that "this last clause amounts to our subscribing to an Orientalization of our race—to the waiving of our birthright."[14] He went on to assert that the Japanese demands were "an insult to our womanhood" and said that "I had rather slay my daughters than see them given over to such an alliance."[15] As did Griffith's film *The Birth of a Nation* (1915), Giesy's novel resorted to the politics of segregation and racial vilification in its attempt to rally the nation. Evoking the specter of Asian men lusting after white women, Giesy appealed to racial purity and female chastity to inspire racial hatred.

To overcome this fictional military threat, Giesy followed in the footsteps of London and Norton by having salvation come in the form of a scientist. In the beginning of the novel, a young inventor named Meade Stillman unsuccessfully attempted to sell the "Stillman aero-destroyer" to the government. The airship, which was extremely expensive, was finally recruited by the government toward the end of the novel. Stillman emerged as the hero, quickly dispatching the Japanese and winning the girl. As in "The Unparalleled Invasion" and *The Vanishing Fleets*, Caucasian ingenuity and technological prowess proved too much for the yellow peril and President Gilson was saved from the prospect of having a Japanese son-in-law. In all of these stories, scientists and inventors were represented as racial heroes who defended America's status as a white nation and helped reinforce the global expansion of the white race. At the same time, these stories represented racial conflict as inevitable as they exhorted white readers to remain vigilant against an attack that was sure to come.

The emergence of science fiction as a self-conscious genre during the 1920s played a significant role in proliferating yellow peril stories. Fantastic stories about science and technology had been around for some time; however, such stories were produced by isolated authors or published only sporadically in magazines.[16] Hugo Gernsback's *Amazing Stories: The Journal of Scientifiction*, which premiered in April 1926, was the first monthly publication dedicated to fantastic stories about science and technology. In the first issue, Gernsback celebrated the emergence of the genre of "scientifiction" and articulated his vision of what the genre was and how it should develop. Gernsback traced what he saw as the prehistory of the genre that he defined as "the Jules Verne, H. G. Wells, and Edgar Allen Poe type of story—a charming romance intermingled with scientific fact and prophetic vision."[17] Through his editorials, story blurbs, and fan forums, Gernsback played an influential role in defining and marketing science fiction.[18] The overwhelming success of *Amazing Stories* spawned a host of imitators. When Gernsback lost control of *Amazing Stories* and started *Science Wonder Stories* in 1929, he coined the term that we still use for the genre: science fiction.[19]

In the August 1928 issue of *Amazing Stories*, Gernsback published Philip Francis Nowlan's story "Armageddon 2419 A.D.," which introduced the hero Anthony Rogers and his world of the future. Within six months, Nowlan had teamed up with artist Dick Calkins to produce a nationally syndicated comic strip based on his story.

Nowlan changed the name of his hero from Anthony to Buck and called the strip *The Adventures of Buck Rogers in the 25th Century*.[20] The strip became wildly popular, running for decades and leading to countless imitations. It was also the first science fiction comic strip, bringing rocket ships and ray guns and atomic bombs to the doorsteps of countless Americans for the first time.

The strip was an extended future-war story about a "Mongol" invasion of the United States, and Buck's adventures took place among the remaining white Americans who fought the Mongols for control of the continent. The racial character of the conflict in *The Adventures of Buck Rogers* was overt from the start. In the opening cells of the strip, which were published on 7 January 1929, Buck slipped into a centuries-long sleep when he was exposed to strange gases in a mine shaft; the original story called the gases "radioactive," but this detail was left out of the strip. When Buck awoke from his slumber in the third frame, he came out of the cave to the sight of a white woman flying through the air. The woman was fleeing an attack by a pack of flying men, and the first words Buck heard in this future world were the woman's cry: "Half-Breeds!"[21] Buck was thrust immediately into the middle of a future war where white women were threatened by predatory nonwhite men. The racial status of the woman's attackers as "half-breeds" showed that this world had already seen a certain amount of undesirable racial mixing. After Buck saved the woman in the second installment, he learned that he had slept for five centuries and had awakened in the year 2430. The woman, whose name was Wilma, told him about the Mongol invasion that had destroyed the great American cities and driven Americans into the countryside. The Mongols, who were technologically sophisticated and utterly ruthless, were little more than a hodgepodge of standard yellow peril stereotypes.

The Adventures of Buck Rogers merged the familiar race war of yellow peril stories with the science fiction frontier scenario of the type Edgar Rice Burroughs made famous. The fight against the Mongols and miscegenation was also the fight to overcome the harsh American environment and build a civilized nation. The Mongols had won the war and occupied most of what used to be the United States, so Buck joined with the growing rebel movement to throw off America's foreign oppressors. The strip used a heavy dose of frontier imagery to romanticize Buck's adventures: during the first year of the strip, Buck had to use his Boy Scout training to survive on a number of occasions. In one instance, Buck made a fire by rubbing sticks together. Dressed in animal hides, he also fashioned a bow and arrow by hand and used it to kill a bear that was charging Wilma.[22] On another occasion, Buck was stranded in the desert. While things looked grim, a thought bubble emerged from Buck's head depicting men in buckskin clothing following a wagon train. Buck said that "the 'never-say-die' spirit of my pioneer ancestors urged me to carry on."[23] Buck was eventually rescued by a group of Navajos. These stock frontier images served to connect the struggle of the Americans of 2430 with the American struggles of the past. As the ingenuity of white scientists reasserted itself, Buck led the way in the struggle to reconquer the continent. The future war with the Mongols led to a new frontier, where Americans like Buck had the opportunity to repeat the heroic exploits of their "pioneer ancestors" against a nonwhite enemy.

In 1934, Alex Raymond created a comic strip to compete with *The Adventures of Buck Rogers* for King Features Syndicate. The strip, *Flash Gordon*, was an immediate success.[24] It chronicled the adventures of Flash Gordon and his adventures in space. As in *The Adventures of Buck Rogers*, the world of *Flash Gordon* was dominated by the yellow peril. However, in the universe of *Flash Gordon*, the yellow peril was embodied in one man: Ming the Merciless. When Flash landed on Ming's home planet Mongo, he led the opposition to this "tyrant of the universe."[25] The Ming character was a futuristically enhanced version of English novelist Sax Rohmer's character Dr. Fu Manchu. In a number of stories from the 1910s through the 1930s, Rohmer helped popularize this specific version of the yellow peril embodied in one mad satanic-looking superscientist.[26] With his evil genius, Dr. Fu Manchu combined the learning of Western science with the perceived mysticism and moral depravity of the east to create monstrosities of various sorts. His ultimate aim was, of course, to overthrow the white world and create a race of beings with mixed blood.[27] In this sense, Rohmer was expounding on the familiar theme that science and technology is dangerous when it falls into the hands of the wrong person (or race). Rohmer's novels formed the basis for several Fu Manchu films, a comic strip, and even a 1950s television show. By modeling his *Flash Gordon* comic strip after Rohmer's Fu Manchu novels and *The Adventures of Buck Rogers*, Raymond was using a familiar formula to achieve his success. Universal Pictures purchased the film rights to a number of King Features comic strips, believing that their popularity would guarantee an audience for their films. In 1936, Universal produced the first of three movie serials based on the *Flash Gordon* comic strip; they were wildly successful and made "Flash Gordon" even more of a household name.[28]

As did Dr. Fu Manchu, Ming the Merciless continually attempted to master his white adversaries and enslave or destroy the Earth. In the movie serials, Ming was particularly interested in Dale Arden, the white women and love interest who accompanied Flash on his adventures. Time after time, Ming captured Dale and attempted to force her into marriage, but Flash always thwarted his schemes at the last moment. The racial coding of the movie serials reflected that of the comic strip, with Flash and Dale serving as models of white virility and beauty. Flash Gordon's timely heroics preserved the virtue of the white heroine and prevented miscegenation.

Flash was aided by the brilliant Dr. Zarkov, a scientist who provided the brains to back up Flash's brawn. In the 1936 movie serial *Flash Gordon*, Ming went to great lengths to capture Dr. Zarkov and exploit his scientific prowess. *Flash Gordon* followed the standard stereotype that asserted that Asians were not inventors and needed to rely on technologies created by whites. Just as Flash thwarted Ming with superior valor and strength, so Zarkov outinvented Ming and his evil (but white) scientists. The true threat Ming posed was technological: What would happen when an evil man like Ming got his hands on scientifically superior weapons? Ming's procurement of ultimate weapons, from deadly rays to death dust, forced Earth-dwellers to turn to Flash Gordon and Dr. Zarkov for salvation.

These science fiction texts provided an important part of the cultural matrix of the 1930s and 1940s that Americans used to make sense out of contemporary events. Americans could read about Japanese aggression on the front pages of their newspapers and then turn to the comics and follow a number of strips that talked about a future race war against the "Mongols." They could see films or read novels and essays that made race war their primary focus. Many American children grew up following the adventures of Buck Rogers and Flash Gordon, including countless young soldiers who fought in World War II. By the time the first atomic bomb dropped on Hiroshima on 6 August 1945, Americans had been hearing about white scientists developing ultimate weapons to destroy the yellow peril for at least forty years, and they had been defining their national identity in terms of racial warfare since the earliest beginnings of the country itself.

When the Japanese attacked Pearl Harbor on 7 December 1941, many Americans believed that the long-standing predictions about an invasion from the yellow peril had finally come true. Unlike the war in Europe, the racial dimension of the war in the Pacific was a primary way of making sense of the conflict for many Americans. In comparison to the responses of Americans to the Nazis, the hatred Americans demonstrated toward the Japanese exposed the contradictions and complexities of the race issue in the United States during the 1940s. Many Americans (including officials in the U.S. government) attacked the Nazi ideal of the "master race" and denounced Nazi policies of racial exclusion. Yet even as the U.S. critiqued Nazi racism, it was rounding up Japanese Americans and placing them in internment camps. U.S. racism was not only unexamined, it was promoted in the popular press. Ernie Pyle, the famous American war reporter, seemed to sum up the sentiments of many Americans (especially white soldiers) when he characterized the Japanese as alien and disgusting. As Pyle stated in one of his reports from the Pacific theater, "In Europe we felt that our enemies, horrible and deadly as they were, were still people," but "the Japanese were looked upon as something subhuman and repulsive."[29] After looking at some Japanese prisoners, Pyle commented that "they gave me the creeps, and I wanted a mental bath after looking at them."[30] To white Americans like Pyle, race mattered: it was a biologically important category that was necessary for understanding the war. The belief that the enemies in Europe were "people" meant that those whose families came from the enemy countries—German Americans and Italian Americans—were not subject to mass interrogation and incarceration; only those who posed a demonstrated security risk were detained, and these were handled on a case-by-case basis.[31] This contrasted starkly with the treatment of Americans of Japanese descent.

The argument that Japanese Americans posed a threat to the country was not supported by evidence. In a now-famous report to the State Department in November of 1941, Special Representative Curtis B. Munson concluded that people of Japanese ancestry posed no significant security risk to the United States.[32] Intelligence professionals such as FBI director J. Edgar Hoover and Lieutenant Commander K. D. Ringle of the Office of Naval Intelligence rejected the idea that the internment of Japanese Americans was necessary to maintain the security of the West Coast. Both men had experience in breaking Japanese espionage rings and knew that the Japanese did not trust Japanese Americans and relied instead on whites to conduct much of their spy work. In the aftermath of Pearl Harbor, there was absolutely no evidence of sabotage by Japanese Americans, who in fact had come to the defense of the islands in great numbers in the face of the Japanese onslaught. However, none of this prevented Secretary of the Navy Frank Knox from announcing to the media that "effective Fifth Column work" played a role in the Pearl Harbor attack.[33] This implicated Japanese Americans in the attack and fed racist sentiment that was already at a fevered pitch in the country.[34]

Two powerful examples of this racism can be found in the popular magazines *Newsweek* and *Life* from the weeks following Pearl Harbor. Two-thirds of the "Home Affairs" section of the 22 December 1941 issue of *Newsweek* was devoted to a boxed section entitled "How to Tell Your Friends from the Japs."[35] Two photos above this headline showed headshots of what were supposedly representative "Chinese" and "Japanese." The tone of the article was anthropological, and the photos were presented as specimens that would help clarify the differences between the Chinese allies and the enemy Japanese. A young Chinese man was shown with a slight smile on his face, standing in front of a board with Chinese writing. The impression given was that the man was a friendly scholar of some sort. The photograph of the scowling Japanese man in military uniform at the top of the page gave the impression that the Japanese were warlike and angry compared to the amiable Chinese. Two pictures at the bottom of the page repeated this smile-frown pattern, though the Japanese man was shown in a traditional robe instead of a military uniform. The text began with a qualification: "There is no infallible way of telling [the Chinese and Japanese] apart, because the same racial strains are mixed in both. Even an anthropologist, with calipers and plenty of time to measure heads, noses, shoulder, hips, is sometimes stumped."[36] The article evoked the "science" of determining racial groupings by measuring skulls to show how similar the Chinese and Japanese were racially, foregrounding the common argument that the Japanese and Chinese were "brothers" who shared a common "Mongol stock."[37] While asserting their racial proximity, the article tried to give some basic ways of telling the groups apart. The list included assertions such as the statement that "Chinese, not as hairy as Japanese, seldom grow an impressive mustache."[38] It also referred to the pictures with the comment that "the Chinese expression is likely to be more placid, kindly, open; the Japanese more positive, dogmatic, arrogant."[39] Such statements reflected not only the political relationship of each group with the United States at the time but also the degree to which racial categorization was entrenched in the thinking of Americans. Despite the fact that most anthropologists rejected such racial classifications by the 1940s, the article presented the Chinese and Japanese as so close to one another biologically that it was nearly impossible to tell them apart (thus the old stereotype that "they all look alike"). The emphasis on superficial markers of identity demonstrates the degree of ignorance in 1940s America about the cultural differences between the Chinese and Japanese. Yet the author was careful to make clear that the Chinese and Japanese were separate from Americans, implicitly reinforcing the concept that the United States was a white nation.

The purpose readers may have had for trying to distinguish between those of Chinese and Japanese ancestry remained unmentioned in this item from *Newsweek.* A similar article from the same week in *Life* magazine made that purpose abundantly clear. The article "How to Tell Japs from the Chinese" stated that "U. S. citizens have been demonstrating a distressing ignorance on the delicate question of how to tell a Chinese from a Jap. Innocent victims in cities all over the country are many of the 75,000 U. S. Chinese, whose homeland is our stanch [*sic*] ally. . . . To dispel some of this confusion, *Life* here adduces a rule-of-thumb from the anthropometric conformations that distinguish friendly Chinese from enemy alien Japs."[40] *Life* reported that racially motivated attacks against Asians were widespread in the United States following the Japanese assault on Pearl Harbor. While the article showed empathy for the "innocent victims" of Chinese ancestry, it did not condemn the attacks outright. Instead, it simply said that on some occasions, presumably white "U. S. citizens" were attacking the *wrong* Asians. By providing a guide for telling "Japs from the Chinese," *Life* attempted to point Americans at the *right* people to attack: people of Japanese ancestry. In this sense, both articles gave an implicit endorsement to racially motivated attacks against Japanese and Japanese Americans despite the fact that they had nothing to do with the assault on Pearl Harbor.

While the *Life* article commented that "physical anthropologists [are] devoted debunkers of race myths," it invoked anthropology to lend scientific authority to the racial and cultural stereotypes it endorsed. Two large pictures dominated the first page. The top picture showed a Chinese man with a pleasant expression on his face. The bottom picture, a close-up of Japanese general Hideki Tojo, emphasized the familiar image of the glowering Japanese soldier. Both pictures had handwritten annotations on them with lines that pointed out supposedly significant aspects of the subjects' faces. The Chinese man was diagramed as having a "higher bridge," a "parchment yellow complexion," and a "longer, narrower face." General Tojo was diagramed as having a "flatter nose," an "earthy yellow complexion," and a "broader, shorter face."[41] The captions referred to the Chinese man as a "public servant" from the "North Chinese anthropological group."[42] General Tojo's description emphasized that "facial expression [is] shaped by cultural, not anthropological factors."[43] However, the article presented Tojo's expression as characteristic of the Japanese, who "show the humorless intensity of ruthless mystics."[44] The article conflated and mobilized racial and cultural stereotypes to demonstrate the supposed nonthreatening nature of the Chinese while it depicted the Japanese as violent religious fanatics. Both articles attempted to focus public animosity against all people of Japanese descent. In this sense, the news media was both reflecting and reinforcing popular sentiments and official policies that led to the Japanese American internment.

The movement for the exclusion of people of Japanese ancestry from the United States was a major part of West Coast politics in the years before World War II.[45] The increasing threat the Japanese military posed that culminated in the attack on Pearl Harbor gave these racist arguments a new life on a national stage. Bolstered by widespread racist attitudes in the public, the media, the government, and the military, the push for the internment of Japanese Americans was eventually successful. On 19 February 1942, President Roosevelt signed Executive Order 9066. This order gave Secretary of War Stimson and his military commanders (including DeWitt) the power to begin immediately with the removal of Japanese Americans from the West Coast.[46] While many whites in the United States deplored the internment and fought against it, the tide of racial animosity overwhelmed them. During three and a half years of bitter warfare in the Pacific, this widespread racism became more firmly entrenched in American life. Drawing on the popular yellow peril rhetoric of the past half century, government officials and media reports vilified the Japanese as a racial threat to white America. Despite the U.S. war against the racism of the Nazis in Europe, loyal American citizens of Japanese descent were denied their civil rights and imprisoned with their families for no other reason than their race.

Chapter 7

"A Very Pleasant Way to Die"

Science Fiction, Race, and the Official Representation of the Atomic Bomb

"God damn you all; I told you so!"

—H. G. Wells, when asked late in life what he wanted on his tombstone

On 6 August 1945, President Harry Truman issued a press release announcing to the world the use of the atomic bomb in an attack earlier that day on Hiroshima. The text of the press release read like the announcement of a science fiction prophecy come true. The atomic bomb was a reality, the yellow peril was suddenly defeated, and the Manhattan Project scientists were heroes. Americans were confronted with the fact that as of 6 August 1945, they truly lived in "a science-fiction world."[1] Truman immediately attempted to deflect any criticism about the bombing of Japanese civilians. In the opening line of his announcement, he referred to Hiroshima as "an important Japanese Army base."[2] He referred to the invasion by the Japanese as justification for the use of an ultimate weapon: "The Japanese began the war from the air at Pearl Harbor. They have been repaid many fold."[3] By putting the blame on the Japanese before revealing the nature of the new weapon, Truman asserted that the militaristic Japanese had brought the terrible destruction of the atomic bomb upon themselves. In this way, he rhetorically absolved the United States of any moral or social responsibility for the attack. An onslaught of reporting and commentary about this new ultimate weapon ensued. Race was a central issue in the response to the attacks, just as it had been throughout the war in the Pacific theater. Beginning with Truman's announcement, the U.S. government attempted to control the representation of the atomic bomb, censoring reports it felt might evoke sympathy for the Japanese and perpetuating the stereotyped image of the Japanese as an anonymous horde of fanatical Shinto soldiers. Despite growing concerns about radiation, the U.S. government insisted that the atomic bomb was no different from other explosive weapons. The atomic bomb, it argued, was simply a more efficient explosive that gave the Japanese what they deserved.

The idea of the atomic bomb was not new. Scientists and journalists had been discussing the potential of atomic science since the turn of the century.[4] Science fiction authors had been spinning tales about atomic bombs since 1914. The explosion of science fiction pulp magazines, comic strips, and films in the 1930s made stories about radium guns and atomic explosions commonplace. Fictional narratives about white American scientists developing ultimate weapons to crush the yellow peril had been widely distributed for over sixty years. President Truman's announcement about Hiroshima therefore had a familiar ring to it. At the beginning of the third paragraph of the announcement, Truman gave the name of the weapon: "It is an atomic bomb. It is a harnessing of the basic power of the universe. The force from which the sun draws its power has been loosed against those who brought war to the Far East."[5] The president provided a science fiction–style explanation of the new weapon's nature, an explanation that hearkened back to Wells's 1914 description of atomic energy in *The World Set Free*. The idea that scientists had captured the sun placed the weapon in a more everyday and accessible context for Truman's nonspecialist audience. At the same time, the atomic bomb came across as an unprecedented scientific achievement.

Truman emphasized the decisive importance of scientific advancements for modern warfare, saying that "the battle of the laboratories held fateful risks for us as well as the battles of the air, land and sea, and we have now won the battle of the laboratories as we have won the other battles."[6] This echoed Jack London's "The Unparalleled Invasion," in which he talked about biological warfare as "ultra-modern war, twentieth-century war, the war of the scientist and the laboratory."[7] As a young man, Truman had probably read London's story in *McClure's*.[8] Where London's story was projecting a possible future, however, Truman was announcing a new historical fact. As historian Paul Boyer argues, Truman's announcement about the atomic bomb constituted "a psychic event of almost unprecedented proportions."[9] A fantastic science fiction weapon that inhabited pulp magazines, comic strips, and movie serials had suddenly sprung to life and made a direct intervention in history, ending the war with Japan far earlier than expected. Initially, this surprising intervention of the atomic bomb seemed to create a sense of joy among most Americans, including President Truman. When Truman heard about the success of the attack on Hiroshima, he was aboard the USS *Augusta* on his way back from the Potsdam Conference. He was ecstatic as he told the sailors on board the good news.[10]

Much of the joy in the response to the use of the atomic bomb was rooted in the long and painful experience of the war. While sheltered from the attacks that devastated Europe and Asia, most Americans on the home front had lived through prolonged periods of relative hardship and loss. By August of 1945, although the war in Europe was over and the war in the Pacific was nearing its conclusion, most people still believed that the United States would have to engage in a land invasion of the Japanese home islands. As in Europe, air power alone did not seem to be decisive enough to force an unconditional Japanese surrender. That perception changed dramatically when the American B-29 nicknamed "Enola Gay" dropped the uranium bomb dubbed "Little Boy" on Hiroshima. The front page of the *Los Angeles Times* on 7 August 1945 reported that comments by Secretary of War Stimson and President Truman about the atomic bomb "renewed speculation . . . again as to whether Japan may be completely crushed by air attack without invasion."[11] On 9 August 1945, an American B-29 named "Great Artiste" dropped a plutonium bomb dubbed "Fat Man" on the Japanese port city of Nagasaki. Within a week, the Japanese surrendered and victory in the Pacific theater of the war was declared. After the Japanese surrender, retrospectives on the war in the news media followed the lead of the U.S. government and emphasized the numbers of American and Japanese lives that had been saved by the atomic bombs. Despite initial estimates from Hiroshima and Nagasaki of hundreds of thousands of casualties, a Gallup Poll taken between August 10 and August 15 of 1945 showed that 85 percent of Americans approved of the use of the atomic bomb on Japanese cities.[12] Another Gallup Poll taken between August 24 and August 29 showed that 69 percent of Americans believed that "it was a good thing" that the atomic bomb had been developed.[13] These polls were consistent with the generally positive initial treatment of the atomic bomb in the news media.

The degree to which Americans were conscious of the science fiction nature of the war's conclusion became clear in the media coverage following the attack on Hiroshima. John W. Campbell Jr., the driving force behind the "golden age" of science fiction and the editor of *Astounding Science Fiction*, found himself being interviewed by such elite publications as *The New Yorker*.[14] The United Press released a story on August 8 that (mistakenly) claimed that H. G. Wells had forecast the development of atomic bombs "12 years ago in his book, 'The Shape of Things to Come'" (Wells had in fact predicted the development of atomic bombs thirty-one years before in *The World Set Free*).[15] The story, which the *Los Angeles Times* ran on page two between a number of other atomic bomb–related stories, centered on Wells's characteristically ambivalent response to the Hiroshima attack. Given the celebratory tone of the articles surrounding it, Wells's comments seemed to be relatively critical of the newly realized technology. With the development of the atomic bomb, science fiction writers suddenly were acknowledged as prophets, visionaries, and critics. An editorial by Campbell in the November 1945 issue of *Astounding* noted that "during the weeks immediately following that first atomic bomb, science fiction writers were suddenly recognized by their neighbors as not quite such wild-eyed dreamers as they had been thought, and in many soul-satisfying cases became the neighborhood experts."[16] This newfound status for science fiction writers, whose pronouncements were now sought after by mainstream publications as well as their neighbors, signaled a growing perception among Americans that they lived in a science fiction world.

An editorial in the August 20 issue of *Life* magazine explicitly acknowledged the familiarity of the atomic bomb: "After all, this [atomic] bomb has been inevitable for a long time. American kids, fans of Flash Gordon, reacted to the news with peanut-butter stares which seemed to say, 'What's all the excitement?' or, '*We've* had it for years.'"[17] Science fiction was characterized as a genre that used to belong to children but now had direct relevance for the adult world after the bombing of Hiroshima. The atomic bomb was seen as a weapon that had sprung from stories like *Flash Gordon*. Captain Robert A. Lewis, the co-pilot of the "Enola Gay," made a similar connection when he commented that "even though we had expected something terrific, what we saw made us feel that we were Buck Rogers twenty-fifth-century warriors."[18] Like the editor of *Life*, Captain Lewis immediately identified his experience of the atomic bomb with science fiction. As a genre, science fiction seemed to have gained a measure of legitimacy overnight. While still not considered good art, it had gained a relevance and an acceptance that it had never known.

Scientists were also represented as war heroes who had won "the battle of the laboratories." Scores of stories in the news media profiled the men and women who contributed to the development of the atomic bomb. As had earlier stories of the soldiers in the trenches, post-Hiroshima stories portrayed the scientists who created the atomic bomb as heroic patriots. On August 8, stories about the B-29 crews that dropped the atomic bombs ran on the same pages as profiles of the atomic scientists and their secret laboratories. Once again, these stories seemed to have a science fiction twist: where Flash Gordon had the European scientist Dr. Zarkov to help him defeat Ming the Merciless, G. I. Joe now had American scientist J. Robert Oppenheimer (as well as European scientists such as Edward Teller) to help him defeat the evil Japanese emperor.[19] Like the atomic bomb, the heroic scientist seemed to spring from the world of science fiction to make a direct intervention in history.

The joy that accompanied the conclusion to the war was mixed with a continuing anger toward the Japanese, much of which was expressed in explicitly racist terms. Yellow peril stories had been common before the war; after Pearl Harbor, these stories fueled the hysteria over the presence of people of Japanese ancestry in the United States, a hysteria that ended in mass internment. After Hiroshima, many news stories contrasted the racially tolerant Allies with the racist Nazis, but these stories ignored the rampant racism that was evident in American life. In an August 1946 interview, a 67-year-old white farmer from Virginia commented that "the man that made that [atomic] bomb was a man after my own heart. I love him. I don't care if he was a nigger. I'd love his neck."[20] This bizarre mixture of elation and racism was a fairly common reaction to the new ultimate weapon. A December 1945 poll published in *Fortune* revealed that most Americans approved of the attacks on Hiroshima and Nagasaki and that 23 percent wished that the U.S. had dropped even more atomic bombs on Japan.[21] As Boyer points out, "many newspaper letters expressed regret that atomic bombs had not been used to destroy all human life in Japan."[22] The fact that many felt that the supposedly racially tolerant United States should commit genocide against Japan was not seen as a contradiction. It was seen as a desire to bring justice to the Japanese for their many war crimes. An editorial in the August 8 *Los Angeles Times*—entitled "Howls of Jap Anguish Betray Heavy Bomb Damage"—criticized the Japanese for their hypocrisy, citing the "rape of Nanking" and Pearl Harbor as atrocities they had committed that left them no room to complain about the cruelty of the American attack.[23] However, some of the satisfaction most Americans felt about the attacks on Hiroshima and Nagasaki clearly came from racist impulses. The racist aspect of this anti-Japanese animosity was perhaps clearest in editorial cartoons that showed buck-toothed, slant-eyed "Japs" being blown into the sky or threatened by the atomic bomb.[24] The Japanese had been represented as savage and animalistic throughout the war, and the post-Hiroshima representations were no exception to this rule.

In the U.S. government's protracted battle to control the story of the atomic bomb, the news media was the front line. The military controlled the press releases and all other information about the atomic bombings, and the occupational force in Japan severely limited access to Hiroshima and Nagasaki throughout 1945. The occupational force (including the civilian-controlled Civil Censorship Detachment) also engaged in a strict regime of censorship about the atomic bombings, mainly to ensure that reports placed blame for the horror of the war on the Japanese.[25] In the official narrative of the atomic bomb, the U.S. government did everything it could to promote the revenge aspect of the Hiroshima and Nagasaki bombings. The "Japs" had committed innumerable war crimes, this narrative went, and therefore they deserved what they got.[26] The government also attempted to squelch or refute reports about the effect of the atomic bombs on humans, especially the devastating and lingering impact of radiation. Instead, it attempted to focus media attention on descriptions of the atomic blasts, the effect of the blasts on inanimate objects, and the crimes of the Japanese military. The official narrative described the effects of the atomic bomb as similar to the effects of earlier weapons; according to the government, the atomic bomb was just more concentrated and efficient than other weapons. This narrative was disseminated through White House and War Department press releases and statements from leading military officers. By limiting stories of radiation and human suffering, the government hoped to limit sympathy for the Japanese. This helped to reinforce the depiction of the victims at Hiroshima and Nagasaki as an anonymous Japanese herd, a racialized image that had been perpetuated throughout the war.

To help establish credibility for its press releases, the military hired William L. Laurence, the *New York Times* Pulitzer Prize–winning science writer, as the official reporter of the Manhattan Project. Laurence was allowed to witness the July 16 atomic bomb test of the Trinity project in New Mexico and the Nagasaki bombing raid; he used his experiences and access to shape all the articles the government released about the development and use of the atomic bomb. In addition, Laurence wrote the original draft of the president's press release about Hiroshima.[27] Throughout his articles and his best-selling book *Dawn over Zero* (1946), Laurence continued to present the bombings of Hiroshima and Nagasaki as justified revenge against the Japanese.[28] In *Dawn over Zero*, Laurence wrote, "Does one feel any pity or compassion for the poor devils about to die? Not when one thinks of Pearl Harbor and the Death March on Bataan."[29] Laurence added his voice to the chorus of officials and commentators who absolved the United States for the still-unknown horrors of the atomic bomb by pointing to Japanese atrocities during the war.

The government seemed most concerned with suppressing or refuting stories that discussed human suffering in Hiroshima and Nagasaki. Rather than detailing what had happened to Japanese civilians, the official U.S. government reports from Hiroshima and Nagasaki in the year following the attacks emphasized the strategic damage to buildings, bridges, and other infrastructure. When bodies were discussed, the tone of the language was detached, objective, and medical. The first wave of stories about the atomic bomb in the news media was based on press releases Laurence had written; though most of the newspaper stories were not credited to him, Laurence's releases were reprinted with only occasional and minor changes.[30] On 7 August 1945, newspapers around the country ran Laurence's account of the 16 July Trinity test in New Mexico on the front page. A report on the front page of the *San Francisco Chronicle* focused on "the ball of fire, many times brighter than the mid-day sun" that went "billowing skyward" when the atomic bomb was detonated at the Trinity test site.[31] The report listed a steel tower that was "vaporized," a huge sloping crater, a "heavy pressure wave," and a "huge multi-colored cloud" as the other effects of the blast.[32] A front-page article in the *Los Angeles Times* on the same day described a "blinding flash" and a "multi-colored cloud" that went "mushrooming" into the New Mexico sky.[33] The tone of both articles was one of scientific detachment and reverential awe at the power of the new weapon. The flood of such stories left no room for considerations about the impact of the blasts on human bodies.

On August 8, the first eyewitness accounts of the Hiroshima attack from the crew of the Enola Gay began to appear in the newspapers. Navy Captain William Parsons talked about a "ball of fire," and a "mountain of smoke [that] was going up in a mushroom with the stem coming down."[34] On August 11, the Associated Press released a story about the eyewitness accounts of the Nagasaki attack. As had the earlier stories of Hiroshima, the descriptions focused on the "immense fiery ball" and "column of billowing smoke" caused by the explosion.[35] The August 12 *San Francisco Chronicle* devoted the upper right quarter of the front page to a picture of the "smoke cloud" taken by the American military at Hiroshima with the caption, "Monument to Victory."[36] Within a week, the narrative sequence of an atomic attack had become familiar: it began with a flash of light, followed by a ball of fire, a shock wave, and a huge mushroom cloud. This official account of the atomic attack was firmly and unapologetically from the perspective of the bombers, the people who had deployed the weapon and watched its effect from a distance. By inundating the news media with such accounts from the bombers' point of view, the government helped ensure that the few voices that expressed concern about the effects of the atomic bomb on Japanese civilians were pushed to the back pages or left out of the news altogether.

Once the dust had settled and the Japanese had surrendered, the U.S. government began to filter reports and pictures of the damage from Hiroshima and Nagasaki to the media. Compared to earlier pictures published of Berlin, Tokyo, and other bombed-out cities, the pictures from Hiroshima and Nagasaki were not remarkable. A retrospective article on the war in the 20 August 1945 issue of *Life* magazine was characteristic of the early media coverage of the atomic bombings. Entitled "The War Ends," the article was like many *Life* articles: dominated by large photographs and written text that served mainly as context for the striking images. The article began with a large picture, an artist's rendering of the smoke that billowed from the bombing of Hiroshima, with text that glossed the events of the final days of the war.[37] The next page showed a large photo of the mushroom cloud over Hiroshima, which the text described as "a major Japanese port and military center."[38] The text then quoted members of the B-29 crew as they described "a terrific flash of light" and the subsequent cloud of "white smoke . . . on a mushroom stem."[39] The next page showed a photo of the mushroom cloud over Nagasaki and gave a nearly identical description of the attack. This account was in tune with the official narrative of the atomic bomb; it asserted the military nature of the targets, obscuring the fact that tens of thousands of civilians lived in the cities. At the same time, the article focused on the "flash of light" and "mushroom" cloud produced by the blast itself.

The article concluded with aerial pictures of Yokohama and Kobe, which had been firebombed in early 1945, followed by before and after pictures of Hiroshima.[40] The photographs were taken from the point of view of the bombers ten of thousands of feet in the air, and the descriptions suggested that firebombing had caused much more damage than the atomic bombs. This aerial point of view simply showed structures that were burning or eradicated. The article presented the destruction caused by firebombing and by the atomic bombings as identical in kind: the atomic bomb was simply a bigger and more efficient bomb with no unique or unusual effects. This too was keeping with the official representation of the atomic bomb. The U.S. government had a virtual monopoly on the information and images of the atomic attacks, and the selected materials it fed to the media ensured that the news coverage would continue to vilify the Japanese and obscure the impact of the war on Japanese civilians. Japanese casualties were described only with numbers and the targets were repeatedly described as military in nature. Nothing in the information coming from the U.S. government grounded the atomic attacks in the individual experiences of the victims; only the stories of the bombers were told. This helped ensure that the celebratory official narrative of the atomic bomb and its effects continued to drown out other possible narratives that might reflect badly on the decision makers, scientists, and soldiers of the United States and its allies.

Despite the efforts of the government to control the emerging narrative of the atomic bomb, cracks began to appear early on in the celebratory narratives published by the news media. Japanese news reports, which were excerpted in American newspapers, characterized the Hiroshima bombing as "designed to massacre innocent civilians."[41] The Japanese reports included eyewitness accounts of the aftermath of the atomic bombings. One such account, quoted in the 20

August 1945 issue of *Newsweek*, graphically described the bodies of some of the victims: "All around I found dead and wounded. Some were bloated and scorched—such an awesome sight—their legs and bodies stripped of clothes and burned with a huge blister."[42] *Newsweek* dismissively framed the description as part of a "vivid program" that was characteristic of the "Jap press and radio" response to the attacks. *Newsweek* also emphasized that the story was told by a "Jap corporal," a fact that supported the official claim that Hiroshima and Nagasaki were military targets. The *Life* article "The War Ends" (discussed above) also contained descriptions of atomic bomb injuries excerpted from this same Japanese source.[43] While graphic, the descriptions in these articles did not represent the atomic bomb as different from other weapons used during the war. The burns and blisters on the bodies of the Japanese victims could have been made by incendiary bombs just as easily as by atomic bombs. The overt hostility toward Japanese news sources in the American press reflected the anger and racism that still flowed unabated through media accounts of the war in the Pacific. Despite the dismissive tone of the articles, they provided the first eyewitness accounts of the atomic bomb's effects on human flesh. Over the next year, this trickle of eyewitness accounts would grow and begin to undermine the government's official position.

In the months after the official surrender of the Japanese, reports began to surface about the unique effect of the atomic bomb: radiation sickness. In the face of such reports, government and military officials expanded the official narrative of the atomic bombings to include denials about radiation. These denials focused on three issues: the number of deaths caused by initial radiation, the suffering involved in radiation sickness, and the threat of lingering radiation in Hiroshima and Nagasaki. In late 1945, a number of sensational articles and reports about Hiroshima and Nagasaki emphasized the lasting effects of the atomic bomb. *New York Times* reporter William Lawrence, one of the first reporters allowed to visit Hiroshima, noted in a 5 September 1945 article that a strange sickness was afflicting the residents of the city and killing over 100 people a day.[44] A report in the September 17 issue of *Time* magazine noted that "since the atom bomb hit

Hiroshima, Jap reports have played on the U.S. conscience with reports of weird, agonized deaths of civilians who had appeared untouched by the explosion."[45]

It wasn't long before radiation was cited as the source of the mysterious illness that had killed seemingly uninjured survivors weeks after the blast. An article in the September 24 issue of *Life* magazine entitled "New Mexico's Atomic Bomb Crater" reported that "the Japanese hinted strongly that parts of Hiroshima and Nagasaki had become radioactive. Rescue workers who came into the cities some time later, [the] Japanese reported, were killed by harmful radiations."[46] These reports were denounced by some members of the military—most notably by General Leslie Groves, the military head of the Manhattan Project—as unsubstantiated "Japanese propaganda" designed to manipulate world opinion and generate sympathy for the defeated Japanese people.[47]

At the request of the White House, General Groves and lead Manhattan Project scientist J. Robert Oppenheimer led a group of reporters through the Trinity test site crater in New Mexico to demonstrate that lingering radioactivity couldn't kill humans, as the Japanese claimed.[48] The article in *Life* noted that "the New Mexico crater was still definitely radioactive. It nevertheless offered strong evidence that the Japs were wrong."[49] The ambivalence in this article indicated the growing skepticism that many were feeling toward the official narrative of the atomic bomb. The reporter was still willing to accept the argument of General Groves and the War Department, which said that "most of the Japanese had been killed by blast and heat."[50] He was also willing to accept the argument that "a few may have died of radioactive effects suffered at the instant of the explosions[,] but none died from radioactivity afterward."[51] Yet the facts of the matter—such as the safety precautions the reporters had to go through to protect themselves from the lingering radiation—seemed to contradict the official narrative and leave the reporters wondering if they were getting the whole truth.

General Groves continued to dismiss the impact of lingering radiation during his testimony before the Senate Special Committee on Atomic Energy on 25 and 26 November 1945. General Groves had assembled a "special group" under the command of his deputy, General Farrell, for the specific task of studying the effects of the atomic bomb at Hiroshima and Nagasaki. In his testimony before the Senate, General Groves claimed that the investigation of this "special group" showed that "there was no radioactivity damage done to any human being excepting at the time that the bomb actually went off, and that is an instantaneous damage."[52] Before General Groves could continue with his comments, Senator Brien McMahon, the chair of the committee, interrupted to question if there would be "anything morally wrong" if the atomic bomb did leave lingering radiation. Clearly, Senator McMahon did not have a problem with irradiating Japan.[53] After making clear that he had no problem with irradiating Japan either, General Groves moved on to dismiss radiation as a major cause of death at Hiroshima and Nagasaki. Not content to merely leave it at that, however, the general testified that "the radiation casualty can be of several classes. He can have enough so that he will be killed instantly. He can have a smaller amount which will cause him to die rather soon, and as I understand it from the doctors, without undue suffering. In fact, they say it is a very pleasant way to die."[54] General Groves not only denied that radiation sickness was a significant cause of death, he also implied that those who actually died of it were the lucky ones. In this way, General Groves continued the pattern of representing the atomic bombings as morally unproblematic and as no different from the conventional bombings of other Japanese cities.

While the War Department continued to deny the large number of radiation deaths, the dangers of lingering radiation, and the significance of radiation sickness, a growing number of credible eyewitnesses began to contradict its claims. In testimony before the Senate Special Committee on Atomic Energy on 6 December 1945, Dr. Philip Morrison described in detail the horrific effects of radiation sickness on civilians he witnessed during his visit to Hiroshima. General Groves was doubtless displeased by Morrison's testimony; he was part of the group Groves had assembled to study Hiroshima and Nagasaki. This was probably not the kind of result General Groves had been hoping for.[55] A transcript of Morrison's testimony was reprinted in the 11 February 1946 issue of *The New Republic*, where his credibility was underscored by his role as "an atomic physicist who worked on the bomb project at Chicago and Los Alamos and on the Marianas."[56]

Despite such credible accounts, military conservatives such as Major Alexander de Seversky continued to argue that "the effects of the atom bombs . . . had been wildly exaggerated" and that radiation sickness was only a minor cause of death at Hiroshima and Nagasaki.[57] De Seversky and Groves continued to press the government's official narrative that emphasized Japanese culpability in the Hiroshima and Nagasaki attacks and dismissed any argument or fact that might evoke sympathy for the victims of the atomic bombs. Finally, two powerful sources emerged to challenge the official narrative of the atomic bomb: the United States Strategic Bombing Survey's official report on Hiroshima and Nagasaki, and John Hersey's landmark news story "Hiroshima."

The United States Strategic Bombing Survey (USSBS) originated from a directive by President Roosevelt to conduct an impartial survey of the impact of the aerial attacks on Germany. After the war in the Pacific ended, President Truman requested that the USSBS conduct a similar survey of Japan. Consisting of over 1,150 people, the USSBS staff included a number of military and civilian experts on architecture, economics, engineering, medicine, and several other fields. They established sub-headquarters in Hiroshima and Nagasaki to expedite their analysis of the effects of the atomic bombs.[58] The USSBS released some preliminary findings in late February 1946 that were reported in such magazines as *Time* and *Life*. The 6 March 1945 issue of *Time* listed a number of the effects of atomic bombs on human bodies and noted that the USSBS's findings contradicted earlier comments by "military conservatives."[59] An article in *Life* showed medical drawings of the human body being penetrated by gamma rays and listed a number of the symptoms of radiation sickness.[60] These reports gave information that certainly didn't seem to jibe with the "pleasant" death General Groves had described. At the same time, the clinical detachment of the accounts lacked any kind of grounding in individual experience and therefore read much like a medical textbook. The suffering of the victims was still excluded in favor of the "objective" voice of scientific authority (see Figure 4).

On 30 June 1946, the USSBS released its final report, *The Effects of Atomic Bombs on Hiroshima and Nagasaki*. The complete text of the report was republished in the 5 July 1946 issue of *The United States News* magazine and received a fair amount of publicity. Even though the publicity for the report was overshadowed by the atomic bomb tests at Bikini atoll in early July, its findings were startling and refuted the dismissive claims of the War Department regarding radiation.[61] The first fourteen pages of the report repeated the official narrative of the atomic bomb, discussing familiar subjects like blast effects and damage to infrastructure. On page fifteen the report turned to the issue of radiation:

> Most of the immediate casualties did not differ from those caused by incendiary or high-explosive raids. The outstanding difference was the presence of radiation effects, which became unmistakable about a week after the bombing. . . . Colonel Stafford Warren, in his testimony before the Senate Committee on Atomic Energy, estimated that radiation was responsible for 7 to 8 percent of the total deaths in the two cities. Most medical investigators in the areas feel that this estimate is far too low; it is generally felt that no less than 15 to 20 percent of the deaths were from radiation.[62]

Colonel Warren was the chief medical expert in General Groves's "special group" that was sent to Hiroshima and Nagasaki.[63] The authors of the USSBS report explicitly attacked the claims of General Groves and his allies and emphasized the unique nature of the atomic bomb as a weapon. Where General Groves, Major de Seversky, and Colonel Warren dismissed radiation as a cause of death, the USSBS report asserted that it was a major cause of death. The report also graphically detailed the delayed effects of initial exposure during an atomic blast. While no individual cases of radiation sickness were discussed in detail, the report thoroughly analyzed the delayed onset of the illness and provided a frank and disturbing account of radiation's effects on the human body.

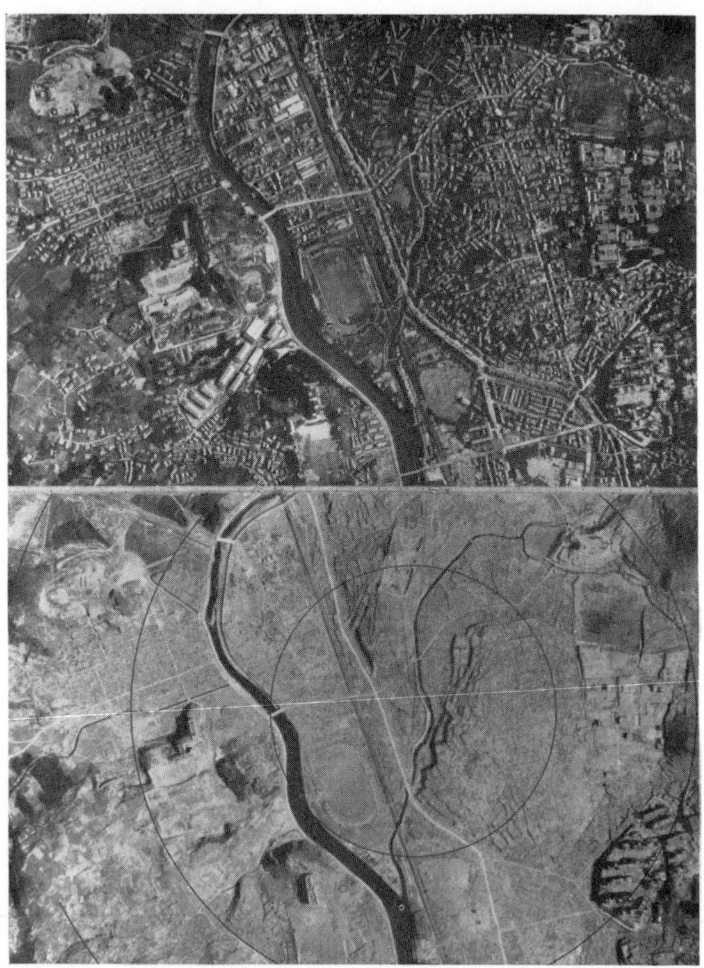

Figure 4. These aerial photographs from the USSBS report entitled *The Effects of Atomic Bombs on Hiroshima and Nagasaki* (1946) show Nagasaki before and after the attack. These images were virtually identical to many that had appeared in popular publications right after the war. This report was written from the point of view of the bombers and did not address the subjective experience of the victims of the attack.

Even though it confronted the issue of radiation sickness head on in the written text, the USSBS report gave only one photo of a Japanese victim of the atomic bombs. The photo, which showed some superficial burns on a Japanese soldier, reinforced the official narrative that Hiroshima and Nagasaki were military, not civilian, targets (see Figure 5). The discrepancy between the images and the written text of the report was likely due to censorship. The story of Lieutenant Daniel McGovern provided a clearer example of the government's censorship of images of atomic bomb victims. As a young officer in the USSBS, McGovern helped a Japanese film crew led by Akira Iwasaki that was having problems with the American military police. The film crew had been shooting footage of the bombing victims in hospitals at Hiroshima and Nagasaki before being ordered to stop by occupation censors. McGovern argued for the documentary value of the footage shot by the crew and was able to hire them to work for the Americans and complete their project. The black-and-white footage was edited into a documentary entitled *The Effects of the Atomic Bombs against Hiroshima and Nagasaki*. After Iwasaki's crew completed the documentary, it was labeled top secret by the Pentagon and locked away for twenty-two years. An American film crew that was also under McGovern's supervision shot color footage of the bombing victims, and this too was locked away for decades as top secret.[64] These incidents indicated that the military, while willing to allow a written discussion of radiation sickness, was not willing to allow the USSBS to release images or accounts of injured Japanese civilians that might evoke sympathy for their plight.

Because it contained no graphic images or detailed first-person accounts of the victims of the atomic bombs, the USSBS report left the official narrative intact in many ways. While it rejected the claim that radiation was not a significant cause of death at Hiroshima and Nagasaki, the objective medical tone and selective images limited the report's emotional impact. Despite the use of specific examples and anecdotes, the representation of the Japanese as an anonymous herd remained unchallenged. While asserting that the atomic bombs were not necessary for bringing World War II to an end, the report failed to

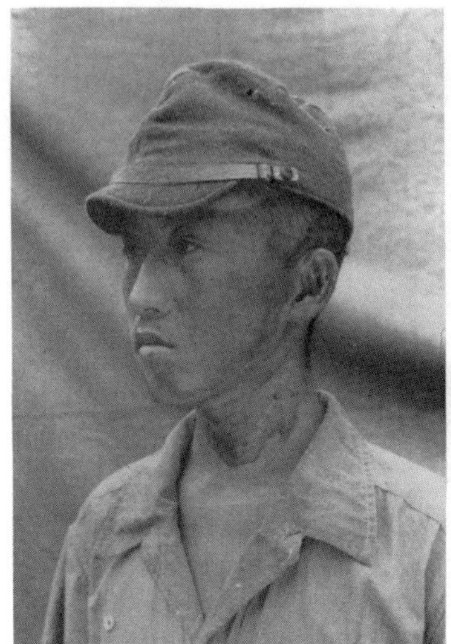

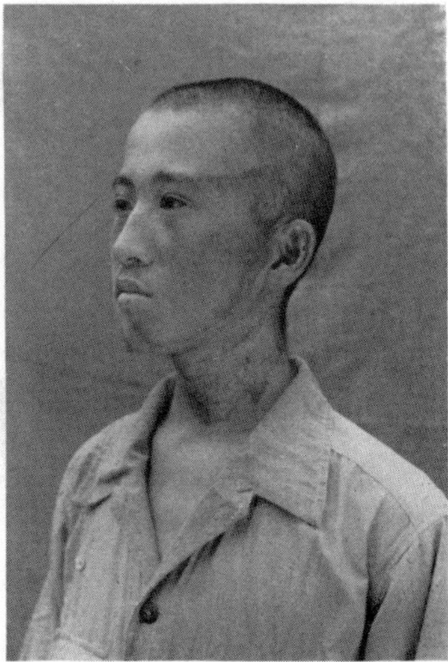

Figure 5. These were the only pictures of atomic bomb damage in the USSBS report to show a human being. The wounds on this soldier were mild compared to the injuries of some in the atomic bombed cities. By showing a soldier, these photos perpetuated the notion that Hiroshima and Nagasaki were military targets. USSBS, *The Effects of Atomic Bombs on Hiroshima and Nagasaki* (1946).

condemn the attacks or personalize the suffering of the victims.[65] It did not contradict the repeated assertion that the Japanese deserved what they got, and it did nothing to undermine the argument that lingering radiation (and what was later termed "fallout") did not exist. Clearly, there were people in the USSBS like Lieutenant McGovern who wanted to challenge the official narrative more strongly. These people must have gotten some satisfaction from the concluding section of the report, which gave a serious warning about the vulnerability of U.S. cities to an atomic attack and attempted to stir readers to a consideration of what an atomic explosion might mean when experienced firsthand. But the limitations of the report format and official censorship prevented a more personal and graphic exploration of the realities of the atomic bomb. That story remained unreported until the publication of John Hersey's "Hiroshima" in August 1946.

Chapter 8

Beyond the Yellow Peril

John Hersey's "Hiroshima"

John Hersey challenged the official representation of the atomic attacks with the publication of "Hiroshima" in the 31 August 1946 issue of *The New Yorker*. A relatively liberal and sophisticated magazine, *The New Yorker* devoted its entire contents to Hersey's story and omitted its usual lighthearted cartoons and humorous editorials. The results were sensational: it was republished in full by several newspapers, ABC radio broadcast a reading of the entire text over four nights, and the book version became an immediate bestseller.[1] Since its initial publication, "Hiroshima" has been required reading for many American students at all levels, and it remains in print to the present day.[2] It is difficult to overstate the importance of Hersey's text in the history of the atomic age and its influence on the way we represent nuclear war. As one reader of *The New Yorker* put it, Hersey's text showed us "what one [atomic] bomb did to people as distinct from a city, the Japanese people[,] or the enemy."[3] Hersey rejected the official practice of representing the atomic bomb from the perspective of the bombers, instead showing his readers the terror of the atomic attacks from the perspective of its victims. He challenged the argument that there was no lingering radiation in Hiroshima and destroyed the idea that radiation sickness was anything other than horrible torment.

The style of "Hiroshima" was understated and spare. Pulitzer Prize–winning Hersey focused on individual accounts of survivors rather than on the collateral damage the blast caused. Hersey said he was interested in "what happened not to buildings but to human beings."[4] He conducted his research during an April 1946 visit to Hiroshima, where he interviewed dozens of survivors.[5] He also studied available technical information about the atomic bomb, including the reports of the USSBS, and he did not submit his writing to the government for censorship clearance.[6] In the end, Hersey focused on six individuals with stories that resonated with the American audience. Two of the survivors were Christian clergymen whose stories undermined the common wartime representation of the Japanese as a fanatical Shinto horde.[7] A widowed mother and a female office worker showed the vulnerability of civilians struck by the bomb and the effect of the atomic bomb on families. The two doctors in the text had to confront the cost in human life when Hiroshima's infrastructure collapsed; their accounts showed the grisly details of radiation sickness. Through these six perspectives, Hersey explored the unspoken or obscured implications of the detached and impersonal official narrative of the atomic bombings.

By mid-1946, the official narrative was widely familiar. The standard description of the flash of light, the ball of fire, the shock wave, and the mushroom cloud was invariably followed by a detached and scientific-sounding discussion of blast effects, including (after the USSBS report) a discussion of radiation damage to the human body at the time of the initial blast. The title of the first section of Hersey's text, "The Noiseless Flash," seemed to indicate that his narrative would follow the sequence of the official narrative. Instead, Hersey detailed the daily minutiae of the lives that were shattered by the atomic bomb. The beginning of "The Noiseless Flash" introduced the six Japanese victims and described what they were doing "at the moment when the atomic bomb flashed above Hiroshima."[8] Hersey then gave a longer version of each person's activities on the morning of 6 August 1945. The knowledge that the detonation of the bomb was imminent cast an air of drama and pathos over each of their stories.

Hersey described the hopes and hardships of each of his subjects before the attack. Reverend Tanimoto was tired from moving his belongings to a safe zone outside the city. Mrs. Nakamura (the widow) was fretting over the incessant air-raid alarms and worried about how she would protect and provide for her children. Dr. Fujii, relatively carefree, was reading the newspaper in his underwear. Dr. Sasaki was worried about being prosecuted for practicing medicine without a license. Father Kleinsorge (a German) was struggling with diarrhea and his duties at the mission. Ms. Sasaki (no relation to the doctor) was doing family chores before going to work. A story about the atomic bomb, the greatest weapon ever devised, began with the banality of everyday life. Hersey turned the narrative away from the atomic bomb itself and toward an exploration of subjective human experience.[9]

When the flash of light came, it completely shattered the lives of Hersey's subjects. Hersey described the flash six times, once from each victim's point of view. The flash interrupted the stories of their lives, and Hersey heightened this perception of interruption by inserting the flash in the middle of sentences and paragraphs. For example, Mrs. Nakamura saw the flash when she was in her kitchen preparing a meal for her children and watching her neighbor tear down his house: "As [she] stood watching her neighbor, everything flashed whiter than any white she had ever seen."[10] While Hersey parenthetically noted the proximity of each character to ground zero, he made no mention of the fireball that figured so prominently in official accounts. Instead, he described the survivors' immediate perceptions of the shock wave and subsequent damage. Mrs. Nakamura "had taken a single step (the house was 1,350 yards, or three-quarters of a mile, from the center of the explosion) when something picked her up and she seemed to fly into the next room over the raised sleeping platform, pursued by parts of her house."[11] Hersey immersed his readers in a particular human experience of the explosion. The blast did not simply damage a house; it destroyed the widow's home and buried her and her three children in the debris. While Hersey maintained the scientific detail and objective tone of the official narrative (here exemplified by his parenthetical notation of the house's distance from ground zero) he went to great pains to show the story behind the U.S. government's numbers and rhetoric.

At one point midway through the story, Hersey explicitly contrasted his own narrative with the official accounts of Hiroshima. After quoting extensively from President Truman's original announcement about Hiroshima, Hersey commented that "even if [the survivors] had known the truth, most of them were too busy or too weary or too badly hurt to care that they were the objects of the first great experiment in the use of atomic power, which (as the voices on the radio shouted) no country except the United States, with its industrial know-how, its willingness to throw two billion gold dollars into an important wartime gamble, could possibly have developed."[12] Hersey directly undermined the nationalistic rhetoric of Truman's announcement. The specter of scientific experimentation with human subjects still haunted the postwar world: Nazi and Japanese scientists had been widely condemned for such wartime atrocities. In this passage, Hersey directed that criticism at the United States, condemning the Hiroshima attack as a "great experiment" on human subjects. The official narrative of the Manhattan Project—with its representations of heroic scientists, American ingenuity, and economic might—became a hollow and cruel boast in the context of Hiroshima's suffering victims. The heroes who emerged in Hersey's "Hiroshima" were not scientists and bomber pilots but rather the doctors and clergymen who tended the wounded and injured and the victims who somehow managed to live on.

Thornton Wilder's *Bridge of San Luis Rey* (1927), a novel that reconstructed a disaster from several points of view, influenced the structure of Hersey's story.[13] Hersey also drew upon Modernist wasteland imagery to communicate the unnatural and horrific effects of the atomic bomb in a familiar literary language. Hersey's use of wasteland imagery was not surprising: such imagery had become part of the literary canon by the mid-1940s. T. S. Eliot's landmark poem *The Waste Land* had been published by the literary journal *Dial* in early 1922.[14] The publication of Eliot's poem established Modernism within the elite publishing world of New England and thrust Eliot into a position of prestige and economic security in the literary world. Well-known authors such as Ernest Hemingway, F. Scott Fitzgerald, and John Dos Passos developed this imagery throughout the 1920s and the 1930s. However, it would be several years before *The Waste Land* and other Modernist texts were taught as the best of American letters. It wasn't until the rise of the New Critics in American universities from the 1930s through the 1950s that Modernist texts began to be regularly taught in English departments.[15] During this period, American universities were becoming more and more accessible. From 1920 to 1940, the percentage of 18- to 21-year-olds enrolled in American universities jumped from 8 to 16. In addition, the number of public colleges in the United States jumped 1,000 percent from 1890 to 1950.[16] This demographic shift, which was closely related to the increasing emphasis on utilitarian education, provided a much larger audience for Eliot and other Modernists than the elite literary world of New England and Europe. Through its influence on other authors and its canonization in universities, the imagery of *The Waste Land* became a widely recognized shorthand for the isolation, fragmentation, and quiet desperation of the modern world. As a Yale graduate who had done postgraduate work in literature at Cambridge, Hersey would have been involved in the growing debates during this period about the validity and implications of the Modernist enterprise.[17]

Hersey's use of literary techniques was masked by his spare and objective nonfiction prose. Hersey juxtaposed several images of fire, death, and desolation with images of water and rebirth. However, the images did not add up to the natural life-death-rebirth cycle of *The Fisher King*, the myth that Eliot acknowledged as one of the primary sources for *The Waste Land*.[18] As in Eliot's poem, the cycle of nature seemed out of balance; the sources of life (such as water) caused illness and death rather than rebirth. Throughout *The Waste Land*, Eliot used dust as a metaphor for sterility; without water, the desiccated ground could not bring forth life. This was foregrounded in one of the most famous lines of the poem, where a narrative voice warned, "I will show you fear in a handful of dust."[19] At the same time, images of excessive amounts of water repeatedly caused death in the poem. The imbalance of water and dust in *The Waste Land* was symptomatic of a world that had become broken. Physically, morally, and culturally, the modern world seemed to be irreparably damaged in some way.

Hersey exploited this imagery in his descriptions of the effects of the atomic bomb. When he mentioned the mushroom cloud, the oblique nature of the reference emphasized its effects on the survivors rather than engaging in a detailed description. Immediately after the attack, Reverend Tanimoto noticed that "under what seemed to be a local dust cloud, the day grew darker and darker."[20] The shadow of what American readers would have recognized as the atomic cloud engulfed the people of Hiroshima and initiated a horrible struggle for survival. Instead of serving as a "monument to victory," the cloud symbolized the hopelessness and death that threatened to consume the main figures in the story.[21] Hersey never used the metaphor of a mushroom, instead referring to the cloud as "a local dust cloud," "clouds of dust," and "a local column of dust."[22] The images of the dust cloud were juxtaposed with descriptions of excessive and unnatural rain. Reverend Tanimoto noticed that "houses nearby were burning, and when huge drops of water the size of marbles began to fall, he half thought that they must be coming from the hoses of firemen fighting the blazes. (They were actually drops of condensed moisture falling from the turbulent tower of dust, heat, and fission fragments that had already risen miles into the sky above Hiroshima.)"[23] Hersey's parenthetical insertion revealed the unnatural aspect of the rain: the marble-sized drops had emerged from the atomic bomb's dust cloud. Later, "abnormally large" drops of rain fell on victims as they lay in an evacuation area.[24] Hersey implied that the rain was radioactive and therefore was not natural life-giving water. Instead, it was an artificial and perverted carrier of death. As a form of radioactive fallout, the rain itself became a source of radiation sickness.

In Hersey's account, centers of natural life became deathtraps for those attempting to survive. A number of the survivors of the initial blast fled to a park that became an evacuation center. Hersey described the park in idyllic pastoral terms that contrasted starkly with his description of the devastated city: "[Asano Park] was far enough away from the explosion so that its bamboos, pines, laurel, and maples were still alive, and the green place invited refugees . . . partly because the foliage seemed a center of coolness and life."[25] But the refuge the park provided was only temporary, as the abnormally large drops of radioactive rain soon began to fall.[26] As Mrs. Nakamura and her children arrived at the park, they had a very unpleasant experience: "They all felt terribly thirsty, and they drank from the river. At once they were nauseated and began vomiting, and they retched the whole day."[27] For Mrs. Nakamura and her children, the water brought no relief from the terrible radiation sickness they were developing. Instead, it precipitated their vomiting and revealed the advancing symptoms of radiation sickness. Through his description, Hersey used wasteland imagery to challenge official denials of fallout and lingering radiation. Instead, he showed how the atomic bomb had turned idyllic nature into a killer.

The specter of death by water that hung over *The Waste Land* is present in other ways in "Hiroshima." As victims fled the fires that engulfed the city, they were confronted with the danger of drowning. The second section of "Hiroshima"—entitled "The Fire"— echoed the third and fourth sections of *The Waste Land*, which were entitled "The Fire Sermon" and "Death by Water," respectively. The third section of Eliot's poem began with the lines, "The river's tent is broken: the last fingers of leaf / Clutch and sink into the wet bank. The wind / Crosses the brown land, unheard."[28] These lines were followed by a number of images that lamented urban decay, decadence, and abandonment. The section closed with the image of Carthage in flames and repeated the word "burning" five times.[29] The fourth section of *The Waste Land*, which was only ten lines long, focused on the image of a sailor who had drowned in the sea. The jarring incongruity of these sections again showed nature out of balance: water did not quench the fires of the burning city or heal "the brown land" but rather engulfed and destroyed life. In the second section of "Hiroshima," the unnatural rain that sprang from the dust cloud did not quench the flames of the burning houses. As the conflagration led to increasingly vicious winds and strange weather phenomena, water posed another deadly threat to the initial survivors of the blast. Dr. Fujii's home was destroyed and blown into the river, and he awoke to find himself pinned between two beams that held his head above the water. He soon realized that he would drown when the tide came in if he did not free himself. Ironically, Dr. Fujii was threatened by drowning while flames begin to grow all around him. Hersey used the irony of these images to show how the atomic bomb was a technology that violated the natural order.

Later, Reverend Tanimoto encountered a group of wounded civilians lying near the river. The people were too weak to move and were in danger of drowning with the rising tide. Reverend Tanimoto went to great pains to ferry them to safety across the river. However, when he looked in on them afterward, he discovered that "the tide had risen above where he had put them; they had not had the strength to move; they must have drowned. He saw a number of bodies floating in the river."[30] Eventually, the fire reached the park as well. Reverend Tanimoto, in one of his many acts of heroism, organized a group of men to battle the flames. While the men used water from a nearby rock pool to successfully stave off the fire, the nearby river became a deadly trap for many of the victims: "As Mr. Tanimoto's men worked, the frightened people in the park pressed closer and closer to the river, and finally the mob began to force some of the unfortunates who were on the very bank into the water."[31] A number of people drowned as a result of trying to escape the fire. The river and the fire formed the proverbial "rock and a hard place" in the imagery of the narrative. As in *The Waste Land*, fire and water became sources of death; as a direct result of the atomic bomb, the fire and the water extended the devastation of the attack. In their weakened condition, many victims found the river as deadly as the fires and devastation they tried to escape. Hersey portrayed the atomic bomb as the destroyer of the balance of nature, a force that turned the entire city of Hiroshima into a literal and metaphorical wasteland.

As the victims of the atomic bombing wandered through the city, they were surrounded by a devastated urban landscape and marched along in a manner that was eerily reminiscent of *The Waste Land*. In the opening section of Eliot's poem, a narrator described a procession of people through the landscape of London: "Unreal City, / Under the brown fog of a winter dawn, / A crowd flowed over London Bridge, so many, / I had not thought death had undone so many."[32] Eliot described the mass of Londoners walking to work as a procession of the walking dead. His footnote to this passage connected these lines to Dante's *Inferno*, an allusion that equated the London Bridge with the bridge between life and death and the Londoners with the damned who suffer for eternity in hell. The description of the Londoners also set the mood for their procession: "Sighs, short and infrequent, were exhaled, / And each man fixed his eyes before his feet."[33] The depression, isolation, and resignation of this description heightened the sense of pathos and quiet desperation that permeated Eliot's poem. Each individual, keeping "his eyes before his feet," seemed transfixed and helpless in his own hellish misery.

Throughout "Hiroshima," Hersey used strikingly similar images to describe the procession of wounded as they attempted to flee the city. The first glimpse of these images came from the point of view of Dr. Fujii, who was confused by the nature of the weapon that had struck the city: "[Dr. Fujii] and his friend observed something that puzzled them, and which, as doctors, they discussed: although there were as yet very few fires, wounded people were hurrying across the bridge in an endless parade of misery, and many of them exhibited terrible burns on their faces and arms. 'Why do you suppose it is?' Dr. Fujii asked."[34] Later, Reverend Tanimoto saw a similar procession as he attempted to find his wife and baby: "He was the only person making his way into the city; he met hundreds and hundreds who were fleeing, and every one of them seemed to be hurt in some way. The eyebrows of some were burned off and skin hung from their faces and hands. Others, because of pain, held their arms up as if carrying something in both hands. . . . Many, although injured themselves, supported relatives who were worse off. Almost all had their heads bowed, looked straight ahead, were silent, and showed no expression whatever."[35] Hersey repeated similar descriptions of the victims at several points in the text. The numerous bridges that connected the separate sections of Hiroshima became passages to the wasteland of suffering and death. Dr. Fujii later observed that "now not so many people walked in the streets, but a great number sat and lay on the pavement, vomited, waited for death, and died."[36] The cumulative effect of these images was much the same as the description of the Londoners in *The Waste Land*; the flight of Hiroshima's suffering victims took on the unnerving aspect of a procession of the damned. Hersey described the mood of the victims as they walked silently with "their heads bowed" and their eyes "straight ahead." Isolated in their extreme suffering, the victims ignored the calls for help from the ruins that surrounded them. Hersey added to the poignancy of the images by describing how the injured silently helped relatives whose suffering was even greater. The victims' ignorance about the cause of their suffering compounded the horror and pathos of the procession. In the context of this wasteland imagery, Dr. Fujii's question became much more than simple curiosity about the cause of the wounds. The reader, who knew very well what had caused the injuries, was invited to ask, "Why did this have to happen?"

In perhaps the most gruesome and moving passage of the text, wasteland imagery played a central role in emphasizing the obscenity of the attack on Hiroshima. The Christian clergymen, Reverend Tanimoto and Father Kleinsorge, attempted to ease the suffering of many of the victims they encountered by bringing them water. In Christian iconography, water is a source of purification and succor; in the ceremony of baptism, water serves to wash away the sins of individuals and to bring them peace. The water that the two clergymen brought, however, seemed inadequate to the scale of suffering they encountered. Reverend Tanimoto experienced this at an evacuation center:

> Mr. Tanimoto's way around the fire took him across the East Parade Ground, which, being an evacuation area, was now the scene of a gruesome review: rank on rank of the burned and bleeding. Those who were burned moaned, "*Mizu, mizu*! Water, water!" Mr. Tanimoto found a basin in a nearby street and located a water tap that still worked . . . and he began carrying water to the suffering strangers. When he had given drink to about thirty of them, he realized that he was taking too

> much time. . . . Then he ran away. He went to the river again, the basin in his hand. . . . There he saw hundreds of people so badly wounded that they could not get up to go farther from the burning city. When they saw a man erect and unhurt, the chant began again: "*Mizu, mizu, mizu.*" Mr. Tanimoto could not resist them; he carried them water from the river—a mistake, since it was tidal and brackish.[37]

This "gruesome review" again evoked Eliot's procession of the damned, abject in their suffering. Like many of the characters in *The Waste Land*, the victims in this passage longed for water; however, the water provided only temporary relief or even worsened their condition. As Reverend Tanimoto moved through the landscape of Hiroshima, he was continually confronted with masses of people whose condition was signified by a single word: "water." No matter how much water the clergyman brought, the suffering continued. Several passages like this humanized the collapse of the city's infrastructure. The scale of the disaster overwhelmed even Christian mercy in Hersey's narrative, a turn of events that drove home the immorality of the attack.

Hersey's "Hiroshima" seemed to capture the unique and horrifying consequences of life in the modern world. The atomic bomb had changed the political and cultural landscape of the United States, and to many it now seemed only a matter of time before American cities began to suffer the same fate as Hiroshima. By grounding his account of the attack in the subjective experiences of several individuals, Hersey forever changed the debate about nuclear weapons. While many did (and still do) feel that the attacks on Hiroshima and Nagasaki were justified revenge for the war crimes of the Japanese military, Hersey's text made such sentiments seem particularly cruel and uninformed. The official propaganda of the U.S. government about its use of nuclear weapons began to meet growing skepticism, and Hersey's "Hiroshima" became a touchstone for those who challenged the wisdom and necessity of the emerging arms race with the Soviet Union.

Hersey's story shifted the perspective most Americans used to think about nuclear weapons: after the publication of "Hiroshima," the majority of nuclear war stories were written from the point of view of the victims instead of the bombers. While the official narrative of the atomic blasts remained familiar, most nuclear war stories used the flash of light, the atomic fireball, the shockwave, and the mushroom cloud only as a brief precursor to the main body of the narrative. Exploring survival in the wasteland after an attack became the dominant mode of storytelling about nuclear war. For many Americans, the *hibakusha*—the Japanese survivors of the atomic bombs—became archetypes of the human condition in the atomic age. What happened to them could (and probably would) happen to us; their story would soon be our own. In the growing climate of nuclear fear, "Hiroshima" emerged as the nonfiction basis for countless fictional explorations of American culture. The wasteland of "Hiroshima" had transformed the narrative landscape of America, and now Americans had to imagine how they too would survive.

PART III

THE NUCLEAR FRONTIER

RACE AND THE REPRESENTATION OF FUTURE WAR, 1945–1959

Chapter 9

Official Fictions

Future-War Stories After Hiroshima

U.S. military officials began to spin visions of future conflicts before World War II was even over. Their stories focused on what technologies and strategies the United States needed to develop to win the next major war. These future-war stories resembled the original story of atomic warfare, H. G. Wells's *The World Set Free* (1914), in a number of particulars. However, unlike Wells's novel, the future-war stories put out by military officials and science fiction authors were focused on strategic goals. They ignored the individual suffering and horror of such warfare, focusing instead on the details of rocket trajectories, defensive fortifications, and retaliatory strikes. One early and well-known military prophet of strategic war fiction was General H. H. "Hap" Arnold, the head of the U.S. Army Air Forces at the conclusion of World War II. During a press conference that was reported on the front page of the *New York Times* on 18 August 1945 General Arnold spoke about "robot, jet-propelled atomic bombs, which will be guided by television and find their targets by radar."[1] General Arnold emphasized that the United States had the lead in developing these new technologies and claimed that "these Buck Rogers things I'm talking about . . . are not so Buck Rogerish as you might think."[2] General Arnold explicitly reinforced the feeling that Americans were living in a science fiction world: the fantastic inventions chronicled in science fiction stories such as *The Adventures of Buck Rogers in the 25th Century* were becoming a reality.[3] General Arnold's comments showed how some military men were self-consciously moving into the realm of science fiction in planning for the next war. In talking about things like "robot, jet-propelled atomic bombs," General Arnold was both engaging in a science fiction–style story of future war and warning about what he saw as realistic threats that the United States would face in the future.

At the heart of these strategic fictions was the desire to preserve the civilization of the United States. Strategic fictions generally imagined an America of the future that had reorganized its infrastructure and military to make less inviting targets for nuclear weapons. However, the vision of the American people as civilized was consistent: repeated images of white middle-class domestic life showed who these strategic fictions were really trying to protect. Strategic fictions bought into the assumption that to be American was to be white; nonwhites were beneath consideration. In opposition to the explicit militarism of strategic fictions, a number of future-war stories began to appear in 1946 that can be classified as critical. Both types of future-war fiction represented nuclear war as something that should be prevented, but they disagreed about how to do that. Strategic fictions claimed that deterrence through overwhelming military power was the only way to prevent war, whereas critical fictions saw such a military buildup as the surest path to a nuclear apocalypse.[4] They predicted that the civilization of the United States would be destroyed if the militarists had their way and focused on the horrific effects of nuclear attacks on civilians in order to represent nuclear war as immoral and pointless.

With the memory of Pearl Harbor fresh in the minds of Americans, stories about future sneak attacks by an enemy that used atomic bombs were particularly effective. After the invention of the atomic bomb and the beginning of the Cold War with the Soviet Union,

Americans began to develop what Spencer Weart termed "nuclear fear."[5] A number of factors contributed to nuclear fear and the obsession with future war in the late 1940s. Not least of these was the increasing tension with the Soviet Union: a series of disagreements in 1945 and 1946 about issues such as spheres of influence, economics, and atomic energy made a confrontation with the Soviets seem inevitable.[6] Politicians, military leaders, and scientists predicted that the American monopoly on the atomic bomb would soon end.[7] As early as 4 September 1945, the *New York Times* ran a front-page story on Russian designs to enter a race with the United States for atomic power.[8] Such stories seemed to have an impact on public opinion; a March 1946 Gallup Poll indicated that 69 percent of Americans believed that the United States would be in another war within twenty-five years.[9] Another Gallup Poll conducted on the same dates that asked a series of questions that measured American feelings about current tensions with Russia found that 71 percent of Americans surveyed disapproved of Russian postwar policies.[10] In an April 1946 Gallup Poll, 42 percent of Americans surveyed indicated that they already believed another country was manufacturing atomic bombs; Russia was cited as the most likely culprit by those surveyed.[11] A survey by sociologists Leonard Cottrell and Sylvia Eberhardt conducted in mid-1946 found that two-thirds of the Americans they interviewed believed that "there is a real danger that atomic bombs will . . . be used against the United States."[12] At the same time, Cottrell and Eberhardt found that many Americans believed that science would save us from the bomb; 55 percent of those surveyed thought that an adequate defense for the atomic bomb would be worked out.[13] In spite of widespread doubts and fears about scientific progress after two terrible wars, many clung to a belief that science could still contain and counteract its new monsters. While a significant number of Americans in 1946 believed that an atomic war with the Soviets was on the horizon, they did not necessarily believe that such a war would bring the end of the world. The strategic fictions of the late 1940s fed off and fueled the mixture of fear and hope about future wars that characterized the early days of the nuclear age.

Before the end of World War II, planners in the White House saw that the United States would have to maintain an unprecedented level of peacetime military mobilization to obtain its foreign policy objectives of containing Soviet communism and expanding American influence. But an ongoing postwar military mobilization in the face of the Soviet threat was at odds with the propaganda of the Office of War Information (OWI), which had used the promise of peacetime prosperity to garner support for the war effort. In 1943, advisors in the White House ordered the OWI to study ways to convince the population that continued mobilization and an active foreign policy was needed after the defeat of Germany and Japan.[14]

The first wave of post-Hiroshima future-war stories also seemed geared to support the OWI's goal of preparing Americans for a protracted period of military readiness. These early strategic fictions took one version of the lessons of Hiroshima and Nagasaki to heart and argued that the American military needed a new approach. While they analyzed the possibilities of active defenses to atomic bombs, these stories generally asserted that such defenses were unlikely. Instead, they pushed for a strategy that would maintain a strong military presence as a deterrent and a system of passive civil defense that included the dispersal of American cities. Drawing on the recent memory of Pearl Harbor, these future-war stories continued the tradition of a sneak attack by a loathsome enemy that more often than not turned out to be the Soviet Union. American military officers were more vocal than anyone else with their predictions about future wars, and their stories received wide circulation as the United States headed into the beginning of the Cold War. Through speeches, official reports, and press conferences, military officers addressed the public and attempted to scare up money for their favorite programs and steer the direction of American military preparedness.

A couple of months after his comments about "Buck Rogers" warfare, General Arnold submitted a report to the secretary of war that *Life* developed into a future-war story for its 19 November 1945 issue.[15] "The 36-Hour War" was presented in the usual *Life* format of large striking images (in this case paintings) with minimal text underneath. The images in "The 36-Hour War" would have been at home in the pages of a science fiction pulp magazine. The first image, which represented the atomic bombing of Washington, D. C., foregrounded a large rocket zooming over a distant gridlike cityscape. A large atomic fireball blotted out the center of the city.[16] The two following pages showed a panoramic depiction of the rocket attack. The bottom half of the painting showed North America from the perspective of "3,000 miles above the Pacific" with the stars of outer space hovering in the background.[17] Long arcs, which represented the trajectories of the rockets, circled the horizon and ended with small flashes at various points in the United States. The text at the bottom of the page quoted General Arnold: "With present equipment an enemy air power can, without warning, pass over all formerly visualized barriers and can deliver devastating blows at our population centers."[18] This quote was followed by a description of the picture: "LIFE's artist has shown the U.S. as it might appear a very few years from now, with a great shower of enemy rockets falling on 13 key U.S. centers."[19] The pictures dramatized the elimination of geographic defense barriers brought about by new technologies like the German V-2 rocket and projected how future versions of these rockets could combine with the atomic bomb to make Earth seem like a much smaller and deadlier place. As the quote from General Arnold emphasized, previous barriers to attacking the United States—namely the Atlantic and Pacific oceans—no longer provided adequate protection in the new age of long-range bombers and rockets. The didactic point of the story was clear: the United States needed to maintain and improve its armed forces and remain vigilant against enemy attack. As the title of the story implied, the United States might not survive another Pearl Harbor–style sneak attack and might lose the next war within thirty-six hours if action was not taken to improve weapons and defenses.

The final six pages of the story showed the response of a mobilized and prepared America to the surprise rocket attack. One illustration showed a room full of military men watching a large radar screen that followed the trajectory of the rockets. The next image showed a close-up of an American defense rocket going to intercept an incoming enemy rocket. Despite the hopefulness of the image, the text warned that "our defensive machines stop few attackers."[20] While it evoked the belief of many Americans that science could create a defense against atomic bombs, the story incorporated a skeptical vision of such a defense. Significantly, there was no active defense against the atomic bomb in the story; there was only an active defense against a particular method of delivering the atomic bomb (via rockets), and even that defense was represented as pretty shaky. In this way, the story reinforced the perception that the atomic bomb was an ultimate weapon that was inescapable once deployed.

The story underscored the inescapability of an atomic attack by calling for passive defense and an overpowering offense as the way to prevent or win the next war. General Arnold's vision of the optimal military posture was represented in a two-page illustration that showed a decentralized America redesigned "for minimum vulnerability" that was prepared to "take immediate offensive action with overwhelming force" or "counterattack."[21] The image featured a vast subterranean military base. Within the base, which was described as an "underground rocket-launching site and atomic bomb factory," thousands of workers lived a self-contained lifestyle.[22] Power plants, ventilation systems, manufacturing plants, assembly areas, storage facilities, firing tubes, and "living areas" constituted the base's primary features. While General Arnold said that the United States should "devise every possible active defense against an atomic bomb attack," the thrust of the story clearly indicated that pursuing a passive defense and an overwhelming offense was the more realistic and effective way to respond to the threat of such an attack.[23] General Arnold's vision of the future echoed the bleak picture Wells had painted thirty-one years before of inescapable weapons that grew ever more powerful in *The World Set Free*.[24] In Wells's novel, this inevitably led to an all-out war that no nation won. (The war in fact led to the end of all nations.) In General Arnold's future-war story, the scenario ended with a national triumph: by being able to both minimize the destruction received from the enemy's blow and maximize the retaliatory punishment, the United States was able to win the "36-Hour War." The uncritical patriotism and victorious ending of the story became standard for American strategic fictions in the postwar years. In the hands of men like General Arnold, these fictions became a central part of the national security strategy itself as the government attempted to gain support for military spending and specific versions of strategic development.[25]

Even though the United States won the future war of the story, the final two images in "The 36-Hour War" must have left some Americans with doubts about the nature of the victory. The penultimate image showed "enemy airborne troops" who had invaded "a small U.S. town."[26] Wearing a strange outfit that included a gas mask and goggles, one of the enemy troops stood over the dead body of a buxom blond woman (presumably a telephone operator) as he repaired a telephone line next to a switchboard.[27] While the story made no explicit mention of radioactivity, the soldier's suit signified the toxic nature of the atomic attack. This detail contradicted the ongoing denials of the U.S. government regarding lingering radiation and fallout at Hiroshima and Nagasaki.

The dead woman presented a disturbing symbol of violation: civilians like this woman, the story showed, were now vulnerable to an enemy attack. In part, the image of the dead woman served to evoke outrage at the attack: she was presented as a full-figured blond white woman whose blouse was torn partly open. Like so many future-war stories that came before it, "The 36-Hour War" used the violation of this idealized white American woman to galvanize white male readers into a virile vigilance against enemy invasion. At the same time, the story portrayed an America that was *already* vigilant and prepared, which made the deaths of American civilians seem inescapable: even a prepared America would suffer heavy civilian casualties. The dubious nature of the American victory was underscored by the final image. While the text on the previous page ended with the upbeat words "the U.S. wins the atomic war," this final image showed U.S. technicians as they tested "the rubble of the shattered city" for radioactivity.[28] These technicians, like the enemy troops, wore gas masks and strange suits as they took measurements with their instruments outside the New York Public Library. Again, this image contradicted the government's position in late 1945 that there was no lingering radioactivity or fallout from the atomic attacks on Hiroshima and Nagasaki. If the atomic bomb left no lingering radioactivity, what were these technicians doing and why were they wearing protective suits?

However, like the images that were coming back from Hiroshima and Nagasaki, the image of a destroyed New York showed collapsed buildings instead of the bodies of the dead. The only civilian victim shown in the entire story was the female operator, and because her body exhibited no signs of burns or radiation sickness, it was unclear whether she was killed by the atomic bomb or by more conventional means. While the final image of a destroyed New York was disturbing, the absence of burned bodies and victims of radiation sickness made the victory of the United States seem sanitary.[29] The text asserted that "some 40,000,000 people have been killed," but the images did not represent this mass slaughter in any way.[30] The choice not to represent any kind of subjective experience of the victims or the effect of the atomic bomb on their bodies preserved the official perspective of the bombers and made the number of dead simply a military abstraction, a strategic calculation in the mathematics of atomic warfare.

One of the most disturbing things about this story was the way in which institutional authority—more specifically, General Arnold's position as head of the Army Air Forces—was mobilized to make the story seem not like fiction but rather like inevitable and inescapable fact. Arnold's story was an unrealized fictional account of what might come to pass. In 1945, it was clearly an example of science fiction, here mobilized as an official fiction to scare up support for Arnold's vision of how the military should develop in the future; his story began as an official report to the secretary of war. With the help of *Life* magazine, it was disseminated to a huge audience that usually did not read official military reports. The story mobilized its "official" status to lend credence to the importance of overwhelming offensive capabilities, passive civil defense, and the doctrine that eventually developed into the stalemate called mutual assured destruction.[31] This vision of what General Arnold termed "real security against atomic weapons in the visible future" dominated the thinking of the U.S.

government for the next forty years.[32] General Arnold's story attempted to scare Americans into accepting an ongoing military buildup as an essential precaution in the postwar world and provided a preview of the streamlined wartime propaganda machine that the government would continue to use throughout the early decades of the Cold War.

Many visions of future war that came from science fiction writers during 1945–1946 were strikingly similar to that of General Arnold. Science fiction authors who wrote future-war stories had gained a wider audience than ever before. Since the emergence of science fiction as a self-conscious genre in the 1920s, science fiction publishing had consisted mainly of short stories and serial novels in pulp magazines. Before World War II there had been a boom in the publication of science fiction pulp magazines, but paper shortages during the war had spelled the end for many of the lesser magazines in the genre.[33] After the revelation of the atomic bomb, though, the genre rode a new wave of popularity. The rise of cheap paperbacks in American book publishing helped the genre reach new audiences in the form of anthologies of the best pulp stories. Science fiction novels that had been published serially in pulp magazines were now collected and released in their complete form.[34] Stories that "predicted" the atomic bomb were especially popular, so much so that upscale magazines such as *Life*, *Colliers*, and *The New Yorker* began to publish future-war stories of the type that used to appear only in pulp magazines. Much early postwar science fiction seemed to toe the official government line with regard to the atomic bomb and its importance to the strategies of future wars. John W. Campbell Jr., editor of *Astounding Science Fiction* and a towering force in the genre, commented in a series of post-Hiroshima editorials that "the civilization we have been born into, lived in, and been indoctrinated with, died on July 16, 1945, and . . . the Death Notice was published to the world on August 6, 1945."[35] In the course of analyzing the new world, Campbell asserted that cities were obsolete and that unless a defense could be found for the atomic bomb, "there won't be any United States twenty-four hours after the next war starts."[36] This notion of sudden death from above and the need for decentralization became a common theme in the stories Campbell published and inspired. These stories helped stoke the growing sense of fear of nuclear war and fed into the U.S. government's attempts to continue spending vast sums of money on defense. If the United States did not keep expending money on new defenses, Campbell's hyperbolic announcement that the atomic bomb had killed civilization might actually come true.

Will Jenkins, who usually published under the pen name Murray Leinster, provided the most developed strategic future-war story written in this period by a science fiction author. *The Murder of the U.S.A.* was dedicated to Campbell. Released by Crown Publishers in 1946, it was one of the first science fiction works to benefit from the genre's wave of relative popularity in the aftermath of World War II. The novel told the story of World War III from the point of view of a common soldier named Lieutenant Sam Burton. In many ways, *The Murder of the U.S.A.* seemed like a more detailed version of "The 36-Hour War"; it espoused the idea of an ongoing military buildup as the only way to survive in the atomic age. The military base where Sam worked was a secret rocket bunker called a burrow. The burrow seems very similar to the subterranean rocket base in "The 36-Hour War." It included an atomic bomb manufacturing plant, a rocket-launching platform, a living area, a nuclear reactor, and a number of other features that made it self-sufficient. The purpose of the "Atomic Counter-Attack Force" of secret burrows was to ensure that the country could launch a devastating counteroffensive in the event of a sudden Pearl Harbor–type attack.[37] The world of Jenkins's novel displayed an idealized vision of nuclear deterrence and the doctrine of mutual assured destruction.[38] The burrows were a deterrent that had established world peace: every country with the technological capability to do so had built a number of burrows and had sworn to use atomic rockets to annihilate any aggressor.

Unfortunately (and inevitably) the peace was broken when an anonymous enemy managed to launch an undetectable Pearl Harbor–style attack that "murdered" the United States. Like the official narrative of the bombing of Hiroshima and Nagasaki, Jenkins's description of the death of America's cities focused on blast effects. The victims of the attack died suddenly after seeing "instantaneous flares of light a thousand times brighter than the sun" that were followed by "an intolerable radiant heat."[39] Jenkins offered no description of the effect of the bombs on humans other than a passing mention of the atomization of victims' bodies.[40] The casualties were also given as an abstract number: "One-third of America's population never knew anything about the war at all. One instant they were alive; the next, they weren't."[41] Like the official narrative of the atomic bomb and General Arnold's vision of future war, the novel represented the deaths caused by the atomic bomb in terms of numbers. The deaths came so quickly that there was no time for suffering; the American victims were anonymous targets who died a painless death.

Despite the abstract nature of the "murder" of so many Americans, the novel argued that these actions were horrible enough that the enemy nation deserved to be wiped from the face of the Earth. In a subsequent attack on individual burrows—attacks that came only when the enemy succeeded in locating one of the secret American bases—the United States launched defensive rockets to try to intercept the incoming enemy rockets. As in "The 36-Hour War," the defensive rockets were rarely effective. However, members of Sam's burrow found a way to make them effective enough to intercept three successive salvos by the enemy. Eventually, Sam's colleagues pieced together enough information from the downed rockets to establish the identity of the enemy. As in "The 36-Hour War," the name of the enemy was not revealed. Nonetheless, the text ended with the United States launching a massive counterattack designed to make an example of the aggressor and turn the enemy's country into "a waste of bomb-craters."[42] In a thinly veiled defense of the attacks on Hiroshima and Nagasaki, Sam justified this final overwhelming destruction of enemy civilians on the ground that they were criminals: "[The enemy] may feel that the murder of America was not their doing; that their leaders are the criminals. I say only that in allowing themselves to be enslaved they became criminals. If they are allowed to go free they will become criminals again."[43] Sam made this speech while trying to convince the other nations of the world that the utter annihilation of the enemy country was necessary.

By the time this novel was written, criticism of the atomic attacks on Japan had become increasingly common. One of the main arguments critics made was that the atomic bomb did not distinguish between civilians and military combatants. Sam's argument dismissed such distinctions as misguided and asserted that an entire nation was responsible for war, not just the leaders or the military. Through Sam's speech, Jenkins echoed the common World War II argument that there was no such thing as a Japanese civilian. Using the logic of Sam's speech, it seems clear that Jenkins was among those who believed that the United States should have continued to drop atomic bombs on Japan until every Japanese was dead: if we did not completely eradicate them, they would attack again in the future. In this way Jenkins provided an atomic age argument for genocide that justified atomic warfare instead of condemning its folly.[44]

While Jenkins vilified the enemy civilians, he painted a sentimental and romantic picture of the American civilians destroyed in the enemy's surprise attack. In his speech to the world, Sam said of the murdered Americans that "some of them were old, but they had committed no crime against our enemy. Some were men and women in the prime of life, with children whom they guarded joyously. They had done no injury to our enemy. And there were young men and women whose lives were hardly begun, and boys playing baseball and climbing trees, and girls playing with their dolls, and very little girls having tea-parties, and there were babies sleeping in utter contentment. . . . But they are dead. Our enemies murdered them."[45] Jenkins presented American civilians as innocents engaged in wholesome activities within middle-class families. Sam cloaked the American victims of the attack in sentimental rhetoric as a way to heighten the perceived barbarity of the enemy murderers. In *The Murder of the U.S.A.*, the enemy deserved destruction because of its sneak attack on peaceful Americans.

Although he was quick to assert the cruelty of the enemy, Jenkins failed to show the horrible impact of the atomic bomb on the human body. While these effects were not fully understood at the time Jenkins wrote the novel, he could have drawn on the ample reports in the news media to make an educated guess: this would have made the enemy seem that much more barbaric. Instead, Jenkins maintained the strategic perspective of the bombers and depicted the next atomic war as somewhat terrible but ultimately sanitary and winnable.[46] The scale of the destruction and the impact on civilians remained abstract and Jenkins asserted that the combination of deterrence and huge underground rocket bases could bring another moral and military victory for the United States in the next war.

Military fictions of strategic war remained relatively unchanged for decades after the stories of General Arnold and Will Jenkins.[47] However, as more information emerged about the horror and suffering Japanese atomic bombing victims experienced, critical future-war stories arose that challenged the perspective of strategic fictions. These stories translated the subjective and personal lessons of the atomic bomb victims into an American context. Instead of worrying about how to win the next war or prevent it with an overwhelming military deterrent, critical future-war stories warned against nuclear proliferation and condemned the immorality of the weapons themselves. The first of these critical stories was Philip Morrison's "If the Bomb Gets Out of Hand." The story was Morrison's contribution to the anthology *One World or None*, which included articles by such luminaries as General Arnold, J. Robert Oppenheimer, and Albert Einstein. The anthology was a call for peace and unity as well as a warning about the dangers of future atomic wars. Published by the Federation of American Scientists in March of 1946, *One World or None* sold 100,000 copies and received favorable reviews from a number of quarters.[48]

Morrison was a well-known Cornell physicist who had worked on the Manhattan Project. His story, which was entitled "If the Bomb Gets Out of Hand," began the anthology and provided the only piece of fiction in the volume. It started with a first-person account of his experiences in Hiroshima as a member of the U.S. army mission to "study the effects of the atomic bomb."[49] Most of the description was already familiar; it focused on the collapse of Hiroshima's infrastructure that was consistent with the official narrative of the atomic bomb. After nine long paragraphs of this familiar account, the direction of the narrative suddenly changed. Rather than continue with the strategic accounting of the Hiroshima bombing, Morrison acknowledged to his American readers that such accounts were "abstract and remote."[50] Morrison explained that in order to drive his point home, he would translate the experience of Hiroshima into the context of a familiar American city: "The streets and buildings of Hiroshima are unfamiliar to Americans. Even from pictures of the damage[,] realization is abstract and remote. A clearer and truer understanding can be gained from thinking of the bomb as falling on a city, among buildings and people, which Americans know well. The diversity of awful experience which I saw at Hiroshima, and which I was told about by its citizens, I shall project on an American target."[51] Because Morrison wanted to arouse in readers a desire to prevent any future atomic war, the victims of the atomic bomb that he described were not the vilified Japanese enemy but the citizens of New York.

The New Yorkers in Morrison's story were anonymous individuals engaged in everyday activities when the enemy struck. However, not everybody died instantly: "From the river west to Seventh Avenue, and from south of Union Square to the middle thirties, the streets were filled with the dead and dying. The old men sitting on the park benches in the square never knew what had happened. They were chiefly charred black on the side toward the bomb. Everywhere in this whole district were men with burning clothing, women with terrible red and blackened burns, and dead children caught hurrying home to lunch."[52] This description of an atomic bombing was very different from that given in strategic fictions. Instead of ignoring the deaths of civilians or asserting that they would die instantly, Morrison focused on the lasting human misery the atomic bomb inflicted. He paid particular attention to the unique horror of the atomic bomb: death by radiation sickness. Morrison refuted official reports that radiation sickness was not a major cause of civilian deaths and the preposterous assertion that such a death was "relatively pleasant," noting that "the most tragic of all the stories of the disaster is that of the radiation casualties."[53] Morrison described how thousands of New Yorkers who believed they had survived the blast ended up dead and how people far away from the center of the blast received lethal doses of radiation. These victims "died of unstoppable internal hemorrhages, of wildfire infections, of slow oozing of the blood into the flesh. Nothing seemed to help them much, and the end was neither slow nor very fast, but sure."[54] Morrison used this image of the suffering victims to emphasize his point that even if the United States could develop an active defense against atomic missiles, if even a few atomic bombs slipped through that defense the effect would be devastating.[55] Morrison asked his readers to weigh the cost in human life and suffering that any future atomic war would bring. With his dramatization of the collapse of a center of American civilization, Morrison encouraged Americans to do whatever was necessary to prevent the deployment of the atomic bomb.

After the publication of John Hersey's "Hiroshima" in late August of 1946, an increasing number of future-war stories explored the perspectives of atomic bomb victims as a way to argue for the prevention of atomic war and the protection of civilization. Leonard Engel and Emanuel S. Pillar dedicated their 1947 novel *The World Aflame: The Russian-American War of 1950* "to all those who realize that another war can be only a disastrous adventure which may lead to personal, national and world suicide." The narrator of the story was a character named Ed Craig, a reporter for a national media organization who had witnessed firsthand the major events of the war. As Craig recounted the events of the war, the influence of Hersey's "Hiroshima" became explicit: "Entire sections of Chicago appeared to be evaporating into pillars of dust which were rising into the atom cloud overhead. Behind these pillars, the sky was red with flame. . . . This was Hersey's Hiroshima—ten times worse—in my own country."[56] The authors mapped the events of Hersey's story onto Chicago, using the familiarity of Hersey's account as a shorthand to dramatize the horror of the atomic war. After this short description of the explosion, Craig described the collapsing infrastructure and the casualties of the blasts. Engel and Pillar were not satisfied with a simple description of the blast or an assessment of its strategic implications. As Craig narrated the impact of the atomic blast on its victims, the story clearly echoed the wasteland imagery of Hersey's "Hiroshima": "Now a fearful procession of the burned and injured was coming out of each of these streets. . . . Several of the wounded were vomiting as they walked—a first effect of the immense doses of gamma radiation to which they had been exposed. . . . Hair and eyebrows were entirely gone. Huge patches of skin hung from their hands and faces. Their clothes were charred shreds."[57] Disfigured and maimed from terrible burns, the civilian victims of the atomic bomb began their long and painful journey toward radiation sickness and death. As Hersey had in "Hiroshima," Engel and Pillar depicted the procession of victims in the city as a procession of the damned. While much of the narrative focused on the strategy and unfolding events of the war, the numerous graphic descriptions of human suffering never allowed the reader to lose sight of the horror brought by the atomic bomb. For Engel and Pillar, the strategies of atomic warfare brought about the collapse of American civilization, turning it into a wasteland of pain and misery.

As the war progressed, Craig described the standard litany of strategic concerns in atomic warfare. First, new Soviet rockets made an active defense against the atomic bomb impossible. Instead, the United States had to resort to extreme civil defense measures to limit the damage of the Soviet attacks. These included establishing martial law, dispersing cities throughout the country, and building underground bunkers to house industries and civilians. The media (including Craig) were given responsibility for convincing the public of the necessity for these and other civil defense measures. With the emphasis on total and global war, the concept of the citizen was exchanged for the concept of the citizen-soldier. This underscored the danger of atomic bombs to civilians: there was no such thing as a civilian in an atomic war because the destructive nature of the atomic bombs did not discriminate. Where the future-war stories of Jenkins and Morrison left the enemy unnamed, Engel and Pillar expressed the popular belief that the Soviet Union would be our enemy in the next atomic war. As had Jenkins and General Arnold, they also explored the impact of rockets on atomic warfare. While the Soviet enemy in the story developed and deployed its atomic rockets before the United States did so, Engel and Pillar were not simply trying to arouse fears about national security to secure support for the military. Like Morrison, they were attempting to critically assess the horrors of the atomic age and the impact of atomic warfare on civilians. However, they did not offer any alternatives to military deterrence in their story.

With concern growing about the threat of a global atomic war, strategic and critical future-war stories provided the two major poles in the developing arguments over how best to prevent another Hiroshima. Military officers and conservative science fiction authors insisted that overwhelming offensive might was the only possible deterrent, but their narratives virtually ignored the horrible impact of atomic weapons on the human body. Critical future-war stories focused instead on human suffering and used the horrors of civilian casualties to argue against the proliferation of nuclear weapons. Both kinds of future-war story had the effect of making the collapse of civilization seem like it might be inevitable. Throughout the 1940s and 1950s, these two modes of imagining nuclear warfare proliferated in the United States and became a national obsession. With the ultimate weapon now realized, were we on the verge of destroying the world? How would we survive the next great war? Under the burden of such weighty questions, many began to wax nostalgic and imagine that nuclear war might return us to a simpler time in American history.

CHAPTER 10

SURVIVAL AND SELF-HELP

CIVIL DEFENSE, WHITE SUBURBIA, AND THE RISE OF THE NUCLEAR FRONTIER

The idea that the United States is essentially a white nation has a long history. During the early Cold War, this idea became a central aspect of both strategic policy and anti-proliferation fantasies regarding nuclear weapons. The sympathetic heroes of strategic government propaganda and critical science fiction were always white, and author after author colonized the lived experience of the Japanese *hibakusha* to imagine what would happen to the white middle class in the event of a nuclear Pearl Harbor. The cover of the 1948 Bantam Books paperback edition of Hersey's *Hiroshima* provided a clear example of this colonization of experience: the painting on the cover showed a young white couple walking down a road that was bordered by grass and trees.[1] The young man was dressed in casual green slacks and a green jacket; he had his arm around the waist of the young woman, helping her along as he looked back toward the distant atomic explosion on the horizon. The young woman was wearing a long green jacket, a light green blouse, and a knee-length red skirt; her clothes were torn and tattered in several places and her hair fell in front of her face as she looked at the ground in front of her. On the first page, there was a note that acknowledged the strangeness of having this picture on the cover of a book about an atomic bombing in Japan. Under the heading "About the Cover," the note said:

> When Geoffrey Biggs, a master of shadow and light technique in art, brought in his startling illustration for the cover of *Hiroshima*, everybody wanted to know: "Where'd you get those people . . . why *those* two?"
>
> Biggs said he thought back to that August morning in a certain big industrial city and he imagined how *universally* terrifying that situation was, how it could strike fear into *anybody's* bones. "And I just drew two perfectly ordinary people—like you or me—and had them portray alarm, anxiety, and yet wild hope for survival as they run from man-made disaster in a big city—a city like yours or mine."

The way Biggs represented a young white couple as universal "ordinary people" showed the thorough acceptance of racist ideology in the 1940s. Never mind that the book was about Japanese atomic bomb victims: to be normal was to be white, and the true importance of the Hiroshima attack for men like Biggs was that such an attack could also happen to normal white Americans. Though the editors noted the strangeness of the image, the fact that they put it on the cover indicated that they accepted Biggs's argument on some level. Between 1946 and 1959, most future-war stories in the subgenre that I call nuclear frontier fiction used a similar ideological position to imagine the horror of an atomic bombing of the United States. The characters of these stories who fled from nuclear destruction resembled this white couple, who still held a "wild hope of survival." The white atomic bomb survivors of American future-war stories were not simply thrust into a degrading struggle for survival, however; the nuclear frontier allowed them to shed their civilization-induced weaknesses and be reborn. Like the storied colonists of old, the white frontiersmen and the white frontier families of nuclear fiction came to embody "American" virtues as they fought to overcome the corruption of modern civilized life and the savagery of the nuclear frontier.

Nuclear frontier stories usually relished the prospect of civilization being destroyed; this distinguished them from the strategic and critical future-war stories of 1946 and 1947. However, the desire to destroy the corrupt modern world and build a new world was consistent with centuries of apocalyptic literature from Europe and the Mediterranean. This apocalyptic imagination ran deep in the literature of the United States from its beginnings; authors such as Charles Brockden Brown and Edgar Allan Poe provide two clear examples of the American obsession with the collapse of civilized order.[2] Within a year after the publication of Hersey's "Hiroshima" (1946), a number of nuclear frontier stories began to appear in both science fiction and mainstream magazines. In nuclear frontier stories, the authors did not dedicate the bulk of the narrative to describing atomic blasts, outlining strategies, or vilifying the enemy. Instead, they followed Hersey's lead and focused on specific individuals who struggle to overcome the horrors of atomic war and the subsequent collapse of civilization. For the people in Hersey's text and the characters in nuclear frontier stories, the primary goal was survival: the destruction of civilization threw them into a Darwinian confrontation with savage nature. This return to a basic struggle to survive was portrayed as one of the ironic horrors of the atomic bomb; the ultimate weapon and sign of progress was precisely what brought about a devolution that reduced humans to an animalistic state.[3] Nuclear frontier stories were defined by their landscape, which combined the wasteland imagery of literary Modernism with the frontier imagery of the nineteenth century in various combinations. With cities reduced to rubble-strewn wilderness, the survivors had to battle with manifestations of savagery in order to establish a new America out of the wreckage of the old.[4] Drawing on Darwinist formulations of progress and the frontier, most nuclear frontier stories repeated the racism of Darwin's arguments that depicted superior Europeans winning the struggle to establish a new and better civilization.

Probably the earliest nuclear frontier story was Ray Bradbury's "The Million Year Picnic," which was first published in the summer 1946 issue of *Planet Stories*. The story followed an American family from New York City as they went on a fishing trip while vacationing on Mars. Soon, however, the mysterious actions of the father and mother betrayed that this was no ordinary trip. The father, a former state governor, had used his influence to arrange it so his family was "the first colonial family" sent to Mars.[5] The family had brought enough provisions to last for several years, which they stored safely away from their ship. A passing enemy rocket destroyed their rocket (along with those of the four other families on Mars) and the Earth was consumed by a devastating war the politically connected father had anticipated. The point of view in the story was not strategic—it did not discuss the details of the war—but rather described one family's attempt to survive the inevitable war by escaping to Mars.[6] By describing them as "the first colonial family," the story evoked the notion of a frontier family stepping out into a new land. With the indigenous Martians already dead, this family had to struggle with the Martian environment as it attempted to establish a new life.

After the father's radio went silent, he brought the family—three blond freckled boys and a "slender and soft" wife with "spun-gold" hair—to an abandoned Martian city that would be their new home.[7] As people did in Fredrick Jackson Turner's account of the frontier, the white family began to shed the aspects of their previous civilization in order to build something new. After the family set up camp for the first night, the father burned a number of documents that were associated with the civilization they had left behind:

> The papers crinkled like an old man's skin and the cremation surrounded words like this:
>
> *Government Bonds, Political Maps, Religious Quarrels, Beliefs, Sciences, Prejudices of the Pan-American Unity, Stock Report for July 23, 2044*, THE WAR DIGEST.
>
> Dad had insisted on bringing these papers, for this purpose. He sat there and fed them into the fire, one by one, with satisfaction, and told them what it all meant.
>
> "I'm burning a way of life, just like that way of life is being burned clean of Earth right now."[8]

By having a main character burn these documents, Bradbury showed disgust with the corruption of many modern institutions. The proof of such corruption was the fact of the war: as the text implied, only corrupt institutions and a corrupt civilization could lead humanity to commit such a horrible act of self-destruction. As did H. G. Wells in his original narrative of nuclear apocalypse, *The World Set Free*, Bradbury represented civilization as unworthy of being saved. The father in "The Million Year Picnic" echoed the argument of Wells's novel: "'Science got too far ahead of them too quickly, and the people got lost in a scientific wilderness . . . putting emphasis on wrong things; on machines instead of the thought of how to run the machines. Wars got worse and killed them. . . . That way of life proved itself wrong, and it strangled itself with its own hands.'"[9] Bradbury was critical of the pace of scientific development and, like Wells, he pointed to the irony of a technological civilization destroyed by its own creations. Once the last aspects of the civilization were stripped away by the atomic bomb and the frontier campfire, the family had an opportunity to start over. As it was in earlier frontier narratives, the family was clearly described as white; in facing a new start with a new colony surrounded by wilderness, they were reliving the origins of the United States. They had returned to the quintessential American moment, the supposedly pure origins at the frontier after the corruption of civilization had been stripped away from white settlers.

"The Million Year Picnic" not only repeated the problematic racial Darwinism of earlier frontier narratives but also reflected the growing emphasis on the white nuclear family that dominated postwar culture. After two decades of domestic instability caused by the Depression and World War II, many Americans devoted themselves to establishing stable and traditional homes in the 1940s and 1950s. The new instabilities of the Cold War further reinforced this drive for tradition and domestic security.[10] The growing attraction of the domestic ideal dovetailed with the growth of white suburbia during the 1940s and 1950s. Urban centers had long been associated with civilization in American culture. Since the beginning of European colonization, European Americans had defined themselves in opposition to what they saw as the corrupt civilizations of Europe. The American landscape was central to the notion of American exceptionalism, providing Americans with the opportunity to renew themselves through the conquest of nature and savagery. With the symbolic closing of the frontier in 1890 and the explosion in urban populations in the early twentieth century, many believed that the United States was headed toward a catastrophe. Without the frontier, many Americans felt that the United States would fall victim to the same sort of overcivilization and decadence that had corrupted Europe.

Turner defined the frontier in 1893 as "the meeting point between savagery and civilization."[11] Located between rural wilderness and urban civilization, the suburbs were a modern version of the frontier. Many white families fled urban civilization in the years following the war, flocking to the traditional American values they felt they would find in the suburbs. By the 1940s, urban centers in the United States were commonly represented as homes to a modern form of savagery. Early in the century a popular literature arose that addressed the life of urban slums in the same manner that *National Geographic* treated "savage" foreign cultures. This literature generally focused on the strange mix of cultures, ethnicities, and races in the urban centers of the United States. As it looked at the immigrant-filled slums, this literature criticized the inherently degrading conditions of urban life in industrial America. The most famous example of this literature was Upton Sinclair's *The Jungle*, which was published serially in 1905 and released as a book in 1906. Sinclair compared immigrant workers in the Chicago meatpacking industry to savages fighting against the forces of nature. Sinclair was a socialist who called for changes in the conditions of workers in industrial America, and his jarring and graphic accounts of the Chicago meatpacking industry quickly led to government reforms. However, instead of rejecting the entire "savage versus civilized" formula embedded in the notion of progress, Sinclair's descriptions of the urban jungle degraded the very people he was attempting to help. The main figure in Sinclair's story began as something of a noble savage, but under the pressure of heartless capitalism he became what Sinclair described as a degraded and corrupt savage. Sinclair's account of immigrants made them appear to be simple preindustrial natives who needed to be lifted up by civilized socialists. With the writing of men like Sinclair, a vision of the American city emerged that viewed civilization as an urban jungle that was full of dangerous savages. To live in the city was to brave the threatening mix of foreign cultures and nonwhite races that festered in its heart.[12]

Many white families that moved to the suburbs in the 1940s and 1950s were fleeing the perceived savagery of the modern city. The move to what historian Kenneth T. Jackson called the "crabgrass frontier" was fueled by an explosion in mass-produced housing that made single-family homes affordable to millions of middle-class Americans after the war. Most new developments had an official policy of selling only to whites, which led to widespread economic, cultural, and racial homogeneity in the suburbs of the 1940s and 1950s. This also increased the segregation of many American cities and the sense that only poor minorities populated urban centers. Despite the cultural diversity of the United States, the cultural conformity and racial homogeneity of the suburbs led many to believe that the entire country was uniform in its attitudes and ideas.[13] With the explosion of suburban communities during the post–World War II period, white middle-class suburban America emerged as a major cultural and political force; as Andrew Grossman notes, both President Truman and President Eisenhower saw "this constituency as vital for developing and nurturing the Cold War domestic political consensus."[14] Within this social and political context, frontier narratives became a popular way of expressing the trials of the white suburban family. Surrounded by forces that threatened to destroy it, the white suburban family fought against the savagery of the city and the dangers of the nuclear age in its quest to uphold "traditional" American values.

Despite this trend in American culture, not all nuclear frontier stories focused exclusively on the family. Instead, many stories evoked the image of the lone white frontiersman struggling through the wilderness to survive.[15] Drawing inspiration from the early American frontier stories of James Fenimore Cooper, these frontiersman stories focused on the white man who had devolved and gone half "savage" in order to survive. One of the earliest and most representative of these nuclear frontiersman stories was Stuart Cloete's two-part piece "The Blast," which appeared in the 12 and 19 April 1947 issues of *Colliers*. Cloete was a young South African novelist living in New York, and he lent both his name and his background to the protagonist of his story. Like most atomic attack narratives in this period, "The Blast" described at length the political circumstances of the attack and the effect of the atomic bomb on the infrastructure of New York. The character Stuart Cloete had to struggle through a social and physical wasteland characterized by rape, murder, cannibalism, and complete lawlessness. While ostensibly a critique of early Cold War politics, "The Blast" uncritically repeated the Darwinist concept of the frontier and Turner's glorification of the frontiersman. As the story progressed, Cloete detailed his process of becoming a frontiersman. He began as an author, an overcivilized man who lived in a stylish penthouse apartment. After the atomic war ended, he and his wife had to go through the slow process of adapting to the postatomic wilderness: they changed their style of dress, killed and ate their pets, and learned to hunt for food. At one point Cloete described his wife's transition "from a rather fastidious young american [*sic*] girl to a primeval savage."[16] Cloete's own transformation became complete with the advent of a plague that killed the remaining survivors in the city, including his wife. Only Cloete survived, and the plague left him with a metaphorically significant coat of hair that made him look like "an old silver-gray gorilla."[17] After this point, Cloete moved from his apartment building to a cave, which he described as "man's natural habitat."[18] Not only did Cloete return to the frontier, he also made a move down the evolutionary ladder. In order to survive, and indeed as a result of his struggle for survival, Cloete became a hairy primeval caveman, killing his own food and breeding dogs to help him with his hunting. Like Frederick Jackson Turner's colonist, he had to strip away the trappings of civilization in order to confront nature. Cloete's return to a savage lifestyle on the nuclear frontier reinvigorated him, as his struggle with nature—including gigantic beasts mutated by radiation—helped him slough off his years of lethargy from his sedentary city life.

However, Cloete went to great pains to point out that he did not go completely savage. This became most apparent toward the end of the story, when he met up with a war party of Comanche and Kiowa who were exploring the ruins of New York. Cloete referred to them explicitly as "Noble Savages," though he qualified this term as a likely by-product of his "Fenimore Cooper-conditioned mind."[19] These "Indians" were untouched by technology, having been on what amounted to a nature preserve at their reservation. Once civilization collapsed, they begin to reconquer the continent. Cloete joined up with them and began to hunt and live among them. Throughout the text, Cloete continued to use large rifles to hunt, though he killed with his bare hands on several occasions. When the Indians wanted Cloete to show them how to use his big hunting rifle, he refused, warning them against the use of such technology: "I could see nothing to be gained by such instruction, so I tried to explain to them that this was white man's magic and so strong that it had destroyed all the white men in the world except me, turning its forces against them in retribution for their own misuse of its powers."[20] Cloete was both criticizing the arms race and the politics of the early Cold War and demonstrating uneasiness about technology in general.

The way he coded technology as the product and property of white men is particularly problematic. In the Darwinist logic of Turner's frontier thesis, the superior white toolmakers displaced and destroyed the inferior and technologically inept Native Americans. While "The Blast" provided an ironic reversal of the westward progression of civilization, it kept Darwin's racial hierarchy with regard to technology intact. The Indians in Cloete's story were seen as essentially primitive, unable to produce any rifles of their own and only capable of using small rifles that they found. When they needed to count or tabulate anything, they turned to two white girls who were accompanying them for help. Cloete's critique of civilization relied on this racist image of the pure noble savage, the primitive who could not use technology or count, who was still unassimilated and living on the reservation.

The critical edge of "The Blast" was dulled not only by Cloete's problematic use of racial savagery but also by the text's happy ending. As the text drew to a close, Cloete was contemplating the possibility of marrying the two young blond blue-eyed white women the Indians brought with them. Of course, these women were immediately attracted to Cloete, and he rode off into the sunset as a nuclear frontier version of both Adam and Cooper's Leatherstocking: he was the frontiersman with a long rifle living among the savages who would likely begin repopulating the planet with white men and, by extension, the white civilization he had rejected. Despite Cloete's ambivalence about reseeding the planet with white offspring, the sexual fantasy involved in this happy ending counteracted the impact of the horrors he had endured earlier the text. The suffering made Cloete stronger, returning him to a simple and idyllic frontier life that allowed him to spend his golden years in a sexual relationship with two nubile young blondes.

Bradbury's "Million Year Picnic" and Cloete's "The Blast" both represented life after an atomic war as liberating. They depicted atomic warfare, despite its horrors, as something that destroyed a corrupt civilization and returned the survivors to an adventurous frontier existence. On the nuclear frontier, individuals could control their own lives without the constant helpless fear of nuclear annihilation. As the Cold War developed and the threat of nuclear war grew increasingly ominous, more and more authors turned to the trope of the nuclear frontier to imagine how the next war could actually make life better.

This optimism was certainly not the only response to nuclear war, however; scores of narratives from this period focused on the unmitigated horrors of nuclear weapons. With the popularity of family-centered discourse in the post–World War II United States, many narratives naturally focused on the threat nuclear weapons posed to the nuclear family. The specter of sterility and mutation was one of the primary family-centered fears that arose in the aftermath of the atomic bombing of Japan. A number of early reports from Hiroshima and Nagasaki cited disturbing problems with fertility among the survivors of the atomic bomb. The United States Strategic Bombing Survey's official report on Hiroshima and Nagasaki noted that "pregnant women within a mile of ground zero showed an increased number of miscarriages, and there was in most cases a low sperm count among men in the same area."[21] This connection was not new for science fiction authors: as early as 1941, Robert Heinlein had cited the dangers of radioactivity for fertility in his short story "Solution Unsatisfactory." Heinlein's story presented a particular twist on this problem—radioactively induced mutation. The radiation mutant, perhaps the most common character type of nuclear-themed stories, became a locus for fears about reproduction after World War II.[22]

A number of science fiction authors in the 1940s and 1950s used the trope of mutation and the imagery of the nuclear frontier to question both the morality of nuclear proliferation and the ideal of the white nuclear family itself. Stories such as Bradbury's "Million Year Picnic" showed the white nuclear family coming closer together on the nuclear frontier, but many post-Hiroshima stories showed the white family disintegrating because of damaged or altered genes. In his first published story, science fiction writer Poul Anderson presented a bleak view of both the nuclear family and the "progress" brought by the atomic bomb. The story, "Tomorrow's Children," was co-authored by F. N. Waldrop and was published in the March 1947 issue of *Astounding Science Fiction*.[23] The story focused on Colonel Hugh Drummond, a pilot who had flown his atomic-powered "stratojet" all over the atomic war–ravaged Earth to survey the damage. As the story opened, Drummond was returning from his trip and was confronted with protocols of military security. The omniscient narrative voice shifted to the perspective of Drummond in assessing the importance of those protocols: "He gave the signal again on his transmitter, knowing with a faint spine-crawling sensation of the rocket batteries trained on him from the green of those mountains. When one plane could carry [within it] the end of a city, all planes were under suspicion. Not that anyone outside was supposed to know that that innocuous little town was important. But you never could tell. The war wasn't officially over. It might never be, with sheer personal survival overriding the urgency of treaties."[24] The narrative voice established a world of strategic future war much like that of General Arnold and Will Jenkins. However, Drummond's ambivalence about military security interrupts the strategic narrative. Rather than simply asserting the strategic necessity of military security, the omniscient narrative voice transformed into Drummond's more informal internal voice and showed the urgency and primacy of basic survival. With the collapse of civilization, the struggle for personal survival absorbed the time of those still left alive. In the face of such widespread global destruction, nobody cared enough about the war to even formulate a peace treaty. Having seen the misery brought about by the war, Drummond chafed at the absurdity of obeying military security protocols that were a part of a world that no longer mattered. While still maintaining a practical wariness—"you could never tell"—Drummond provided a subtle critique of the military obsession with national security and winning an atomic war in the face of widespread suffering.

Set two years after the end of a global war, "Tomorrow's Children" focused primarily on the attempt of Drummond and General Robinson—the remaining military leaders of the United States—to reestablish and rebuild civilization. General Robinson also had another agenda: to maintain the genetic purity of the human race and ensure that evolution unfolded at a natural rate, not the unnatural rate generated by radiation. Human mutations were growing in frequency, and Drummond doubted that this would be possible. But General Robinson had a pregnant wife and could not face the fact that his own child might be a mutant. Drummond saw the implications of the mutations and attempted to warn General Robinson: "'It's wrecking our culture. . . . People are going crazy as birth after birth is monstrous. Fear of the unknown, striking at minds still stunned by the war and the immediate aftermath. Frustration of parenthood, perhaps the most basic instinct there is. It's leading to infanticide, desertion, despair, a cancer at the root of society.'"[25] Mutation came to be seen as a threat to the family, and the family in turn was seen as the heart of civilization. The radioactive dust and postwar diseases that ran rampant in "Tomorrow's Children" threatened the very essence of American society as it was defined by men like General Robinson.

The general's home provided a final bastion of the European American domestic ideal with its warm water, comfortable beds, and attentive (and pregnant) housewife. The only hope the general saw for saving this domestic ideal lay in eugenics, and he hoped to preserve white families like his own at the expense of the mutated others. Drummond attacked the general's plan, arguing that it was "repeating the old *Herrenvolk* notion."[26] Drummond went on to reject racism altogether: "No, the only way to sanity—to *survival*—is to abandon class prejudice and race hate altogether, and work as individuals. We're all . . . well, Earthlings, and subclassification is deadly."[27] Anderson and Waldrop showed how racism in the face of nuclear war was actually threatening the very survival of the species. To survive, they argued, humanity needed to give up racism and put a premium on all human life, regardless of racial differences or mutations. When his son was born with "rubbery tentacles" for limbs, the general had to confront the fact that his idealized notion of humanity was an impractical myth.[28] Through Drummond's arguments, Anderson and Waldrop criticized the idea that the white nuclear family was at the center of civilized order. They showed the racism implicit in the glorification of the white domestic ideal and showed how intolerance could threaten the entire world in the nuclear age. At the same time, their critique of nuclear proliferation and civilization did not rely on the notion of the savage. Unlike Cloete and countless others, Anderson and Waldrop's vision of the nuclear frontier refrained from romantic depictions of frontier life, keeping the focus instead on the horrors of atomic war and the evils of racism.

Throughout the 1940s and 1950s, a growing number of science fiction authors took aim at the idealized white nuclear family and the developing military industrial complex. Women science fiction authors such as Judith Merril, Alice Eleanor Jones, and Carol Emshwiller wrote stories that showed the horrors of nuclear war through fractured domestic relationships. Merril's fiction took particular aim at the absurdity of civil defense in a nuclear war, positing the necessity of peace activism to prevent such a war from ever occurring.[29] Merril's classic "That Only a Mother" was perhaps the most well known mutation story of the 1940s; originally published in the June 1948 issue of *Astounding Science Fiction*, it centered on a young mother named Margaret Marvell who lived in a future time of prolonged war fought with atomic weapons. Most of the narrative was from Margaret's point of view; we see her daily routine, her impressions of her new baby, and her letters to her husband Hank. Margaret's consciousness was riddled with anxiety about her new baby and she seemed unable to escape her fear of genetic defects triggered by radiation. Even the newspaper she read was filled with reports of genetic mutations that were similar to those "near Hiroshima and Nagasaki in 1946 and 1947."[30] Despite the child's ability to speak at an early age, all seemed normal when Hank came home on leave from his job as a nuclear weapons designer. From Hank's point of view, the baby was a deformed limbless mutant "that only a mother" could love. The story ended with Hank clenching his hand around the baby to kill it in a fit of hysteria. As Lisa Yaszek argues, Merril's story showed how atomic warfare produced not only mutant children but also "mutant fathers" who killed their children instead of protecting them.[31] Merril returned to the theme of atomic war threatening the family in her 1950 novel *Shadow on the Hearth*, which again showed atomic war driving parents to extremes such as infanticide. Merril's work asserted that there was nothing positive or progressive about nuclear weapons and that they in fact threatened the very fabric of American culture and humanity as a whole by mutating children and destroying family relationships. At the same time, Merril pointed to the problems of a family ideal and a social order driven by patriarchy: the military men and the fathers (who were both embodied in Hank) created a world that was destroying itself. Only alternative arrangements generated by mothers and those devoted to peace could prevent this mad patriarchy from destroying the world.[32]

The U.S. government's strategic narratives did not go away in the late 1940s. Though they were less prevalent after 1945 and 1946, strategic narratives continued to appear in mainstream media. General George C. Kenney, the commander of the Strategic Air Command (SAC), put forward his vision of what a war with the Soviets would look like during a speech to the Maine State Federation of Women's Clubs. General Kenney's story, which began with a Pearl Harbor–type sneak attack by the Soviets, was picked up in the 17 May 1948 issue of *Newsweek*; the magazine wrote that Kenney "all but scared the wits out of an audience of women."[33] General Carl Spaatz, chief of staff of the U.S. Air Force, went into more detail about the official vision of the next war in two articles published in *Life* magazine on 5 July and 16

August 1948. Both General Spaatz and General Kenney used their future-war stories to induce fear in their audience and encourage increased military expenditures for air power and atomic weaponry. At the same time, they reassured their audiences that an atomic war with the Soviet Union was winnable if the United States continued to build its military power. The development of a strong federal civil defense agency in the late 1940s led to another explosion of strategic narratives. These official fictions attempted to counter the critical fictions of people such as Anderson and Merril with the arguments that atomic bombs were not that dangerous and that the white nuclear family would emerge from World War III stronger than before.

Planning for civil defense was not a pressing priority for the United States in its initial stage after World War II. Responsibility for civil defense fell to the National Security Resources Board (NSRB), which in late 1948 issued a report to Secretary of State James Forrestal advising only minor modifications to the civil defense planning used during World War II.[34] The report, *Civil Defense for National Security*, discussed atomic bombs as an inevitability but represented the threat of a large chemical attack as equally likely. This seeming lack of urgency in the nation's civil defense plans contrasted starkly to the debates in the news media and academic journals about how to best defend against an atomic attack. From late 1945, a host of military officers, urban planners, science fiction writers, and other assorted commentators proposed their own ideas for how to survive in the face of an atomic Pearl Harbor. From General Arnold's underground rocket bunkers to Engel and Pillar's decentralized cities, the American public was bombarded with visions of planning for the next war.

The United States Strategic Bombing Survey (USSBS) issued the first serious assessment of U.S. readiness to defend against an atomic attack. In the final section of its official report on Hiroshima and Nagasaki in 1946, the USSBS laid out the major steps the United States needed to take to minimize the effectiveness of an atomic attack. Like many Americans, USSBS investigators had become concerned about the implications of the attacks on Hiroshima and Nagasaki for the future security of the United States. In the words of the report, "The Survey's investigators, as they proceeded about their study, found an insistent question framing itself in their minds: 'What if the target had been an American City?'"[35] In assessing the damage of the attacks, the investigators cited several factors that made American cities vulnerable to atomic attack: most American buildings were susceptible to the blast effects of an atomic explosion, they wrote, and American cities were inviting targets because of their high population density and "crowded slums."[36] The investigators proposed three passive measures to help minimize the effectiveness of an atomic attack: building bomb shelters, decentralizing cities, and organizing a national civil defense. The ideas behind these measures were straightforward: bomb shelters would help civilians survive the initial blast effects of the atomic bomb (including the high doses of radiation) that killed tens of thousands of people in Hiroshima and Nagasaki. Decentralizing the "activities and population" of cities would make them less inviting targets and would limit the effectiveness of an attack.[37] A coordinated national civil defense would help a city cope with the damage to its infrastructure because resources from surrounding areas and undamaged cities could be mobilized more effectively.

The entire contents of the USSBS report were published in the 5 July 1946 issue of the *U.S. News and World Report*. The issue also ran an article entitled "What Atom Bomb Means to U.S.: Revision of Plans for Defense" that summarized and analyzed the findings of the USSBS report. This article set a reassuring tone by asserting that "a U.S. city fearing an atomic attack would prepare to defend itself in the same way it would prepare for fire bombs or ordinary explosives, rather than in some new, fantastic way."[38] While noting the atomic bomb's unique effects such as X-rays, radiation sickness, and "increased sterility," the article asserted that many stories about the destructiveness of the atomic bomb were "myths."[39] Evacuating cities and developing underground bunkers were cited as practical ways to "avoid large-scale loss of life" in an atomic attack.[40] It raised the specter of fallout, described as "a deadly rain of radioactive particles from the dust blown out of the city," as a potential hazard to suburban and rural populations but argued that "farmers and others on the outskirts of the Japanese cities" were unharmed by fallout or other effects of the atomic blasts.[41] In this way, the article undercut the sober assessment of the USSBS, tempering its findings with assertions that were more in line with the earlier declarations of military conservatives and the White House. Though it presented the atomic bomb as having some unique properties, the article dismissed the idea that civil defense preparations needed to change in any significant way. Instead, the article asserted that deterrence was the most desirable method of defense: "The ability to retaliate may prove to be the only really effective defense in the end."[42] This focus on building overwhelming offensive military capabilities and devaluing civil defense became a central component of the U.S. strategy in the 1950s.

In the late 1940s, a number of experts and commentators attempted to expand the practical ideas for civil defense outlined by the USSBS. In the May and October 1948 issues of *Bulletin of the Atomic Scientists*, Tracy B. Auger argued for new city planning methods that would minimize the effects of an atomic attack. Auger developed a vision of what he called cluster cities that were relatively small and were dispersed throughout the countryside. As "an outstanding city planner," Auger was concerned that this new method of city planning would preserve "urban values," or the social and economic advantages of urban life.[43] At the same time, Auger saw this new method of city planning as a way to eliminate urban slums and their complicated social problems: "[Cluster cities] would minimize the danger of fifth column activity base on internal unrest by substituting wholesome living conditions for the slum and near-slum environments in which so many millions of Americans are now forced to live."[44] Auger associated urban slums with radical social subversion, and while he was sympathetic to those who were forced to live in slums, his allusion to "fifth column" activity promoted his urban vision as a solution to internal threats to American democracy.

While Auger did not explicitly refer to race in these articles, race played a central role in debates about the problems of inner-city slums in America during the 1940s and 1950s.[45] Associating fifth-column activities with slums reinforced the idea that the urban jungle was overrun with savage minorities who posed a threat to national security. Auger's solution of cluster cities would introduce slum inhabitants to "wholesome" living, which included increased access to "open country," ready sources of fresh food, and "relaxation from the increasing pace of living."[46] Auger's pastoral vision of the modern atomic age city aimed to integrate the values of the city with those of the country, in effect turning all American cities into vast suburbs. The elimination of cities—especially the potentially dangerous racial problems associated with slums—was a common element of civil defense narratives during the 1950s. The survival of the idealized white suburban family came to represent a major aspect of the strategy of the United States for winning an atomic war, at least in the official propaganda of the period.[47]

Despite the ongoing debates about how best to protect cities from an atomic attack, civil defense did not emerge as a pressing national priority until 1949. The most important development that brought civil defense to the forefront was the Soviet Union's successful test of an atomic bomb in August of that year. When Truman announced this news to the world on September 23, preparedness for an atomic attack became the dominant focus of public anxiety and official policy.[48] Late 1949 also saw the victory of the communists in China, and the communist threat seemed even more pressing with the outbreak of the Korean War in the middle of 1950. These three major events fueled the rapid development of the new Federal Civil Defense Administration (FCDA), which took over civil defense responsibilities from the NSRB in January of 1951.[49] Over the next ten years, the FCDA and its successor, the Office of Civil and Defense Mobilization, played a major role in shaping narratives about nuclear weapons. The FCDA continued the wartime tactics of the Office of War Information (OWI) and in fact employed a number of people who had worked in the OWI during World War II. The FCDA's wartime model of propaganda involved a carefully orchestrated relationship with private sector media organizations. Magazines, radio stations, television networks, movie studios, and the Ad Council participated willingly in the FCDA's propaganda campaign; they produced civil defense materials, self-censored their stories, and even staged "spontaneous" discussions of nuclear issues for a mass audience.[50] These supposedly independent media organizations helped disseminate strategic visions that envisioned the white suburban family as the hero of the nuclear frontier and that represented the white middle-class suburban home as the front line in the nuclear war to come.[51]

In order to perpetuate and manage fear of nuclear war, the FCDA and its allies focused their propaganda on military discipline and frontier-style readiness. The center of the FCDA's philosophy was "self help"; there was a broad political consensus that American civil defense should avoid a centralized communist-style system and instead reflect the "American" characteristics of volunteerism and self-reliance.[52] Implicitly at first and explicitly in the mid- to late 1950s, the imagery of the frontier was used to capture and idealize these American characteristics as the keys to survival. In response to the crisis that emerged in late 1949 and worsened in 1950, the NSRB developed *Survival Under Atomic Attack*, the first of several civil defense publications designed to reassure Americans about the dangers of an atomic attack. This booklet was distributed to millions of Americans throughout the country by both the NSRB and the FCDA.[53] The "facts" and tone of the booklet were aimed at refuting popular representations of the effects of the atomic bomb that sensationalized lingering radiation, mutation, and social disintegration. As had the official representation of the atomic bomb in 1945–1946, *Survival Under Atomic Attack* argued that the atomic bomb was not that different from earlier bombs and that life after an atomic attack would quickly return to normal.[54] The booklet began by announcing in very large letters, "You Can SURVIVE. You can live through an atom bomb raid and you won't have to have a Geiger counter, protective clothing, or special training in order to do it."[55] The emphasis on survival followed the lead of Hersey's "Hiroshima," but here the purpose was to reassure Americans that the atomic bomb was not that bad. By asserting that special equipment and training were not necessary for survival, *Survival Under Atomic Attack* made the atomic bomb seem ordinary and fears about its effects seem overblown. Civil defense publications constituted the U.S. government's latest offensive in the battle over the meaning of the bomb. The FCDA became the government's primary organ for disseminating strategic future-war stories, and its official fictions of civil defense attempted to rally support for the government's deterrence model of national defense. When the atomic bomb was represented as just another weapon, nuclear war seemed winnable and the government's drive to build up the military seemed a rational step in winning the next war.

Survival Under Atomic Attack took on the voice of official truth, paternalistically dismissing other arguments as absurd. Throughout the booklet, phrases like "know the bomb's true dangers" and "kill the myths" were highlighted to cast other arguments as hysterical and ignorant.[56] To counter the "myths," the booklet offered fatherly nuggets of wisdom like the following:

> To begin with, you must realize that atom-splitting is just another way of causing an explosion. While an atom bomb holds more death and destruction than man has ever before wrapped in a single package, its total power is definitely limited. Not even hydrogen bombs could blow the earth apart or kill us all by mysterious radiation.
>
> Because the power of all bombs is limited, your chances of living through an atomic attack are much better than you may have thought. . . . Today, thousands of survivors of [the Hiroshima and Nagasaki] attacks live in new houses built right where their old ones once stood. The war may have changed their way of life, but they are not riddled with cancer. Their children are normal.[57]

Here civil defense officials were again pushing the argument that the atomic bomb was not qualitatively different from other bombs: it was only the quantity and efficiency of "death and destruction" that was different. The reference to Hiroshima and Nagasaki demonstrated that civil defense officials were focusing on the family and the home as their main topics for reassurance from their very first publication. The emphasis on normality seemed aimed at news stories and science fiction scenarios that detailed lingering radiation, cancer, and mutated children. The Japanese were seen as once again living lives of domestic bliss, an image that was repeated again and again in civil defense literature throughout the decade.

The FCDA used film as well as print media in its propaganda campaign, and in 1951 it widely distributed a number of short civil defense films produced with the help of Hollywood studios.[58] In the film version of *Survival Under Atomic Attack*, a pipe-smoking father sat on the couch reading the booklet to his wife and pointing out significant details. Like the booklet, the film encouraged the family to be prepared for an atomic attack by keeping their home and yard tidy to prevent fire damage. The wife immediately moved to handle the relevant dangerous domestic appliances when attack sirens sounded by turning off the stove and unplugging the iron. After making sure to close the curtains and unlock the front door for emergency personnel, the family went down to the basement to wait for the explosion. While the film briefly acknowledged that there were others who lived in different types of housing, the primary focus was on protecting this idealized white suburban family home. As historian Laura McEnaney notes, a large number of Americans, especially poor whites and people of color, did not live in single-family homes.[59] This early film made clear that the priority of civil defense was not the protection of all Americans; white middle-class suburbanites were the most politically and socially important Americans to policymakers.[60]

In the same year it released the film version of *Survival Under Atomic Attack*, the FCDA released the most infamous civil defense film of all, *Duck and Cover*. This film, which was clearly designed to appeal to children, opened with a cartoon of Bert the Turtle. Wearing the white helmet of an air raid warden, Bert immediately pulled his extremities into his shell when he heard an explosion. Bert's reaction was shown as the ideal response for children in the nuclear age: when the nuclear attack came, children were supposed to jump under a shelter (such as a desk or doorway) or cover themselves with whatever they could find (such as a sweater, a picnic blanket, or a newspaper). Several live-action scenes showed children and adults modeling this appropriate type of behavior, and a fatherly narrative voice asserted that if the people in Hiroshima and Nagasaki had practiced such behavior there would have been far fewer casualties. Numerous commentators have noted that such civil defense assurances were based on the model of the atomic bombs dropped on Hiroshima and Nagasaki: by 1951, nuclear weapons had become far more destructive, and what might have worked for the Japanese in 1945 would not have worked for Americans in the 1950s.

The main purpose of these assurances, however, was not so much to offer practical advice but rather to help avoid panic in the face of an atomic attack. According to many social science experts of the day, panic might well cause more damage than nuclear weapons during a Soviet attack. Civil defense officials attempted to "inoculate" the public against panic by confronting them with some of the harsh realities of nuclear weapons and at the same time reassuring them about their chances of survival if they followed proper civil defense procedures.[61] This mixed message of fear and reassurance, of a horrible atomic attack followed by the white nuclear family's triumph of survival, was supposed to mobilize citizens into a quasi-military discipline that would lead citizens to support U.S. foreign policy goals and cooperate with civil defense officials.

While civil defense officials spread their stories of triumphant survival through self-help, science fiction authors continued to spin critical stories of survival on the nuclear frontier that challenged the ideas that nuclear war was survivable and that the world would return to normal domestic bliss without much trouble after an atomic attack. Wilson Tucker's *The Long, Loud Silence* (1952) portrayed a particularly dark future after the eastern United States was hit by atomic bombs and biological weapons. The survivors were quarantined because of an ongoing plague, leaving them in a Darwinist struggle to survive as the fractured civilization of the east descended ever deeper into savagery. The line of quarantine was the Mississippi River, and those on the western side shot any eastern survivors who approached the river on sight. As in most nuclear frontier stories, the collapse of civilization led to social disintegration and people resorted to rape, murder, and even cannibalism to satisfy their unchecked desires or to survive. The novel followed the main character, Gary, as he and the rest of the eastern survivors became stripped of all sympathetic and civilized impulses. The landscape of the world after attack was described as an "empty wasteland" that was a "pile of ashes"; both the physical and social environments were devastated by nuclear weapons and biological warfare agents.[62] Gary was the lone frontiersman, struggling to make a life for himself in the harsh environment of the nuclear frontier.

Where Cloete's use of frontier imagery painted a very romantic picture, Tucker's world had a heavier dose of wasteland imagery that gave it a very different feel. While Gary initially resisted resorting to extremes to survive, he eventually developed an animosity toward those on the "safe" side of the United States who had an easy life. Late in the novel, Gary bitterly noted that "the river was a tormenting barrier that divided the nation in halves, unequal halves in which unequal lives were played out on a stage of poverty or plenty. For many—food, drink, chocolates, gasoline, money, neon, flesh, sleep, peace. For some—be quick or be dead, starve slowly or die quickly by violence."[63] Gary noted this after a visit to the west, where he saw the life of civilized leisure he had lost. Because he was a carrier of plague, he knowingly left a wake of devastation and death behind; he fled back to the east only in order to survive, as the authorities were hot on his heels and would kill him if captured. Tucker juxtaposed the relatively easy life of civilization in the west with an extreme form of natural selection in the east in order to provide a warning about atomic (and biological) warfare. Readers were given a glimpse of civilization through the eyes of a man who had gone completely savage, a perspective designed to foster appreciation for a lifestyle that needed to be preserved. Gary's life was a horrible vision of the kind of frontier survival an atomic war would bring.

Paul Brians argues that *The Long Loud Silence* is "unfortunately . . . alienating" because of the "extremely unsympathetic protagonist," but it was precisely this alienation that made the novel so powerful as a critique.[64] The main character did not become a stronger and happier frontiersman like the protagonist of Cloete's "The Blast," nor did he leave his cave to wander off into the sunset with two young blond women.

Instead, the novel ended with Gary living in a cave that was "foul and dead from his refuse."[65] In his attempts to survive among the "savage, steadily dwindling life" of the post-attack wasteland, Gary did find a woman for himself.[66] However, this did not lead to the development of the idealized frontier family of civil defense propaganda or even to a sexual fantasy scenario. Gary knocked the woman unconscious and planned to take her back to his cave, not because of any romantic or lustful feelings but rather because he intended to use her "to trap men" in the "struggle to stay alive."[67] This conclusion to the text showed that Gary had descended down the evolutionary ladder to the level of a degraded caveman. This descent was not seen as something that was reinvigorating like the frontier struggles described by Roosevelt and Cloete. Instead, this image of frontier degradation—where civilization met and was destroyed by savagery—provided an ending that was anything but optimistic and happy. While it still relied on the problematic formulation of civilization versus savagery, the racial connotations of the formulation were not invoked as an essential component of the text. The atomic bomb had not made the world a better place but had led to an unchecked spiral of misery, destruction, and death.

In the 1950s, the debate about the meaning and importance of nuclear weapons continued to rage throughout American culture. A growing number of science fiction authors used the specter of nuclear mutations and the nuclear frontier to attack the notion of the ideal white family and the escalating nuclear arms race. Some science fiction authors were seduced by the promise of the nuclear frontier, and their visions of postwar rebirth lapsed into romantic fantasies that reinforced Darwinist racism and undermined their assertions that nuclear war needed to be avoided at all costs. The U.S. government escalated its use of civil defense propaganda, using its own version of the nuclear frontier to convince the public to support its Cold War policies. The FCDA continued the postwar pattern of lying to the American public about the dangers of nuclear weapons by presenting them as big conventional weapons. While stoking nuclear fear through its images of future war, the FCDA maintained the old position that a nuclear war was winnable. In fact, its propaganda made it appear as though nuclear war might even bring the white suburban family closer together. The racism implicit in this glorification of the white suburban family was not lost on African Americans, and as the 1950s moved forward a growing number of commentators attempted to address the racial dimension of civil defense and the nuclear frontier.

Chapter 11

The Color of Ground Zero

Civil Defense, Segregation, and Savagery on the Nuclear Frontier

The U.S. government's civil defense efforts in the early Cold War benefited from a political consensus on a number of key issues relating to foreign and domestic policy. Drawing on a streamlined propaganda machine like the one used in World War II, civil defense officials engaged in a successful effort to spread their message throughout American culture. However, there were at least two major sources of resistance to the government's official representation of the nuclear age: science fiction and the civil rights movement. Science fiction authors tended to explore the horrors of nuclear warfare in a way that belied the easy reassurances of civil defense officials. Civil rights groups like the NAACP took issue with the racial imagination of civil defense, exposing the fact that the government had no intention of trying to protect all of its citizens equally from future enemy attacks. In the last half of the 1950s, science fiction authors began to catch on to the unique racial problems posed by the nuclear age. These authors became increasingly skeptical about the practicality of civil defense and attempted to address the problems of entrenched racism and segregation. Drawing on the struggles and observations of the civil rights movement, some of these authors even attempted to desegregate the nuclear frontier. While sympathetic to African Americans and critical of racism, many science fiction authors remained trapped in the nineteenth-century formulation of progress and the connection between race and savagery that was central to the American concept of the frontier. Their adherence to the concept of the savage undermined the progressive race politics in their writing and perpetuated the Darwinist racism of earlier generations.

In the 1950s, the civil rights movement became more aggressive and stepped up its challenges to the many forms of segregation and persecution nonwhites experienced in the United States. The "race problem" was becoming a major issue for federal policymakers, who moved to eliminate some forms of discrimination. Part of the motivation for this came from communist attacks on American hypocrisy: not all citizens of the "freedom-loving" United States shared the same freedoms or enjoyed the same treatment from the government. Poll taxes, Jim Crow laws, and repeated acts of physical violence plagued African Americans who attempted to exercise their right to vote. Lynching was still common and racial segregation was the official policy or unofficial fact of life throughout the country. President Truman vocally supported the cause of civil rights and created a Committee on Civil Rights to investigate racial inequality in the United States. Despite his high rhetoric, however, Truman took little action to improve the status of African Americans. He did sign an executive order in 1948 that desegregated the military, but this important step took over ten years to implement completely.[1] Politically, Truman had to walk a fine line to keep the support of Southern Democrats who were committed to Jim Crow policies.

When it came to civil defense, Truman completely ignored the interests of African Americans by appointing Millard Caldwell, a former governor of Florida who was well known for his support of segregation, as the first head of the Federal Civil Defense Administration in late 1950. This led to an uproar in African American communities, and the NAACP organized an attempt to block the appointment. African Americans were justifiably concerned that appointing such a man to head the FCDA would lead to civil defense planning that protected whites at the expense of blacks. Caldwell oversaw the enactment of policies that produced segregated public bomb shelters and that largely abandoned the sizeable population of African Americans living in major urban centers.[2]

African American resistance to the racist premises and representations of civil defense took many forms. Though the FCDA hired specialists to encourage blacks to participate in civil defense, it was not able to muster much cooperation from African Americans in some major urban centers. Where most national newspapers cooperated with the FCDA by republishing its materials and distributing its message, African American newspapers mostly ignored civil defense or published articles that were critical of the agency.[3] Langston Hughes drew attention to the problem of segregated civil defense in one of his "Simple" stories, which was published on 10 July 1954 in the *Chicago Defender*. Hughes joked that whites would integrate bomb shelters out of fear that their servants would become irradiated and expose them to radiation later on. Hughes's character Simple dreamed of spreading radiation to get back at his enemies.[4] Although the FCDA attempted to mask its decision to leave most African Americans to their own devices in case of a nuclear war, the focus on the white suburban family in most of its propaganda made its agenda clear. The skeptical derision of men like Hughes showed that African Americans were not fooled by the FCDA's reassurances.

Some in the civil defense establishment tried to address the issues of African Americans and invited black leaders to participate in advisory committees and conferences on civil defense. However, the race problem seemed too deeply entrenched to allow for easy government solutions, especially when segregationists like Caldwell held so much power in Washington.[5] In the early 1950s, the growing size and efficiency of nuclear weapons worsened the practical problems and propaganda hurdles of the FCDA. Up until 1952, it had primarily focused on blast-related damage in its preparedness publications, which argued that the initial blast of an atomic attack was the only real danger and that most people in cities could survive that if they took the proper precautions. The revelations of the "Mike" blast on 1 November 1952, the first-ever detonation of a thermonuclear device, forced the FCDA to abandon any hope of saving cities. The blast, which vaporized Elugelap Island and left a vast crater, made clear to FCDA officials that evacuation to suburban and rural areas was the only possible way to save urban residents in the event of a nuclear war.[6] Civil defense planners worried that evacuating blacks from slums and relocating them in the suburbs would cause a backlash from white Americans who had worked hard to maintain segregated housing patterns.[7]

Fallout, which had always been a concern of scientists and medical experts working with nuclear weapons, greatly complicated the problem. The first test of an atomic bomb at Alamogordo, New Mexico, in July 1945 had produced far more fallout than expected, and there was also evidence of fallout at Hiroshima.[8] The U.S. government vehemently denied the danger of fallout in the early years of the Cold War, but this began to change in the middle of the 1950s. Evidence of significant fallout was noticed in a May 1953 Atomic Energy Commission test in Nevada, where radioactive particles were found 100 miles downwind of the actual blast site. In March 1954, Japanese sailors aboard the fishing boat *Lucky Dragon* contracted radiation sickness from the fallout of a hydrogen bomb test the United States had conducted in the Marshall Islands. The *Lucky Dragon* incident sparked an international outcry that had long-term implications for above-ground nuclear testing and civil defense planning. The serious dangers posed by radioactive fallout forced the FCDA to admit that even evacuation to suburban and rural areas did not provide an adequate defense against the effects of nuclear weapons.[9]

With these new developments, civil defense publications began to appeal more explicitly to the need of suburban white families to exercise frontier readiness in the face of a nuclear attack. Perhaps the best-developed narrative of nuclear frontier civil defense came from Philip Wylie, a well-known science fiction author who worked as a consultant to the FCDA. Wylie wrote his novel *Tomorrow!* (1954) after years of frustration with what he saw as government underfunding of civil defense and public apathy about the threat of nuclear war.[10] Wylie dedicated the novel to "the gallant men and women of the Federal Civil Defense Administration, and to those other true patriots, the volunteers." Civil defense volunteers were the heroes of the novel, which told the tale of two midwestern cities—Green Prairie and River City—that were "halves of a happy, urban world, separated by a river."[11] The cities had diametrically opposed attitudes toward civil defense: while Green Prairie diligently carried out civil defense drills that were "the best in the state," River City considered civil defense "a waste of money" that was a government "interference with the rights of the common man."[12] As the novel developed, this ant-and-grasshopper narrative painted Green River as the model of preparation, while it portrayed River City as the embodiment of the ambivalence and denial about the nuclear threat that Wiley despised.

The novel began with an account of the frontier roots of the cities that uncritically repeated late-nineteenth-century formulations of the frontier. In the mythology of the novel, "the pioneers" founded "Fort Abanakas, the first settlement," which "was often attacked by hard-riding Sioux."[13] Next came "the Indian trading post," followed by farmers and merchants who helped develop the cities.[14] Finally, the text connected this history to the present day: "By then, there were families who could look back to four or five generations of unbroken residence in the region. Some of these 'natives' were rich and powerful; some were poor; but most were ordinary people—prospering modestly, loving freedom, hating interference . . . fair citizens and superb neighbors. The Conner family in Green Prairie was such."[15] The evocation of the frontier struggle against the Sioux portrayed the founders of the cities as hearty and tough white settlers. At the same time, it repeated the Darwinist racism that glorified white colonization as a natural step in the march of progress. Wylie represented characteristics such as "loving freedom" as the natural result of the frontier struggle to survive and associated these traits with the Conner family. As leaders in the civil defense organization of Green Prairie, the Conner family embodied the white middle-class ideal that was central to most civil defense propaganda. Wylie asserted that freedom-loving and industrious white people like the Conner family would rise up and help Green Prairie survive the savagery brought by the Russian atomic bombs, just as their pioneer ancestors had fought and survived the savagery and flaming arrows of the Sioux.

Although people like the Conner family of Green Prairie exhibited frontier virtues, the people of River City seemed to have been swallowed by a social wasteland. The biggest figure of moral decay in the novel was Minerva Sloan, a wealthy and influential widow who lived on an estate in River City and opposed civil defense drills. Minerva also embodied "Momism," the infamous philosophy Wylie had first outlined in *A Generation of Vipers* (1942). For Wylie, the coddling of overbearing mothers was turning America into a nation of effeminate, self-involved degenerates.[16] In *Tomorrow!* Minerva wanted to put a stop to civil defense drills in Green Prairie because she found them a personal inconvenience. Also, like some other mothers, Minerva wanted to stop civil defense because "all it does is *frighten* people. . . . Terrorize them by making them react to weapons the Reds probably don't even own."[17] When the attack eventually came, Wylie made clear that the hysterical concern of mothers was misguided and led to immorality and death. Kip Sloan, Minerva's son, was the quintessential product of Momism. Wylie characterized him as spoiled, lazy, and effeminate; all he ever did was listlessly pursue a girlfriend between trips to the country club. During World War II, Kip had been a fighter pilot whose cowardice under fire had caused the death of two of his wingmates.[18] When the Russian attack came, Kip was again useless under fire; his panic led him to run right into the path of a plane spreading biological warfare agents. His cowardice and decadence were punished by a horrible death, and Wylie used his fate as a stark warning for those who refused to participate in civil defense and allowed their mothers to coddle them into lazy immorality.

Wylie also marked the social decay of River City with his descriptions of its segregation and slums. The slums in River City were populated by "colored people" at the center and "Italians, Greeks, Jews and Poles" farther out.[19] For protagonist Charles Conner, the expanding slums exemplified the negative aspects of urban growth that had transformed the area and destroyed his childhood haunts. Wylie used his description of the slums to criticize urban conditions in a way that was similar to the critique of Upton Sinclair and other "urban jungle" writers of the early twentieth century. The slums had emerged when blacks and immigrants had "poured into River City" at the turn of the century to work in its industrial core; their labor had helped "to make America great" and "men like Emmet Sloan rich."[20] Blacks overtook the center of the slum when the descendents of the white immigrants began moving to the suburbs. While Emmet Sloan had been sympathetic to the workers who had made him rich, his widow Minerva resented the hospital her late husband had built for black slum-dwellers. Her resentment was due to her deep racism: Minerva was appalled that Alice Groves, the black woman who managed the hospital, had a Ph.D. from Columbia and spoke better English than her son. She also refused to allow her name to appear "over the doorway . . . of a 'darkie infirmary'" in the slum she referred to as "Niggertown."[21] Wylie used his descriptions of the slums of River City and the racism of Minerva Sloan to point to the problems of modern urban decay. Like urban and civil defense planners before him, Wylie represented these problems as the unhealthy by-products of a highly centralized industrial city. The class and race stratification that propped up rich people like Minerva Sloan was clearly a social evil that was justifiably destroyed when the Russian attack came.

The Russian atomic bomb detonated directly above the slum in the heart of the city. Kip Sloan noticed this when he became trapped downtown while trying to escape. The social wasteland of River City had turned into a post-atomic wasteland much like the one John Hersey described in "Hiroshima" (1946). Kip noted that the people around him were "foreigners, mostly. Their area had not been annihilated, just set on fire here and there. . . . So they were on the move, on the way out of town, Polaks and Hunkies and Latwicks, Yids and Guineas and Micks. Not many Nigs. He even thought . . . there was a reason for the dearth of shines in the stampeded mobs: Niggertown was right on Ground Zero."[22] Wylie used bigoted language to underscore Kip's despicable character. Through Kip's voice, Wylie called attention to the racism that had led to de facto segregation, the housing pattern that caused those in the "Negro District" to be disproportionately affected by the atomic attack. Wylie was pointing to the actual dilemma facing African Americans and civil defense officials in every major urban center in the country during the 1950s: How could African Americans be served by civil defense in a society so heavily segregated and where so many blacks lived in densely populated urban centers?

Unfortunately, Wylie's novel followed the lead of civil defense planners: after Kip's brief observation, Wylie completely ignored the problems of blacks to focus on the survival of whites. African Americans were wiped out by the atomic bomb, and the racial problems that were symptomatic of unhealthy urban development vanished with them. The war ended when the United States destroyed the Soviet Union with a radical new fallout weapon, and the middle-class white households like the Conner family survived to rebuild the city. Near the end of the novel, Wylie spelled out his belief in the relatively decentralized form of American city proposed by men like General Arnold and Tracy Auger. The densely populated cities of America became replaced in the post-attack world of the novel with a smaller and more thinly distributed infrastructure: "The Green Prairie Professional Building had been the first one erected according to the new plan and the first one to invade the 'total destruction' area. It wasn't high, not a skyscraper, only four stories. . . . It was something like a ranch house, but blocks long, with many 'L's' and 'courtyards' between them, with gardens, patios, glassed-in restaurants, even a skating rink in the courtyards. . . . 'Semidecentralized,' they called it, and 'horizontal expansion.' It replaced the vertical growth of the skyscraper age which had let fumed air, heat and darkness and slums accumulate in its canyons."[23] Once again, slums were cited as a negative by-product of bad urban design. Wylie's description marked a new frontier: the traditional values of rural and suburban America began to colonize the new wilderness that was opened up for expansion by the flattening of the inner city. The new buildings embodied these values; they were even designed to look "something like a ranch house." These new ranch houses began to invade the area destroyed by the atomic bomb just like the white pioneers who established Green Prairie had invaded the area inhabited by the Sioux in the previous century. However, the racial dimension of this frontier expansion was problematic in the same way that the expansion of the previous century had been. Twentieth-century pioneers like the Conner family were invading and expanding into the area once populated by African Americans. The removal of African Americans was necessary for Wylie's new idealized version of the American city.

Wylie's vision of urban renewal ultimately represented the attack as a blessing that returned America to its frontier roots and eliminated the social wasteland that had been developing in River City.[24] Wylie asserted that "it had not been so difficult as many had expected to 'sell' the once-crowded city dwellers on the new pattern for living. Most people had detested many aspects of urban living. And even those who clung to old ideas habitually were shaken in their conservatism. For nobody who had lived in a bombed city wanted to spend another hour . . . in such a death trap. . . . Indeed, by this time, unhit cities were considered 'obsolete.' Those that had been bombed provided people with a surge of exhilaration, for the bombing had proved an ultimate blessing by furnishing a brand-new chance to build a world brand-new—and infinitely better."[25] Like the atomic war in H. G. Wells's novel *The World Set Free* (1914), the atomic war in *Tomorrow!* did not spell the end of civilization or progress. Instead, it provided a new opportunity to develop life and civilization along what Wylie saw as more productive lines by getting rid of the "obsolete" old infrastructure. Once African Americans were gone, the new urban world of Wylie's vision could be rebuilt without the racial conflict that had characterized the old urban world. Charles Conner finally married his childhood sweetheart Lenore, who is pregnant by the end of the novel. The Conner family celebrates Lenore's pregnancy because this means that she is not sterile despite having received a heavy dose of radiation in the attack. The happy ending of Wylie's civil defense tale was consistent with the earlier reassurances of the FCDA that an atomic attack was survivable and that white Americans would be able to return to "normal" life and reproduce at will afterward.

Wylie's novel prescribed atomic warfare as an antidote for the ills endemic to the urban life of the 1950s such as slums, racial segregation, and Momism. While Wylie took the time to show graphic details of the horrors of the atomic attack, the social vision and happy ending of the novel implied that atomic warfare was a hardship well worth going through in order to return Americans to a healthy way of life. Though Wylie was clearly sympathetic to the plight of African Americans in the nuclear age, eliminating their race was a precondition for the development of his suburban utopia: his segregated utopian vision overwhelmed any progressive racial politics in the novel.

Within a year after Wylie's novel was released, the FCDA launched its "grandma's pantry" campaign. This campaign was largely aimed at housewives, and over the next few years the FCDA produced several publications that explicitly invoked the rhetoric of frontier preparedness in its descriptions of the ways in which women should prepare their homes in case of nuclear war. The campaign was coordinated with the National Grocer's Association, several pharmaceutical houses, and the American National Dietetic Association. Local supermarkets encouraged local women's clubs to set up "grandma's pantry" exhibits, and even "Betty Crocker" herself threw her weight behind the FCDA's efforts.[26] In 1955, the first publication of this campaign was released. *Grandma's Pantry Was Ready* was a simple two-sided 8.5 × 11–inch flyer with a drawing of a frontier kitchen on its front cover. In the center of the kitchen was a large wood-burning stove; the walls of the kitchen were lined with well-stocked shelves (see Figure 6). The text under the image warned that "most of us take for granted the public services that now guard our family health. But many of these services would be temporarily knocked out by disaster."[27] Here frontier preparedness was championed as a hedge against disaster, but the nature of this disaster was left unspoken. Following the Eisenhower administration's policy of toning down rhetoric that might evoke fear, this pamphlet failed to even mention a nuclear attack or fallout as possible dangers.[28] Of course, by 1955 the FCDA hardly needed to mention these threats in its publications. American culture had been saturated for a decade with warnings about the threat of nuclear war. Still, the overall tone of the pamphlet

Figure 6. This nostalgic image from the FCDA pamphlet *Grandma's Pantry Was Ready* (1955) used the myth of the frontier to romanticize survival in the harsh post–nuclear attack environment.

was one of reassurance; the horrors of nuclear war were not even obliquely referred to in this romanticized vision of frontier life.

The approach of the 1955 FCDA pamphlet *Six Steps to Survival* provided a stark contrast to the approach of *Grandma's Pantry Was Ready*. The FCDA's first publications and films focused on helping families survive the blast effects of an atomic attack, but the publications in 1955 began to focus primarily on the long-term survival of families in fallout shelters. While mentioning briefly that the "whole family" should learn "how to 'duck and cover'" if caught by surprise, *Six Steps to Survival* acknowledged that such procedures were not the best way to survive a nuclear attack.[29] The front flap of the pamphlet showed a gigantic nuclear explosion; in the foreground, a white nuclear family (son, daughter, wife, and husband) held hands and watched the explosion from a presumably safe distance (see Figure 7). This pamphlet stated rather directly that "the best protection against

Figure 7. A white family watches a thermonuclear explosion destroy an urban center from the safety of the suburbs. These images, which come from the first and last pages of FCDA, *Six Steps to Survival* (1955), show the suburban white family ideal that was the primary focus of civil defense in the 1950s.

atomic or hydrogen bombs is—*don't be there*! In major cities, this means pre-attack evacuation."[30] This exhortation was characteristic of the major shift that occurred after the hydrogen bomb tests in the Marshall Islands in the early 1950s and the *Lucky Dragon* incident in 1954. The size of nuclear weapons was constantly increasing, and evacuation was seen as the only way to save those living in the urban core. Civil defense publications were designed to sell the public on this new approach.[31] At the same time, the pamphlet encouraged suburban American families to construct a home fallout shelter and to stock it with enough "emergency food and water to sustain your family for a week."[32] Finally the government was admitting that fallout was a major threat in a nuclear attack, and suburban families who were safely outside the range of the initial blast became the main priority in these civil defense publications. Pamphlets like *Six Steps to Survival* encouraged white suburban families to hunker down in their fallout shelters, and pamphlets like *Grandma's Pantry Was Ready* provided nostalgic and comforting imagery that located fallout shelters on the nuclear frontier. People in the urban core were advised to run, but their prospects for survival in these publications seemed bleak at best.

By 1958, civil defense publications combined the imagery of "grandma's pantry" and the evacuation/fallout shelter rhetoric of just a few years before. In the pamphlet *Between You and Disaster* (1958), the Office of Civil and Defense Mobilization (OCDM, the successor of the FCDA) waxed nostalgic in the opening lines: "Remember grandma's pantry, its shelves loaded with food, ready for any emergency, whether it be unexpected company or roads blocked for days by a winter's storm? Today, when we are vulnerable as always to the ravages of nature as well as the possibility of nuclear attack, every wise and thinking family will likewise prepare for emergencies with the modern equivalent of grandma's pantry."[33] The threats of nature and nuclear attack were cited as good reasons for frontier-style preparedness. The first flap of the pamphlet showed a smiling white family happily stocking the shelves of their bomb shelter. The imagery showed once again the racial imagination of civil defense officials about who would populate the nuclear frontier: with large numbers of blacks and poor people likely to be wiped out in the initial blast, officials focused their planning and propaganda on the politically expedient imagery of the white suburban family. The length of time a family should be prepared to survive without assistance had increased in this pamphlet: "You should assemble a 2-week food supply in your home shelter area, and a 3-day evacuation-survival kit in your family automobile. This precaution might mean the difference between comfort and hardship—even between survival and starvation—in case of enemy attack or a natural disaster."[34] The extension of the stay in the fallout shelter from one week to two weeks reflected the increasing pace of the arms race; hydrogen bombs were growing larger and more deadly all the time (see Figures 8 and 9). Innovations in the delivery of weapons such as long-range bombers, missiles, and attack submarines meant that the warning time civilians would have in the event of an attack was becoming miniscule. As the 1950s came to a close, public and government skepticism about the viability of any form of

Figure 8. Cover of the OCDM booklet *Ten for Survival* (1959). By the end of the 1950s, civil defense officials were focusing more on survival from fallout than on blast effects. However, this image shows how the "duck and cover" mentality remained an important part of civil defense propaganda through the end of the decade.

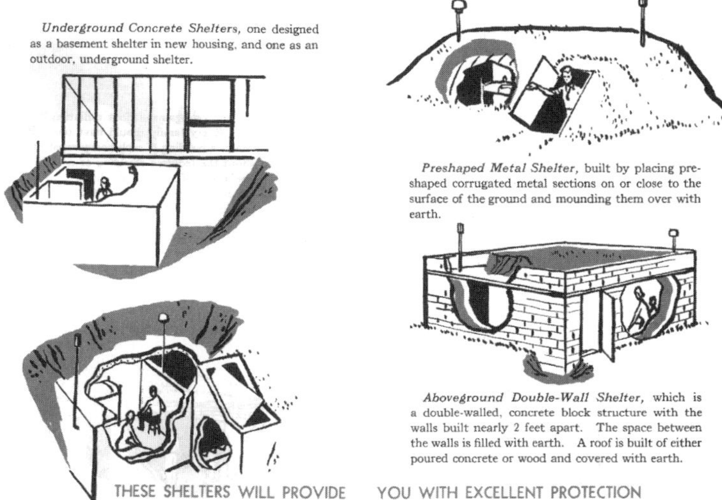

Figure 9. Examples of four fallout shelters the OCDM endorsed in *Ten for Survival* (1959). By the end of the 1950s, the OCDM was encouraging citizens to be prepared to stay in a fallout shelter for at least two weeks in the event of a nuclear attack.

civil defense was growing stronger by the day. A few years after publishing *Tomorrow!*, even Wylie rejected the idea that civil defense was possible in the face of nuclear war and completely repudiated the conceit that a nuclear war was somehow winnable.[35] Future-war stories increasingly reflected this skepticism about civil defense.

A growing number of science fiction novels represented the stark possibility that nuclear war would mean the end of the human race. Englishman Nevil Shute's *On the Beach* (1957) told the story of the last remaining humans in Australia as they slowly succumbed to a toxic cloud of fallout that inevitably killed all life on the planet. Israeli Mordecai Roshwald's *Level 7* (1959) told the story of a military survival shelter that slowly broke down after a nuclear war, killing the last humans on Earth. American Helen Clarkson's *The Last Day* (1959) told a similar story of fallout slowly killing off the residents of an island in New England. These novels were hailed as important works of fiction that showed the extreme dangers of the arms race between the United States and the Soviet Union. In all of these stories, there was no hope for survival after a nuclear war because of the extreme toxicity of fallout.

By contrast, nuclear frontier stories continued to fantasize about the survival of white Americans in the face of such extreme circumstances. Some nuclear frontier stories represented the rise of societies that were radically technophobic. In these stories, the characters usually led a repressed and primitive existence while longing for the ability to pursue science once again. Leigh Brackett's *The Long Tomorrow* (1955) represented the quest of three young teenagers to find an underground research center that had begun to conduct scientific research again. In Brackett's postwar world, there was a strong social taboo against technological development, but the narrative clearly sided with the inquisitive young teens as they boldly set off in their quest for progress. Probably the most famous and highly regarded story in this vein was *A Canticle for Leibowitz* (1959) by southerner Walter Miller Jr. In 1959, Miller collected and released his series of short stories that were originally published between from 1955 to 1957 as a novel.[36] It received a Hugo Award in 1959 and has been hailed as easily "the most effective postcatastrophe story."[37] The quality of the plot, prose, and characterizations have earned the novel a place of respect in the nuclear apocalypse genre. The novel also provided a strong critique of racism and racial segregation. However, as did so many other nuclear frontier stories, the novel depended on the racist specter of the "savage" for some of its critical edge.

Miller's novel offered a bleak version of the nuclear frontier. In the first section of the novel, the world had already been blasted into the dark ages by what was called the "flame deluge." The story revolved around a Catholic order of monks begun by an engineer named Leibowitz. The order tried to preserve knowledge from the destroyed civilization in the face of anti-science riots and savagery. The first image of the novel described the blasted wasteland of the southwestern United States, where a young novitiate named Francis kept his Lenten fast in the desert outside the abbey. With luck, Francis stumbled across an ancient bomb shelter from the period of the flame deluge. While the shelter provided the monks with a treasure trove of artifacts, it also warned the reader about the futility of civil defense. The door mechanism of the shelter only opened outward, and when rubble from the nuclear attack had blocked the door, those in the shelter had been trapped inside and had died a slow death. A few outside the shelters survived, but they didn't necessarily prosper. The world was filled with mutants and savage cannibals; in fact, the first section of the novel ended with Francis getting eaten by mutants after making a pilgrimage to New Rome. Through the eyes of Francis, Miller showed a small, sad, yet endearingly devoted group of men striving to preserve scientific learning in the face of overwhelming ignorance and savagery. The death of Francis underscored the near-futility of their calling, as progress was so slow that it could barely be perceived within the span of one lifetime.

Where the first section of the novel was set in a future dark age, the middle section of the novel was set in a future mixture of the Renaissance and the nineteenth-century American west. As civilizations began to grow in various spots on the continent, a genius named Thon Taddeo made a trek across the country to study the ancient texts in the abbey of Saint Leibowitz. However, the Great Plains, which were occupied by savages, lay between the civilization of the east and the civilization of the west. Although some of the savages in the novel were simply mutants, the savages of the plains were described in a way that clearly invoked race. Though skin color was never mentioned, the description of the leader of the plains tribes made the racial connotations obvious: "Hongon Os was essentially a just and kindly man. When he saw a party of his warriors making sport of the Laredan captives, he paused to watch; but when they tied these Laredans by their ankles between horses and whipped the horses into frenzied flight, Hongan Os decided to intervene. He ordered that the warriors be flogged on the spot, for Hongan Os—Mad Bear—was known to be a merciful chieftain. He had never mistreated a horse."[38] By naming the chieftain of the plains tribes "Mad Bear," Miller evoked famous

Native American names like Crazy Horse and Sitting Bull. The historical situation of Mad Bear's people also equated them with Native American horse cultures, as they occupied the Great Plains and were beset by warring civilizations that wanted their land. Miller's description uncritically repeated common stereotypes that asserted that Native Americans tortured their victims and valued animal life more than human life. Mad Bear's people also drank blood instead of water and considered farmers to be effeminate weaklings. This racialized representation of the nomadic savage served to highlight the scientific mind of Thon Taddeo and the progress he represented. In this sense, Miller's novel repeated the racist frontier narrative of evolutionary progress put forward in the late nineteenth century. Miller made civilization and progress appear to be inevitable outgrowths of human curiosity and ambition and his descriptions of savages functioned to cast the agents of progress in a positive light.

The pattern of progress continued to follow the Darwinist narrative of human history through the final third of the novel. With the world on the brink of yet another nuclear war, political tensions were exacerbated by the expansion of humanity into space. As humans began to colonize space, Miller made a pointed critique of racism:

> Nevertheless, the Asian rulers had sent the first colony ship. Then in the West the cry was heard: "Are we to let the 'inferior' races inherit the stars?" There had been a brief flurry of starship launching as colonies of black people, brown, white, and yellow people were hurled into the sky toward the Centaur, in the name of racism. Afterwards, geneticists had wryly demonstrated that—since each racial group was so small that unless their descendants intermarried, each would undergo deteriorative genetic drift due to inbreeding on the colony planet—the racists had made cross-breeding necessary to survival.[39]

Miller created a scenario where racism became irrelevant because of the struggle to survive. Ironically, racist sentiments led to this scenario, and after the final war, the vestige of humanity that had survived in space was interracial. In this sense, Miller rejected the racist arguments of the late nineteenth century: the conceited "toolmakers" who eventually destroyed the world espoused racism as a part of their corrupt civilization.[40] Miller viewed unchecked science as a blight when put in the service of human ambition and racism, and he used his representation of the nuclear frontier to make a strong critique of contemporary American society.

The sobering fate of human life on Earth in the novel also offered a focused attack on the wrong kind of human progress. With the world in the hands of illiterate bullies and racists armed by science, the progress of humanity ended in another flame deluge. This time, no humans survived. Instead, the Earth now seemed fated to be inherited by mutants who were unfazed by the toxic environment left by the war. Like Shute's *On the Beach* and Roshwald's *Level 7*, Miller's novel ultimately represented global nuclear war as pure folly that could not be survived (at least, not twice). However, Miller preserved a sliver of hope; the order of Leibowitz sent a mission to the multiracial colonies before the final bombs struck. Like Bradbury's "Million Year Picnic" (1946), Miller presented space as the new frontier where humanity would have an opportunity to overcome its shortcomings. The human colonies in space were forced to overcome segregation in order to survive, and Miller showed that hope for mankind lay in racial tolerance and cooperation instead of in racism and selfish conflict. Miller's novel presented a mixed bag with regard to race: though his critique of progress relied at times on the racist concept of savagery, his vision of the future was racially integrated. This was a major step forward from the white suburban utopias of civil defense officials and Philip Wylie.

Progress was slow for the civil rights movement of the 1950s. President Truman gave vocal support to civil rights but did little to change the status quo. President Eisenhower, who took office in 1953, did even less to help African Americans. In 1954, the Supreme Court's decision in *Brown v. Board of Education* promised to transform race relations in the United States because it provided a legal basis for ending segregation. However, President Eisenhower did not like the decision and refused to use his authority to enforce it. Emboldened by the president's inaction, racists throughout the country—especially in the south—dug in to resist.[41] In this context, the support of a white southerner such as Miller was remarkably progressive. His vision of the future showed that desegregation was necessary for survival and that interracial marriages would be required to preserve humanity. The image of nonwhite men raping white women had been used throughout the twentieth century to rally support for segregation. Miller defied this entrenched phobia of racial mixing with his interracial space colonies, a radical move for the 1950s.

Desegregation was key to the last great nuclear frontier story of the decade, Pat Frank's best-selling novel *Alas, Babylon* (1959). The primary plot revolved around a multiracial group of "normal" Americans who worked together to reestablish a rural lifestyle in the fictional town of Fort Repose, Florida. Frank's novel emphasized the frontier tradition of the town that reasserted itself after the global nuclear war. As the title of the book implied, Frank portrayed city life as corrupt, superficial, and justifiably annihilated. One reason the citizens of Fort Repose survived was that they were miraculously spared the fallout from nearby cities and military installations hit by hydrogen bombs. The main reason the families survived, however, was that they abandoned segregation and displayed a frontier spirit of working together in the face of savagery.

Frank romanticized the postwar environment by evoking the Darwinian struggle to maintain civilization on the frontier. Randy Bragg, the main character of the novel, thrived in the new environment, while selfish and greedy characters were naturally eliminated from the gene pool. Frank described Randy as a direct descendant of the navy lieutenant who founded Fort Repose in 1838. The men in Randy's family had been influential and important, keeping up the tradition of their pioneer forefather. As the text opened, however, Randy had become a slacker who was falling victim to the easy life of overcivilization: he was a lazy drunk, a failed politician, and a womanizer. His white neighbors also felt he was a race traitor because of his anti-segregationist political views and his kindness to the Henrys, his black neighbors. After the inevitable nuclear war, Randy emerged as a true leader. Like his pioneer forefather, Randy successfully organized his neighbors and eventually the whole community into a mutually beneficial system of trade and self-defense. Randy helped Fort Repose return to its roots as a frontier town, a bastion of civilization surrounded by savage invaders and a hostile environment.

Frank went out of his way to underscore his belief that Darwinian struggle on the frontier reinvigorated men like Randy. Dan, the town doctor, explained this to Randy when he said, "Some people melt in the heat of crisis and come apart like fat in the pan. Others meet the challenge and harden. I think you're going to harden."[42] Randy repeated this Darwinist logic to his fiancée Lib when explaining what they would have to do to survive on the nuclear frontier:

> "Survival of the fittest."
>
> "What do you mean?" Lib said.
>
> "The strong survive. The frail die. The exotic fish die because the aquarium isn't heated. The common guppy lives. So does the tough catfish. . . . That's the way it is and that's the way it's going to be. . . . We're going to have to be tough. We're going to have to be catfish."[43]

Even though several million people died, Frank represented the return to the nuclear frontier as a blessing to Randy. He became physically fit, settled down with a nice girl, and took his place as leader of the town like his forefathers. In this sense, *Alas, Babylon* repeated Turner's narrative of the frontier: Randy was reinvigorated by the struggle to survive on the nuclear frontier and he became much happier than he was before the war.

Through his descriptions of the war and its aftermath, Frank criticized the ideas and representations of the U.S. government's civil defense establishment. In his description of the mass confusion that ensued as refugees fled bombed-out cities, Randy noted that "this chaos did not result from a breakdown in Civil Defense. It was simply that Civil Defense, as a realistic buffer against thermonuclear war, did not exist."[44] Frank also rejected the idealized white family and the segregationist politics of civil defense. At one point in the story, he argued that racism was an impediment to survival. While visiting the local trading post, Randy was struck by the fact that formerly racist whites now drank out of the same water jugs as blacks and treated them as equals. Randy reasoned that "the economics of disaster placed a penalty upon prejudice. The laws of hunger and survival could not be evaded, and honored no color line. . . . There were two drinking fountains in Marines Park, one marked 'White only,' the other 'Colored only.' Since neither worked, the signs were meaningless."[45] Humanity was thrown back into a state of nature, and the segregation established in the south collapsed along with the technological infrastructure that supported it. Frank used the image of segregated water fountains to show that racism was another harmful by-product of civilization that was destroyed by nuclear war. Frank portrayed the cooperation of whites and blacks as essential for the survival of the community of Fort Repose.

Randy also noted the ridiculousness of segregated education. When Randy's family began home-schooling their kids, the child of his African American neighbors showed up as well: "When Caleb Henry arrived to attend classes with Peyton and Ben Franklin, Randy was a little surprised. He saw that Peyton and Ben expected it, and then he recalled that in Omaha—and indeed in two thirds of America's cities—white and Negro children had sat side by side for many years without fuss or trouble."[46] Frank used Randy's response to chastise southern whites who still staunchly refused to adhere to the Supreme Court's ruling in *Brown v. Board of Education*. Frank used the interracial friendship between youngsters Caleb Henry and Ben Bragg to reinforce his idea that integrated education and integrated communities were key to the future of America.

Unfortunately, Frank's strong attack on segregation was limited by his depiction of the Henrys as unsophisticated and primitive. The Henrys were descendants of the slave who accompanied Randy's pioneer forefather on his original expedition, and they were a source of primitive wisdom and low-tech know-how for Randy throughout the text. Though the Henrys were seen as an essential part of the community, they contributed by providing whites with knowledge about farming, fishing, and making moonshine. Their contributions were portrayed as useful only after the community had lapsed into a state of nature; once whites were reduced to a primitive existence, blacks became their teachers for how to live. In this way, Frank repeated the stereotype of the black savage: the Henrys were noble savages working under the leadership of frontiersman Randy Bragg. Though this vision was certainly not as contemptible as nineteenth-century representations of the savage, Frank equated whites with advanced toolmaking and leadership while he associated blacks with primitive implements and servitude.

Frank's appeal to the imagination of the frontier gave him an interesting vantage point from which to criticize the madness of the arms race and the problems of contemporary American society. By placing his characters on the nuclear frontier, Frank presented his idealized image of American society: desegregated communities of people who live a simple, "real" life devoid of the racial divisions and corruption of modern civilization. However, his appeal to frontier Darwinism limited the anti-racist message of his novel. By representing black people as primitive, he repeated the logic of Darwinist racism in which savages were inherently inferior to whites technologically. At the same time, the romanticized happy ending of the story undermined his critique of civil defense and nuclear proliferation. The United States won the war and the main characters were better off after the destruction of civilization. With such an outcome, why would people want to avoid a nuclear war?

By the end of the 1950s, a happy ending to a story about a global nuclear war seemed naïve at best. With the overwhelming power of the hydrogen bomb, new intercontinental ballistic missiles, an increased understanding of fallout, and the prospect of no warning in the event of an actual attack, stories about survival on the nuclear frontier were lapsing farther into the realm of fantasy. Authors such as Miller and Frank made racism a problematic aspect of this frontier representation: both represented racism as an evil brought on by civilization that became an impediment to survival on the frontier. They also rejected the claims of the FCDA and the OCDM that civil defense was possible and that the white suburban family was the key to postwar survival. Unfortunately, like Bradbury and Wylie before them, Miller and Frank retained some of the problematic aspects of the Darwinist frontier vision of the nineteenth century. By linking race to savagery and primitive wisdom, they yoked their criticism of modern civilization to an outmoded version of Darwinist racism that they otherwise seemed to reject.

Conclusion

In the late 1950s, African Americans increased their activities to bring an end to Jim Crow segregation. Using protests like the Montgomery bus boycott, they built powerful organizational networks that would become increasingly important in the 1960s. Galvanized by the success of the boycott, they continued to organize themselves and their allies to fight for their freedom.[1] Even though the civil rights movement realized a number of successes during the Cold War years, racism continued to pervade American culture. Segregated housing remained an everyday reality in most urban areas, and the attitudes of those who fought against the civil rights movement were not changed overnight. While there was measurable progress in race relations, in the minds of many Americans, the United States was still a white nation. The stereotype of the savage continued to be used to describe African Americans and American Indians, though more positive images began to appear in some mainstream media.

One of the legacies of the stereotype of the savage can still be seen in the Indian sports mascots that emerged in the early twentieth century. The impulse behind these mascots came from the idea that white Americans should retain some of the violent characteristics from earlier stages of cultural evolution. This idea, which was pushed by President Teddy Roosevelt, asserted that engaging in physical competition was a way to maintain individual and national fitness while warding off the dangers of overcivilization. Indian mascots exemplified the unbridled ferocity young men were supposed to emulate as they engaged in athletic competitions. While racist representations have been curbed in many aspects of American life, Indian mascots have proven particularly resistant to calls for reform. One reason for this is simple: most Americans still believe in cultural evolution and accept the argument that fierce "Indian warriors" symbolize primitive virtues that young men (and now young women) should emulate. Modern arguments in favor of Indian mascots generally ignore the problematic history of representations of "savagery" in American culture. Indian mascots were conceived with the assumption that American Indians were inherently less evolved than whites. They usually consisted of racist caricatures who wielded a "savage" tool such as a tomahawk or a spear and inaccurate abstractions of what it means to be an Indian. Some bodies that govern high school and college sports have taken steps to eliminate these racist mascots. However, major professional sports organizations such as the National Football League and Major League Baseball have yet to act.

Just as the stereotype of the savage continues to haunt African Americans and American Indians, the rhetoric of the yellow peril continues to haunt Asian Americans. After World War II, Japan became a stable Cold War ally. However, the 1949 victory of the communists in the Chinese civil war engendered renewed rumblings about the yellow peril. The outbreak of the Korean War in 1950 increased anxiety about the communist threat in Asia. When the Korean War ended, the growing conflict in Vietnam during the 1960s kept this threat at the forefront of public discourse. China's first successful test of an atomic bomb on October 16, 1964, stoked a fire that still rages in American culture. The Vietnam War period was rife with the rhetoric of the savage and the yellow peril as American troops were again sent to protect American civilization from people who were seen as cruel and primitive. A new generation of activists challenged the racial dimension of the Vietnam War, rejecting the notion that communist Asians posed a threat to the United States. On television, George Takei's character Sulu on *Star Trek* provided a vision of a heroic Asian using technology to work alongside whites for the benefit of civilization. This offered a sharp contrast to the steady stream of media images that portrayed technologically unsophisticated North Vietnamese soldiers battling Americans.[2]

Despite the work of Takei and scores of other Asian American pioneers, yellow peril rhetoric still carries immense weight in American culture. This racially motivated representation of the Asian threat took center stage during the Wen Ho Lee espionage case at the turn of the twenty-first century. Lee was a mild-mannered code developer who worked on computer simulations of nuclear explosions at Los Alamos National Laboratories. When the United States discovered that China had made some advances in nuclear weapons design, investigators began a vigorous search for a security leak. Lee was singled out and condemned as a nuclear spy for China by the *New York Times*, the FBI, the Department of Justice, and a number of members of Congress. During late 1999 and 2000, Lee spent 278 days in jail under extreme conditions while the government tried to make its case.[3] The problem with the prosecution's case was simple: it was based on racist assumptions with no supporting evidence. The first racist assumption was that China could not develop its own nuclear capability without stealing from the United States. This was a classic mistake of the man-the-toolmaker myth; this version assumed that whites were superior when it came to developing technology while Asians were only good imitators (and, in this case, sneaky thieves). As a number of experts indicated, there was no conclusive proof that China's weapons advances were based on ideas stolen from the United States.[4] The second racist assumption was that Lee was suspect because he was of Chinese descent; his detention and prosecution exemplified racial profiling at its worst.[5] The government's abuse of power in the case was so egregious that conservative judge James Parker apologized to Lee, saying that the government's prosecution "embarrassed our entire nation and each of us who is a citizen of it."[6] While the fact that Lee was innocent emerged in the end, the fact that so many people bought into the yellow peril myth showed how deeply entrenched racist beliefs remained in American culture.

Beginning with President George W. Bush's speech that reframed the enemies of civilization as an "axis of evil" in 2002, the U.S. government launched a new cycle of yellow peril rhetoric. The weapons programs of dictator Kim Jong Il of North Korea led to calls for harder positions against this supposed threat to American national security. While the government of North Korea is certainly not innocent of many of the charges made against it, the rhetoric that the Bush administration has used to attack it is highly questionable. By including Kim Jong Il in the "axis of evil" during his first major post-9/11 speech, President Bush made it appear that racial others around the world were banding together in their attempts to acquire high technology and use it against the United States. Similar rhetoric has been used by government officials who continue to push for Wen Ho Lee–style investigations of people of Chinese descent. These investigations invariably center on technology and portray people of Chinese descent as spies working for a foreign government bent on stealing American technological secrets.[7] These calls for crackdowns on spying and terrorism committed by those seen as "foreign" ignore demonstrable threats to national security posed by white Americans. By pointing the finger at racial and ethnic minorities, government officials are keeping up the long-standing tradition of casting the United States as a white nation under siege by savages and racial minorities.

Domestic terrorism of the type that led to the April 19, 1995, bombing of the federal building in Oklahoma City is still a problem. In January 2002, the FBI began to investigate members of self-styled militias in New Jersey and Texas. The FBI investigation uncovered large stores of weapons, ammunition, and bomb-making materials as well as white supremacist and anti-government literature. To their credit, the FBI and federal prosecutors were successful in thwarting what could have become another major attack by domestic terrorists. Still, the Bush administration largely ignored what should have been trumpeted as a major success in their ongoing war against terrorism.[8] This silence clearly demonstrated the Bush administration's practice of whipping up support for its policies by evoking the specter of savage racial "others" who threaten the United States. In other words, the Bush administration's "war on terror" is a publicity campaign that makes thinly veiled appeals to racist sentiments in order to induce a sense of fear in white America. As were the civil defense campaigns of the 1950s, this evocation of fear has been used to cow the white electorate and pursue a variety of disparate domestic and foreign policy goals under the guise of "national security." If national security was truly the goal, potential domestic terrorists like those arrested in New Jersey and Texas would be held up as a threat on a par with the Al Qaeda operatives and Chinese spies that dominate White House press briefings and American media outlets.

Anthropologists now reject the concept of the savage and the significance of race, but these ideas are so embedded in our narrative traditions that even the most talented authors and artists have found it difficult to uproot them. Science fiction enjoys a reputation as politically progressive, but the history of the genre with regard to race is mixed. While some science fiction artists have imagined worlds that defy racist stereotypes, many others have reinforced the connection between race, technology, and civilization. The frontier myth has been a dominant theme in science fiction, and men such as Ray Bradbury and Gene Roddenberry have used the frontier landscape to question notions of cultural and racial superiority. Yet the image of the savage has served too often in the genre as a foil for civilized progress. From the green Martians of Edgar Rice Burroughs to the plains horsemen of Walter Miller Jr., the savages of science fiction have helped keep the Darwinist racism of the nineteenth century alive. As videogames such as Fallout and films such as the Terminator series demonstrate, the nuclear frontier remains a popular narrative landscape for modern America. However, it is a landscape that has been carved out of outdated beliefs and failed scientific theories. As we move further into the twenty first century, we must challenge the lingering connection between race, technology, and civilization put forward by authors, media makers, and government officials. The lessons of the nuclear age must not be used to romanticize a racist vision of American identity or to drum up support for policies by appealing to our basest sentiments. They should remind us of the dangers of unchecked racism, militarism, and nationalism and keep us vigilant against the never-ending stream of distortions and outright lies disseminated by our leaders.

NOTES

INTRODUCTION

1. George W. Bush, "State of the Union Address."
2. Ibid.
3. Quoted in Chen, "Bush Urges Unity on Terror," A1.
4. Hudson, "From 'Nation' to 'Race,'" 252–258; Stocking, *Victorian Anthropology*, 10–11.
5. Dower, *War without Mercy*, 148.
6. London, "Yellow Peril," 348.

CHAPTER 1

1. Gould, *Mismeasure of Man*, 68; Will, "American School of Ethnology," 29–31.
2. Horsman, "Scientific Racism and the Indian," 149–150; Nott and Glidden, *Types of Mankind*, ix–x; Stanton, *Leopard's Spots*, 162–163; Will, "American School of Ethnology," 14, 30.
3. Nott and Glidden, *Types of Mankind*, 67.
4. Horsman, *Race and Manifest Destiny*, 135–136; Stanton, *Leopard's Spots*, 163; Will, "American School of Ethnology," 30–31.
5. Following the work of Roland Barthes and a number of cultural critics, I use the term "myth" to mean a specific combination of imagery and ideology that coheres into a relatively stable narrative structure and operates at a very basic level of the cultural imagination. In this usage, myths are narratives that naturalize social relations and order reality at an unconscious level for members of a particular culture. As such, myths routinely migrate across cultural boundaries and manifest themselves in a wide variety of genres and disciplines. The frontier myth was a narrative structure that became central to national identity in the United States. In this chapter and later chapters, I trace the development of this frontier myth as a narrative structure and show how it was entwined with beliefs about race, progress, and national identity.
6. Slotkin, *Regeneration through Violence*.

7. Ibid., 21.
8. Berkhofer, *White Man's Indian*, 4–12.
9. Ellingson, *Myth of the Noble Savage*, 99–100.
10. Horsman, *Race and Manifest Destiny*, 10.
11. Ibid., 12–14.
12. Ibid., 18–24.
13. Hudson, "From 'Nation' to 'Race,'" 247–250.
14. Adas, *Machines as the Measure of Men*, 21–68; Hudson, "From 'Nation' to 'Race,'" 250.
15. Hudson, "From 'Nation' to 'Race,'" 252–258; Stocking, *Victorian Anthropology*, 63–64.
16. Adas, *Machines as the Measure of Men*, 119–120; Dain, *A Hideous Monster*, 9–14; Fredrickson, *Racism*, 56; Gould, *Mismeasure of Man*, 402–405; Stanton, *Leopard's Spots*, 3.
17. Stocking, *Victorian Anthropology*, 10–11.
18. Ibid., 14.
19. Ibid., 11.
20. Berkhofer, *White Man's Indian*, 46–47; Greene, "American Debate," 390–391; Stocking, *Victorian Anthropology*, 11, 15–18.
21. Berkhofer, *White Man's Indian*, 48–49; Fredrickson, *Racism*, 68–69.
22. Slotkin, *Regeneration through Violence*, 268–269.
23. Ibid., 274–276.
24. Ibid., 467–468.
25. Cooper, *Last of the Mohicans*, 17.
26. Slotkin, *Fatal Environment*, 85.
27. Ibid., 91.
28. Cooper, *Last of the Mohicans*, 62.
29. McWilliams, "Historical Contexts of *The Last of the Mohicans*," 400–401.
30. Cooper, *Last of the Mohicans*, 262.
31. Bell, "Beginnings of Professionalism," 24–37; Berkhofer, *White Man's Indian*, 93–95; Slotkin, *Fatal Environment*, 81–82.
32. Lawlor, *Recalling the Wild*, 15–18, 27; Slotkin, *Fatal Environment*, 87–88.
33. Horsman, *Race and Manifest Destiny*, 192–193; McWilliams, "Historical Contexts of *The Last of the Mohicans*," 419; Slotkin, *Fatal Environment*, 172; Zinn, *A People's History*, 136–137.
34. Berkhofer, *White Man's Indian*, 160–162; McWilliams, "Historical Contexts of *The Last of the Mohicans*," 420.
35. Horsman, *Race and Manifest Destiny*, 189–207; LaFeber, *American Age*, 95–97; Zinn, *A People's History*, 125–148.
36. Fredrickson, *Racism*, 43–45.
37. Will, "American School of Ethnology," 14.
38. Gould, *Mismeasure of Man*, 71; Stanton, *Leopard's Spots*, 10–11; Thomas, *Skull Wars*, 38. I use the term "Euro-American" as an adjective to describe aspects of history or culture common to both Europe and America. I use the

term "European American" to refer to Americans whose ancestors originally came from Europe; I use the term interchangeably with the terms "white" and "Caucasian."

39. Fredrickson, *Racism*, 74–76; Gould, *Mismeasure of Man*, 71, 78–82.
40. Thomas, *Skull Wars*, 106–109.
41. Gould, *Mismeasure of Man*, 73–74; Greene, "American Debate," 387–396; Horsman, *Race and Manifest Destiny*, 48–52; Stanton, *Leopard's Spots*, 15–23.
42. Horsman, *Race and Manifest Destiny*, 116–125.
43. Gould, *Mismeasure of Man*, 82–86; Horsman, *Race and Manifest Destiny*, 125–127; Stanton, *Leopard's Spots*, 25–33; Thomas, *Skull Wars*, 38–41.
44. Gould, *Mismeasure of Man*, 93–94; Kaplan and Rogers, "Race and Gender Fallacies," 324–327.
45. Gould, *Mismeasure of Man*, 86–100.
46. Lurie, *Louis Agassiz*, 122–142; Stanton, *Leopard's Spots*, 101–103.
47. Gould, *Mismeasure of Man*, 74–79; Lurie, *Louis Agassiz*, 143–144; Stanton, *Leopard's Spots*, 101–102.
48. Nott and Glidden, *Types of Mankind*, lxxii.
49. Ibid., lxxiii–lxiv.
50. Ibid., lxxv.
51. Ibid., lxxvi.
52. Ibid., lxviii.
53. Ibid.
54. Ibid.
55. Ibid., 67.
56. Ibid.
57. Ibid., 80.
58. Ibid., 53.
59. Horsman, "Scientific Racism and the Indian," 160.
60. Horsman, *Race and Manifest Destiny*, 229–248.

Chapter 2

1. Beer, *Darwin's Plots*, 2.
2. I will be using the second (and final) edition of *Descent*, which Darwin published in 1874; this edition provides the fullest articulation of Darwin's views on human nature.
3. Desmond and Moore, *Darwin*, 579.
4. Clark, *Survival of Charles Darwin*, 107–109; Desmond and Moore, *Darwin*, 466–470.
5. Kuhn, *Structure of Scientific Revolutions*, 10–24.
6. The debate over Dawkins's *The Selfish Gene* (1976) and Wilson's *Sociobiology* (1975) provide two clear examples of the modern version of the controversy over heredity versus environment. See Lewontin's *Biology as*

Ideology (1992) and *The Triple Helix* (2001) for a refutation of the work of Dawkins and Wilson and a discussion of the importance of environment.

7. Clark, *Survival of Charles Darwin*, 120–121; Desmond, *Huxley*, 241; Desmond and Moore, *Darwin*, 462–463.
8. Darwin, *Autobiography of Charles Darwin*, 122–123; Desmond and Moore, *Darwin*, 477. Darwin uses the term "lower animals" to refer to nonhuman animals throughout *The Origin of Species*, *The Descent of Man*, and his other works.
9. Darwin, *Origin of Species*, 458. By the time the sixth edition of *Origin* was published in 1872, Darwin had become bolder and had changed this line to "Much light will be thrown on the origin of man and his history." See Appleman, *Darwin*, 130; Clark, *Survival of Charles Darwin*, 120; Darwin, *Autobiography of Charles Darwin*, 130–131; Stocking, *Victorian Anthropology*, 146.
10. Clark, *Survival of Charles Darwin*, 127–128.
11. Desmond and Moore, *Darwin*, 477.
12. For a more complete discussion of the immediate response to *Origin of Species*, see Clark, *Survival of Charles Darwin*, 120–154; and Desmond and Moore, *Darwin*, 477–499.
13. Desmond, *Huxley*, 282–284.
14. Quoted in Desmond and Moore, *Darwin*, 504.
15. Desmond, *Huxley*, 239–241; Desmond and Moore, *Darwin*, 504.
16. Desmond, *Huxley*, 292.
17. Desmond, *Huxley*, 292–311; Desmond and Moore, *Darwin*, 507–509.
18. Clark, *Survival of Charles Darwin*, 121–122; Desmond, *Huxley*, 299, 312, 315–316.
19. Stocking, *Victorian Anthropology*, 146–185.
20. Desmond and Moore, *Darwin*, 505–506; Fichman, *Evolutionary Theory and Victorian Culture*, 101–103; Stocking, *Victorian Anthropology*, 73–74, 147.
21. Desmond and Moore, *Darwin*, 452–453; Desmond, *Huxley*, 295.
22. Desmond, *Huxley*, 399–401.
23. Clark, *Survival of Charles Darwin*, 180–185; Desmond and Moore, *Darwin*, 579–584.
24. Stocking, *Victorian Anthropology*, 149.
25. Stocking, *Race, Culture, and Evolution*, 45–47.
26. Darwin, *Descent of Man*, 2.
27. Gould, *Mismeasure of Man*, 74, 82.
28. Browne, *Charles Darwin*, 243–244.
29. Darwin, *Descent of Man*, 183.
30. Stocking, *Race, Culture, and Evolution*, 45–47.
31. Darwin, *Descent of Man*, 172.
32. Ibid., 180.
33. Ibid., 186.

34. Ibid., 182.
35. Ibid., 188.
36. Haller, *Outcasts from Evolution*, 78–79; Stocking, *Race, Culture, and Evolution*, 45.
37. Darwin, *Descent of Man*, 121.
38. Ibid., 128–129.
39. Browne, *Charles Darwin*, 244–246; Greene, *Science, Ideology, and World View*, 114, 122–123.
40. Darwin, *Voyage of the Beagle*, 61.
41. Browne, *Charles Darwin*, 255–258; Desmond and Moore, *Darwin*, 140–142.
42. Browne, *Charles Darwin*, 244–246; Desmond and Moore, *Darwin*, 122, 142.
43. Darwin, *Voyage of the Beagle*, 64, 65–66.
44. Ibid., 204.
45. Desmond and Moore, *Darwin*, 574–575, 632.
46. Browne, *Charles Darwin*, 248.
47. Desmond and Moore, *Darwin*, 540–541; Fichman, *Evolutionary Theory and Victorian Culture*, 120.
48. Nott and Gliddon, *Types of Mankind*, 52, 80.
49. Darwin, *Descent of Man*, 55. In this passage, "Americans" refers to Native Americans and "Australians" refers to Native Australians or Aborigines.
50. As discussed in Chapter 1, Darwin's skepticism was justified; twentieth-century scientific studies have shown that brain size is proportional to body size in all humans and provides no measure of intelligence. See Gould, *Mismeasure of Man*, 93–94; and Kaplan and Rogers, "Race and Gender Fallacies," 324–327.
51. I use the characterization "sloppy methodology" to mean that from a modern perspective, the methodology of craniometry was sloppy. As Gould shows, many contemporaries viewed men such as Samuel George Morton as incredibly careful with their quantitative methodology.
52. Stocking, *Race, Culture, and Evolution*, 113–114.
53. Stocking, *Victorian Anthropology*, 145–179.
54. Darwin, *Descent of Man*, 149.
55. Adas, *Machines as the Measure of Men*, 69–198.
56. Ibid., 308.
57. Darwin, *Descent of Man*, 49.
58. Ibid., 132.
59. Greene, *Science, Ideology, and World View*, 115–116.
60. The concept of "man the toolmaker" has also been expressed as "man the tool user."
61. Darwin, *Descent of Man*, 52.
62. Ibid., 53.
63. Ibid., 55.

64. Stanford, *Upright*, 8.
65. Browne, *Charles Darwin*, 7–9, 245.
66. Adas, *Machines as the Measure of Men*, 134.
67. Quoted in Clark, *Survival of Charles Darwin*, 120–121; Greene, *Science, Ideology, and World View*, 100.
68. Darwin, *Descent of Man*, 133.
69. Nott and Gliddon, *Types of Mankind*, 79–80.
70. Greene, *Science, Ideology, and World View*, 107–108, 112.
71. Clark, *Survival of Charles Darwin*, 197–199; Desmond and Moore, *Darwin*, 665–677.

CHAPTER 3

1. Roosevelt, *Winning of the West*, I:xxxi.
2. Ibid., xxxiv.
3. Ibid., xxxiii.
4. Ibid., xxxv–xxxvi.
5. Dalton, *Theodore Roosevelt*, 173–176; Morris, *Rise of Theodore Roosevelt*, 681–686; Slotkin, *Gunfighter Nation*, 82–86, 101–106.
6. Jacobson, *Barbarian Virtues*, 3–5.
7. Slotkin, *Gunfighter Nation*, 60–61.
8. Zinn, *A People's History*, 192–210.
9. LaFeber, *American Age*, 148–149.
10. Zinn, *A People's History*, 253–256.
11. LaFeber, *American Age*, 150–154; Zinn, *A People's History*, 255–295.
12. LaFeber, *American Age*, 158–161; Nash, *Creating the West*, 103.
13. Wrobel, *End of American Exceptionalism*, 30.
14. Ibid., 6–31.
15. Auchincloss, *Theodore Roosevelt*, 10–11; Dalton, *Theodore Roosevelt*, 15, 26–35; Morris, *Rise of Theodore Roosevelt*, 8–10.
16. Dalton, *Theodore Roosevelt*, 37–38.
17. Brands, *T. R.*, 49; Dalton, *Theodore Roosevelt*, 58.
18. Dalton, *Theodore Roosevelt*, 40.
19. Morris, *Rise of Theodore Roosevelt*, 16–19; Roosevelt, *Theodore Roosevelt: An Autobiography*, 14–16.
20. Dalton, *Theodore Roosevelt*, 18; Morris, *Rise of Theodore Roosevelt*, 48.
21. Dalton, *Theodore Roosevelt*, 41; Morris, *Rise of Theodore Roosevelt*, 34.
22. Dalton, *Theodore Roosevelt*, 43; Roosevelt, *Theodore Roosevelt: An Autobiography*, 346.
23. Dalton, *Theodore Roosevelt*, 37–42.
24. Brands, *T. R.*, 65, 72, 92; Burton, "Theodore Roosevelt's Social Darwinism," 103–104; Morris, *Rise of Theodore Roosevelt*, 68, 77.
25. Dalton, *Theodore Roosevelt*, 62.
26. Morris, *Rise of Theodore Roosevelt*, 65–67.

27. Dalton, *Theodore Roosevelt*, 6, 41, 117–118; Morris, *Rise of Theodore Roosevelt*, 16; Slotkin, *Gunfighter Nation*, 33.
28. For a more complete discussion of the frontier writings of Roosevelt and Frederick Jackson Turner, see Slotkin, *Gunfighter Nation*, 29–62. Slotkin's discussion gives much more detail about the works of both men and shows how their ideas developed and changed over the course of their lives. Slotkin also gives a much clearer comparison of the ideas of the two men, who differed a great deal on many issues. I focus on a representative text from each author that portrays the history of the American frontier in Darwinian terms to show a snapshot of the historical moment of the 1890s, one that is key in the development of the American conception of progress.
29. Roosevelt, *Winning of the West*, I:2.
30. Ibid., 2.
31. Ibid., 3.
32. Ibid., 3.
33. Ibid., 3–4.
34. Slotkin, *Gunfighter Nation*, 39.
35. Roosevelt, *Winning of the West*, I:5.
36. Ibid., 6.
37. Ibid.
38. Ibid., 10.
39. Ibid., 4, 10.
40. Ibid., 7.
41. Ibid., 1–2, 4–5, 7.
42. Ibid., 11–12.
43. Ibid., 12.
44. Ibid., 17.
45. Ibid., 11.
46. Ibid., 20–21.
47. Ibid., 8, 13.
48. Slotkin, *Regeneration through Violence*.
49. Slotkin, *Gunfighter Nation*, 38.
50. Jacobson, *Barbarian Virtues*, 130–131.
51. Bogue, *Frederick Jackson Turner*, 100; Ridge, "Introduction," 3–4.
52. Bogue, *Frederick Jackson Turner*, 53, 92–93, 102; Coleman, "Science and Symbol," 24, 28–29; Nash, *Creating the West*, 6.
53. Bogue, *Frederick Jackson Turner*, 107; Nash, *Creating the West*, 9–10.
54. Bogue, *Frederick Jackson Turner*, 116.
55. Ibid., 91.
56. Slotkin, *Gunfighter Nation*, 35–36.
57. Bogue, *Frederick Jackson Turner*, 112.
58. Turner, "Significance of the Frontier," 4, 24.
59. Ibid., 1.
60. Coleman, "Science and Symbol," 25–26; Ridge, "Introduction," 4.

61. Turner, “Significance of the Frontier,” 3.
62. Bogue, *Frederick Jackson Turner*, 92–94; Slotkin, *Gunfighter Nation*, 54–55.
63. Wrobel, *End of American Exceptionalism*, 31, 35–37.
64. Turner, “Significance of the Frontier,” 3.
65. Bogue, *Frederick Jackson Turner*, 109; Turner, “Significance of the Frontier,” 11.
66. Bogue, *Frederick Jackson Turner*, 113.
67. Turner, “Significance of the Frontier,” 3–4.
68. Jacobson, *Barbarian Virtues*, 3–4.
69. Turner, “Significance of the Frontier,” 13.
70. Ibid., 13–14.
71. Roosevelt, *Winning of the West*, I:16–17.
72. Turner, “Significance of the Frontier,” 1.
73. Nash, *Creating the West,* 7.
74. Bogue, *Frederick Jackson Turner*, 117–118.
75. Bogue, *Frederick Jackson Turner*, 113–114; Nash, *Creating the West,* 9–10.
76. Ridge, “Introduction,” 7.

Chapter 4

1. Clarke, “Introduction: The Paper Warriors and Their Flights of Fancy,” in Clarke, *Tale of the Next Great War*.
2. Clarke, *Voices Prophesying War*, 2nd ed., 1.
3. Clarke, *Voices Prophesying War*, 2nd ed., 27; Desmond and Moore, *Darwin,* 579.
4. Clarke, *Voices Prophesying War*, 2nd ed., 48–51; Stocking, *Victorian Anthropology*, 144–185.
5. Clarke, *Voices Prophesying War*, 2nd ed., 8, 27.
6. Franklin, *War Stars*, 19.
7. Clarke, *Voices Prophesying War*, 2nd ed., 2–3, 25–26.
8. Ibid., 29–33.
9. Ibid., 20–24, 31.
10. Ibid., 29.
11. Ibid., 24–25.
12. Ibid., 29.
13. Clarke, “Introduction: The Paper Warriors and Their Flights of Fancy,” 14–15.
14. Chesney, “Battle of Dorking,” 34–35; Clarke, *Voices Prophesying War*, 2nd ed., 31–32.
15. Franklin, *War Stars*, 19–20.
16. Chesney, “Battle of Dorking,” 68–70.
17. Clarke, *Voices Prophesying War*, 2nd ed., 2–3.

18. Ashley, *Time Machines*, 3–4, 6; Clarke, *Voices Prophesying War*, 2nd ed., 1, 27–28.
19. Clarke, *Voices Prophesying War*, 2nd ed., 35.
20. Ibid., 1, 34–35.
21. Quoted in Clarke, "Introduction: The Paper Warriors and Their Flights of Fancy," 15.
22. Clarke, *Voices Prophesying War*, 2nd ed., 35.
23. Ibid., 39.
24. Ibid., 48–50.
25. Ibid., 57. I do not engage in a detailed discussion of the future-war stories in Britain between 1871 and 1897—the years in which "The Battle of Dorking" and *The War of the Worlds* were first published, respectively—as it would detract too much from the heart of my critical response to the concept of nuclear apocalypse.
26. Ashley, *Time Machines*, 6–10.
27. Clarke, *Voices Prophesying War*, 2nd ed., 57–58.
28. For his own account of his early years, see Wells, *Experiment in Autobiography*, 21–158.
29. Foot, *H. G.*, 11; Wells, *Experiment in Autobiography*, 137–139.
30. Wells, *Experiment in Autobiography*, 162.
31. Ibid., 161.
32. Foot, *H. G.*, 16–28; Wells, *Experiment in Autobiography*, 237–346.
33. Foot, *H. G.*, 29–35.
34. Clarke, *Voices Prophesying War*, 2nd ed., 83; Kemp, *H. G. Wells*, 13–14.
35. Manlove, "Charles Kingsley," 228–229.
36. Clarke, *Voices Prophesying War*, 2nd ed., 86; Franklin, *War Stars*, 65.
37. Clarke, *Voices Prophesying War*, 99. This comment appeared only in the first edition, published in 1966.
38. Clarke, *Voices Prophesying War*, 2nd ed., 86.
39. Wells, *War of the Worlds*, 147.
40. Kemp, *H. G. Wells*, 12, 22–23.
41. Wells, *War of the Worlds*, 181.
42. Franklin, *War Stars*, 64–65.
43. Clarke, *Voices Prophesying War*, 2nd ed., 84; Foot, *H. G.*, 38; Franklin, *War Stars*, 65.
44. Wells, *War of the Worlds*, 9.
45. Ibid., 125.
46. Ibid., 128.
47. Ibid., 141–143.
48. Chesney, "Battle of Dorking," 69. In his description of the Germans on this page, Chesney refers to "a hulking lout" who sends out "a cloud of smoke from his ugly jaws."
49. Wells, *War of the Worlds*, 22.
50. McConnell, *Science Fiction of H. G. Wells*, 124–143.

51. Wells, *War of the Worlds*, 128.
52. Ibid., 7, 128.
53. Ibid., 127.
54. Manlove, "Charles Kingsley," 234–237.
55. Gannon, "'One Swift, Conclusive Smashing,'" 42.
56. Kemp, *H. G. Wells*, 12.
57. Ibid., 218.
58. Jacobson, *Barbarian Virtues*, 3–5.
59. Ibid., 5.
60. Franklin, *War Stars*, 132; Gannon, "'One Swift, Conclusive Smashing,'" 37, 39.
61. Frederick Soddy was a well-known English chemist whose 1909 book *The Interpretation of Radium* had a profound influence on Wells. Soddy went on to win the Nobel Prize in Chemistry in 1921.
62. Wells, *World Set Free*, 11.
63. There is often a great difference between the perspective of the narrator and that of the author of a text. In this case, however, Wells's didactic narrative voice—which borders at many points on preachiness—seems to be a relatively transparent expression of the author's thoughts and beliefs. Therefore, for the sake of convenience, I will refer to the narrative voice of the text as if it is the voice of Wells himself.
64. Wells, *World Set Free*, 62.
65. Ibid., 118.
66. Ibid., 17.
67. Ibid., 24.
68. Ibid., 21.
69. Ibid., 33.
70. Ibid., 37.
71. Ibid., 37–38.
72. Ibid., 18, 50–51, 54–62.
73. Ibid., 69.
74. Ibid., 53, 69–72.
75. Ibid., 118.
76. Ibid., 114.
77. Ibid., 117.
78. Ibid., 38, 248–249.
79. Ibid., 87, 95–106.
80. Ibid., 106.
81. Ibid., 107–108, ellipses in original.
82. Ibid., 101–102.
83. Ibid., 103.
84. Ibid., 106–107.
85. Ibid., 218, 222.
86. Ibid., 27.

87. Ibid., 151.
88. Ibid., 210–211.
89. Ibid., 178.
90. McConnell, *Science Fiction of H. G. Wells*, 192.
91. Wells, *World Set Free*, 210.
92. For a general discussion of the Eurocentric assumptions of the scientific community and the relationship between science and colonialism, see Harding, *Is Science Multicultural?*
93. Wells, *World Set Free*, 236–237.
94. Clarke, *Voices Prophesying War*, 2nd ed., 90.
95. Clarke, *Voices Prophesying War*, 2nd ed., 157; Franklin, *War Stars*, 133–134.
96. Szilard to Strauss, 7–8.
97. Einstein to Roosevelt, 9–11.
98. Gannon, "'One Swift, Conclusive Smashing,'" 37–38; Wagar, *H. G. Wells*, 146–147.

CHAPTER 5

1. Thomas, *Skull Wars*, 78.
2. Jacobson, *Barbarian Virtues*, 149–151; Stocking, *Ethnographer's Magic*, 352–354; Stocking, *Race, Culture, and Evolution*, 209–219.
3. Boas, "Methods of Ethnology," 121–122.
4. Baker, *From Savage to Negro*, 119–125; Boas, "Methods of Ethnology," 27; Stocking, *Race, Culture, and Evolution*, 209–219.
5. Thomas, *Skull Wars*, 104–105, 111–112.
6. Stocking, *Ethnographer's Magic*, 352–354.
7. Jacobson, *Barbarian Virtues*, 151.
8. Thomas, *Skull Wars*, 103–110.
9. Jacobson, *Barbarian Virtues*, 105–138; Lutz and Collins, *Reading National Geographic*, 16–27.
10. James, *Science Fiction in the 20th Century*, 14–17.
11. Slotkin, *Fatal Environment*, 64–65.
12. Ashley, *Time Machines*, 36; James, *Science Fiction in the Twentieth Century*, 45–46.
13. Burroughs, *A Princess of Mars*, 13–15.
14. Ibid., 13.
15. Ibid., 33.
16. Ibid., 59.
17. Ibid., 62.
18. Baker, *From Savage to Negro*, 129–130.
19. Baker, *From Savage to Negro*, 132; Guerrero, *Framing Blackness*, 11; Loewen, *Lies My Teacher Told Me*, 26–28.
20. Taylor, "Re-Birth of the Aesthetic," 31.

21. Baker, *From Savage to Negro*, 130–133; Guerrero, *Framing Blackness*, 13–14.
22. Franklin, *War Stars*, 21, 33–37.
23. Labor and Reesman, *Jack London*, 12–13; Lawlor, *Recalling the Wild*, 113–114; Tavernier-Courbin, "*The Call of the Wild*," 239.
24. Budd, "American Background," 27–30.
25. Lawlor, *Recalling the Wild*, 110–111.
26. Peluso, "Gazing at Royalty," 58.
27. Furer, "'Zone Conquerors' and 'White Devils,'" 162–163.
28. London, "Yellow Peril," 346.
29. London, "Give Battle to Retard Enemy," 1 May 1904, *Jack London Reports*, 106.
30. London to Charmain Kittredge, 22 May 1904, *Jack London Reports*, 24.
31. Wu, *Yellow Peril*, 8–11.
32. Daniels, *Asian America*, 29–66, 100–154.
33. London, "Yellow Peril," 343.
34. Ibid., 341.
35. Darwin, *Descent of Man*, 49.
36. London, "Yellow Peril," 344–345.
37. Ibid., 346.
38. Ibid., 347.
39. Franklin, *War Stars*, 37–38.
40. London, "Unparalleled Invasion," 104.
41. London, "Unparalleled Invasion," 105; for the earlier version of this passage, see London, "Yellow Peril," 345.
42. London, "Yellow Peril," 346.
43. Ibid., 348.
44. Darwin, *Descent of Man*, 584.
45. Harding, *Is Science Multicultural?* 26–31.
46. London, "Unparalleled Invasion," 105.
47. Ibid., 105–107.
48. Ibid., 107.
49. Ibid., 109.
50. Ibid., 107–108.
51. Ibid., 114.
52. Ibid., 110–114.
53. Ibid., 114.
54. Ibid.

Chapter 6

1. Quoted in U.S. Commission on Wartime Relocation, *Personal Justice Denied*, 66.
2. Quoted in ibid.

3. Dower, *War without Mercy*, 80–81; Takaki, *Double Victory*, 145–149.
4. Franklin, *War Stars*, 35.
5. Ibid., 41.
6. Norton, *Vanishing Fleets*, 4.
7. Ibid., 5. Inexplicably, Norton refers to the war as "the racial war" in spite of the fact that Japan is allied with Great Britain as well as China. The bulk of the conflict is between the United States and Japan, yet Great Britain—though much less antagonistic and more polite than Japan—enters the fray as the enemy of the United States.
8. Ibid., 4–5.
9. Franklin, *War Stars*, 44.
10. Giesy, *All for His Country*, 102.
11. Daniels, *Politics of Prejudice*, 70.
12. Giesy, *All for His Country*, 153.
13. Ibid., 196–197.
14. Ibid., 197.
15. Ibid.
16. Ashley, *Time Machines*, 1–48; James, *Science Fiction in the Twentieth Century*, 12–36.
17. Gernsback, "A New Sort of Magazine," 3.
18. Ashley, *Time Machines*, 48–54; Westfahl, "'The Jules Verne, H. G. Wells, and Edgar Allan Poe Type of Story.'"
19. Ashley, *Time Machines*, 62–66.
20. Ibid., 62.
21. Nowlan and Calkins, *Collected Works of Buck Rogers*, 1.
22. Ibid., 5.
23. Ibid., 9.
24. Ashley, *Time Machines*, 98; Harvey, *Art of the Funnies*, 124.
25. Harvey, *Art of the Funnies*, 132.
26. Wu, *Yellow Peril*, 164–182.
27. Chan, *Asian American Masculinities*, 41–44.
28. Ashley, *Time Machines*, 98; Kinnard, *Fifty Years of Serial Thrills*, 132–139.
29. Quoted in Dower, *War without Mercy*, 78. Dower's book examines how World War II was seen as a race war by both the United States and Japan.
30. Quoted in Dower, *War without Mercy*, 78.
31. Dower, *War without Mercy*, 80; Takaki, *Double Victory*, 137.
32. U.S. Commission on Wartime Relocation, *Personal Justice Denied*, 52–54; Weglyn, *Years of Infamy*, 34–53.
33. Quoted in U.S. Commission on Wartime Relocation, *Personal Justice Denied*, 55.
34. Ibid., 53–60.
35. "Home Affairs," 33.
36. Ibid.

37. London, "Yellow Peril," 345.
38. "Home Affairs," 33.
39. Ibid.
40. "How to Tell Japs from the Chinese," 81.
41. Ibid.
42. Ibid.
43. Ibid.
44. Ibid.
45. Daniels, *Politics of Prejudice*.
46. U.S. Commission on Wartime Relocation, *Personal Justice Denied*, 49.

CHAPTER 7

1. Bartter, *Way to Ground Zero*, 113–134.
2. Truman, "White House Press Release on Hiroshima," 64. As I shall discuss later, the author of the original draft of this announcement was William L. Laurence, a *New York Times* science reporter who was recruited by the government. A draft of this press release was also discussed with the British. President Truman read it aloud over the radio and the text was distributed under his authority. Therefore, for the sake of convenience, I will discuss the announcement as if Truman was the sole author.
3. Ibid., 64–65.
4. Badash, Hodes, and Tiddens, *Nuclear Fission*, 3–13.
5. Ibid., 65.
6. Ibid.
7. London, "Unparalleled Invasion," 114.
8. Franklin, "Fatal Fiction," 6.
9. Boyer, *By the Bomb's Early Light*, 22.
10. Ibid., 3; "Truman Tells Warship Crew," 2; Walker, *Prompt and Utter Destruction*, 79; Winkler, *Life under a Cloud*, 24.
11. "Man's Most Destructive Force," 1.
12. Gallup, *Gallup Poll*, 521–522.
13. Ibid., 517.
14. Boyer, *By the Bomb's Early Light*, 14.
15. "Wells Says World Has Choice," 2.
16. Campbell, "Atomic Age," 5.
17. "Atomic Age," *Life*, 32.
18. Laurence, *Dawn over Zero*, 219.
19. G. I. Joe was a fictional soldier made popular by journalist Ernie Pyle in his reports from the front during World War II. Pyle's stories often profiled "normal" enlisted men, telling about their hometowns, giving their impressions of the war, and detailing events from their everyday lives as soldiers.
20. Cottrell and Eberhart, *American Opinion on World Affairs*, 68.

21. Badash, *Scientists and the Development of Nuclear Weapons*, 58; Boyer, "'Some Sort of Peace,'" 182.
22. Boyer, "'Some Sort of Peace,'" 183.
23. "Howls of Jap Anguish," 4.
24. For some representative examples, see Boyer, *By the Bomb's Early Light*, 157.
25. Braw, *Atomic Bomb Suppressed*, 133.
26. Lifton and Mitchell, *Hiroshima in America*, 3–114.
27. Weart, *Nuclear Fear*, 98–103.
28. Boyer, *By the Bomb's Early Light*, 185.
29. Laurence, *Dawn over Zero*, 234.
30. Lifton and Mitchell, *Hiroshima in America*, 18–19.
31. "Results of Experiment," 1.
32. Ibid.
33. "Atom-Splitting Test," 1–2.
34. "Superfort Crew Describes Terrific Flash," 1.
35. "Eyewitness of Nagasaki Bombing," 3.
36. "Monument to Victory," 1.
37. "War Ends," 25.
38. Ibid., 26.
39. Ibid.
40. Ibid., 28–31.
41. "Bomb News Withheld," 2.
42. "Targets of Fate," 22.
43. "War Ends," 26.
44. Lifton and Mitchell, *Hiroshima in America*, 48. William Lawrence is not the same man as William L. Laurence. Both men wrote for the *New York Times*, but William L. Laurence was the official reporter of the Manhattan Project during the war while William Lawrence (who later went by Bill Lawrence) was a regular war correspondent. Lawrence tended to be a shade more critical of the atomic bombings in his writing, while Laurence took a more apologist tone.
45. "Atomic Footprint," 68.
46. "New Mexico's Atomic Bomb Crater," 27.
47. Boyer, *By the Bomb's Early Light*, 188–189; Lifton and Mitchell, *Hiroshima in America*, 44–45; Weart, *Nuclear Fear*, 108; Yavenditti, "John Hersey and the American Conscience," 27.
48. Lifton and Mitchell, *Hiroshima in America*, 51.
49. "New Mexico's Atomic Bomb Crater," 27.
50. Ibid.
51. Ibid.
52. U.S. Senate, Special Committee on Atomic Energy, *Atomic Energy*, 1:36.
53. Ibid.
54. Ibid., 1:37.

55. U.S. Senate, Special Committee on Atomic Energy, *Atomic Energy*, 2:233.
56. Morrison, "Beyond Imagination," 177.
57. De Seversky, "Atomic Bomb Hysteria," 27–28.
58. Lifton and Mitchell, *Hiroshima in America*, 82–83; U.S. Strategic Bombing Survey, *Effects of Atomic Bombs on Hiroshima and Nagasaki*, iii.
59. "What Happened," 90.
60. "Atom Bomb Effects," 92.
61. Lifton and Mitchell, *Hiroshima in America*, 83.
62. U.S. Strategic Bombing Survey, *Effects of Atomic Bombs on Hiroshima and Nagasaki*, 15.
63. U.S. Senate, Special Committee on Atomic Energy, *Atomic Energy*, 1:36.
64. Lifton and Mitchell, *Hiroshima in America*, 57–59.
65. U.S. Strategic Bombing Survey, *Effects of Atomic Bombs on Hiroshima and Nagasaki*, 22–23.

Chapter 8

1. Boyer, *By the Bomb's Early Light*, 203–205; Lifton and Mitchell, *Hiroshima in America*, 86–88; Weart, *Nuclear Fear*, 107–109.
2. Huse, *Survival Tales of John Hersey*, 35–36; Yavenditti, "John Hersey and the American Conscience," 24–25. Through countless conversations, I have discovered that *Hiroshima* was required reading at school for many people: some read it in elementary school, many in high school, and many more in college. Several people I've spoken to have been required to read it more than once. While this evidence is anecdotal, the diversity and the number of people who have told me this convinces me that people from a wide variety of economic classes, ethnicities, and educational levels in the United States read this text through at least the 1980s.
3. Quoted in Luft and Wheeler, "Reaction to John Hersey's 'Hiroshima,'" 137.
4. Quoted in Lifton and Mitchell, *Hiroshima in America*, 87.
5. Ibid., 87; Sanders, *John Hersey*, 41.
6. Stone, *Literary Aftershocks*, 6; Yavenditti, "John Hersey and the American Conscience," 35–36.
7. For a discussion of how the Japanese were represented as "Shinto" fanatics by authors in the United States, see Dower, *War without Mercy*, 20–21.
8. Hersey, "Hiroshima," 15.
9. Stone, *Literary Aftershocks*, 6.
10. Hersey, "Hiroshima," 17.
11. Ibid.
12. Ibid., 33.
13. Boyer, *By Bomb's Early Light*, 204–205; Lifton and Mitchell, *Hiroshima in America*, 87; Stone, *Literary Aftershocks*, 6; Yavenditti, "John Hersey and the American Conscience," 34.
14. Rainey, "The Price of Modernism," 290.

15. McDonald, *Learning to be Modern*, 190–191.
16. Ibid., 65.
17. Sanders, *John Hersey*, 13.
18. See introductory note and footnote to line 46 in Eliot, *Waste Land*.
19. Eliot, *Waste Land*, line 30.
20. Hersey, "Hiroshima," 16.
21. "Monument to Victory," 1.
22. Hersey, "Hiroshima," 16, 18, 19.
23. Ibid., 20.
24. Ibid., 25.
25. Ibid., 24.
26. Ibid., 25.
27. Ibid., 24.
28. Eliot, *Waste Land*, lines 173–175.
29. Ibid., lines 307–308, 311.
30. Hersey, "Hiroshima," 30.
31. Ibid., 25.
32. Eliot, *Waste Land*, lines 60–63.
33. Ibid., lines 64–65.
34. Hersey, "Hiroshima," 21.
35. Ibid., 23.
36. Ibid., 24.
37. Hersey, "Hiroshima," 23. Hersey referred to Reverend Tanimoto as "Mr. Tanimoto" in many places in the book.

CHAPTER 9

1. Shalett, "Arnold Reveals Secret Weapons," 4.
2. Ibid.
3. Franklin, *War Stars*, 157.
4. Ibid., 170–174.
5. Weart, *Nuclear Fear*.
6. Chafe, *Unfinished Journey*, 61–66; Franklin, *War Stars*, 156.
7. Grossman, *Neither Dead nor Red*, 30.
8. "Russian Hints Race for Atomic Power," 1, 7.
9. Gallup, *Gallup Poll*, 566–567.
10. Ibid.
11. Gallup, *Gallup Poll*, 578–579.
12. Cottrell and Eberhardt, *American Opinion on World Affairs*, 24.
13. Ibid., 28–29.
14. Grossman, *Neither Dead nor Red*, 24–26, 30–32.
15. Clarke, *Voices Prophesying War*, 2nd ed., 166–167; Franklin, *War Stars*, 157.
16. "36-Hour War," 27.
17. Ibid., 28–29.

18. Ibid., 29.
19. Ibid., 28.
20. Ibid., 31.
21. Ibid., 32–33.
22. Ibid., 33.
23. Ibid., 32.
24. Wells, *World Set Free*, 118.
25. Davis, "Future-War Storytelling," 16.
26. "36-Hour War," 34.
27. Ibid.
28. Ibid., 34–35.
29. Stone, *Literary Aftershocks*, 37.
30. "36-Hour War," 32.
31. Kegley and Wittkopf, *Nuclear Reader*, xvi.
32. "36-Hour War," 32.
33. Ashley, *Time Machines*, 170.
34. Ashley, *Time Machines*, 197; James, *Science Fiction in the Twentieth Century*, 35–37, 84–87.
35. Campbell, "Atomic Age," 5.
36. Campbell, "—but Are We?" 117.
37. Jenkins, *Murder of the U.S.A.*, 7–9.
38. Clarke, *Voices Prophesying War*, 2nd ed., 167; Franklin, *War Stars,* 160.
39. Jenkins, *Murder of the U.S.A.*, 5.
40. Ibid., 160.
41. Ibid., 5.
42. Ibid., 164.
43. Ibid., 163–164.
44. Franklin, *War Stars,* 160.
45. Jenkins, *Murder of the U.S.A.*, 162. This paragraph was attributed to "Steve," but no character named Steve existed anywhere else in the novel. Because the paragraph came between others attributed to Sam, I assume here that the use of the name "Steve" was a typographical error.
46. As John Campbell noted, World War II was the first atomic war. See Campbell, "Concerning the Atomic War," 5.
47. Davis, "Future-War Storytelling," 18–20.
48. Boyer, *By the Bomb's Early Light*, 76.
49. Morrison, "If the Bomb Gets Out of Hand," 1.
50. Ibid., 3.
51. Ibid.
52. Ibid.
53. De Seversky, "Atomic Bomb Hysteria"; U.S. Senate, Special Committee on Atomic Energy, *Atomic Energy*, 1:37; Yavenditti, "John Hersey and the American Conscience," 29; Morrison, "If the Bomb Gets Out of Hand," 5.
54. Morrison, "If the Bomb Gets Out of Hand," 5.

55. Ibid., 6.
56. Engel and Pillar, *World Aflame*, 32.
57. Ibid., 32, 34–35.

Chapter 10

1. Special thanks to my colleague Dr. Alejandra Marchevsky, who found this rare copy of Hersey's text and recognized the significance of the cover art for my argument.
2. Ketterer, *New Worlds for Old*, 3–14.
3. Hendershot, "Darwin and the Atom," 319–320; Wagar, "Rebellion of Nature," 139–141.
4. Wolfe, "Remaking of Zero," 2–14.
5. Bradbury, "Million Year Picnic," 190.
6. "The Million Year Picnic" was revised by Bradbury and became the final chapter of *The Martian Chronicles* (1950). In the original version that I am discussing, the nature of the war was never made explicit, though it was clearly implied that it was an atomic war. In the 1950 version, the fact that atomic weapons had been used in the war on Earth was explicitly stated. Also, in many of his stories in *The Martian Chronicles*, Bradbury demonstrated an acute awareness of the race politics involved with colonization and used the colonization of Mars to engage in a very pointed critique of the conquest of the Americas by Europeans. My point is not to argue that Bradbury was some sort of closet racist but rather to point out how even a man of Bradbury's progressive politics could slip into repeating implicitly racist visions of American identity when evoking the Darwinist imagery of the frontier. Once the atomic bombs had dropped, only the white nuclear family survived.
7. Bradbury, "Million Year Picnic," 184.
8. Ibid., 189.
9. Ibid., 190.
10. May, *Homeward Bound*, 58–91.
11. Turner, "Significance of the Frontier," 3.
12. Jacobson, *Barbarian Virtues*, 121–136.
13. Brinkley, "Illusion of Conformity," 68–70; Jackson, *Crabgrass Frontier*, 232–242.
14. Grossman, "Segregationist Liberalism," 485.
15. Franklin, *War Stars,* 174–175.
16. Cloete, "Blast" (19 April 1947), 75.
17. Ibid., 76.
18. Cloete, "Blast" (12 April 1947), 63.
19. Cloete, "Blast" (19 April 1947), 83.
20. Ibid., 87.
21. U.S. Strategic Bombing Survey, *Effects of Atomic Bombs on Hiroshima and Nagasaki*, 28.

22. Franklin, *War Stars,* 158–159.
23. Brians, *Nuclear Holocausts*, 119–120.
24. Anderson and Waldrop, "Tomorrow's Children," 148.
25. Ibid., 166.
26. Ibid., 168.
27. Ibid., 169.
28. Ibid., 171.
29. Franklin, *War Stars*, 177; Yaszek, "Women History Doesn't See," 37–41.
30. Merril, "That Only a Mother," 351.
31. Yaszek, "Unhappy Housewife Heroines," 102.
32. Ibid., 101–103.
33. "White Star vs. Red," 30.
34. McEnaney, *Civil Defense Begins at Home*, 14.
35. U.S. Strategic Bombing Survey, *Effects of Atomic Bombs on Hiroshima and Nagasaki*, 36.
36. Ibid.
37. Ibid., 41.
38. "What Atom Bomb Means," 16.
39. Ibid., 16–17.
40. Ibid., 16.
41. Ibid., 17.
42. Ibid.
43. Auger, "Dispersal of Cities as a Defense Measure," 131–133.
44. Auger, "Dispersal of Cities—a Feasible Program," 312.
45. Jackson, *Crabgrass Frontier*, 226–229.
46. Auger, "Dispersal of Cities as a Defense Measure," 133–134.
47. Grossman, "Segregationist Liberalism," 482.
48. McEnaney, *Civil Defense Begins at Home*, 13; Weart, *Nuclear Fear*, 128–129; Winkler, *Life under a Cloud*, 67–68.
49. Grossman, *Neither Dead nor Red*, 38–39; McEnaney, *Civil Defense Begins at Home*, 14–15.
50. Grossman, *Neither Dead nor Red*, 45–50.
51. During the 1950s, the term "atomic" began to be replaced by the term "nuclear." This was largely due to the development of the hydrogen bomb, a thermonuclear device with destructive power that dwarfed that of the atomic bomb. The word "nuclear" came to represent the growing scale of destruction that was possible with modern weapons and "atomic" came to refer only to the smaller Nagasaki-type implosion bombs prevalent in the 1940s and early 1950s. Also, "nuclear" was a more scientifically accurate term than "atomic" for the entire class of fission and fusion bombs.

    The Ad Council is a private nonprofit organization that began creating public service advertising for government agencies and other nonprofit organizations in 1942.

52. McEnaney, *Civil Defense Begins at Home*, 21.
53. Grossman, "Segregationist Liberalism," 481; McEnaney, *Civil Defense Begins at Home*, 74; Weart, *Nuclear Fear*, 123, 130.
54. Grossman, *Neither Dead nor Red*, 36–37, 53–54.
55. U.S. National Security Resources Board, *Survival under Atomic Attack*, 3.
56. Ibid., 3, 15.
57. Ibid., 4.
58. Grossman, *Neither Dead nor Red*, 47–48; Weart, *Nuclear Fear*, 130.
59. McEnaney, *Civil Defense Begins at Home*, 147.
60. Grossman, *Neither Dead nor Red*, 76–81.
61. Boyer, *By the Bomb's Early Light*, 329–333; Grossman, *Neither Dead nor Red*, 57–65; Grossman, "Segregationist Liberalism," 481; McEnaney, *Civil Defense Begins at Home*, 29, 34–37; Weart, *Nuclear Fear*, 129–130.
62. Tucker, *Long Loud Silence*, 145, 172.
63. Ibid., 176.
64. Brians, *Nuclear Holocausts*, 327.
65. Tucker, *Long Loud Silence*, 181.
66. Ibid., 180.
67. Ibid., 190.

CHAPTER 11

1. Chafe, *Unfinished Journey*, 86–91; Zinn, *A People's History*, 448–450.
2. Grossman, *Neither Dead nor Red,* 93–97; Grossman, "Segregationist Liberalism," 482–485; McEnaney, *Civil Defense Begins at Home*, 123–124, 141–145.
3. Grossman, *Neither Dead nor Red,* 97–101; Grossman, "Segregationist Liberalism," 487–490; McEnaney, *Civil Defense Begins at Home*, 137–141.
4. Hughes, "Radioactive Red Caps," 54.
5. McEnaney, *Civil Defense Begins at Home*, 134–141, 149–150.
6. Dibblin, *Day of Two Suns*, 256; Lapp, "Civil Defense Faces New Perils." Elugelap was a part of the Marshall Islands, a chain of islands in the Pacific ocean where the military conducted tests on nuclear weapons from 1946 through the end of the 1950s. "Mike" was the code name for the fusion bomb project.
7. McEnaney, *Civil Defense Begins at Home*, 149.
8. Lifton and Mitchell, *Hiroshima in America*, 42–45, 55.
9. Lapp, "Civil Defense Faces New Perils"; McEnaney, *Civil Defense Begins at Home*, 48; Winkler, "A 40-year History of Civil Defense."
10. Dowling, *Fictions of Nuclear Disaster*, 51; Seed, *American Science Fiction*, 15; Weart, *Nuclear Fear*, 131–132, 229–230.
11. Wylie, *Tomorrow!*, 5.

12. Ibid., 47.
13. Ibid., 3–4.
14. Ibid., 4.
15. Ibid., 5.
16. May, *Homeward Bound*, 74.
17. Wylie, *Tomorrow!*, 59.
18. Ibid., 150.
19. Ibid., 84, 175–176.
20. Ibid., 175.
21. Ibid., 176, 179.
22. Ibid., 295.
23. Ibid., 360.
24. See Bartter, "Nuclear Holocaust as Urban Renewal" for a more complete discussion of the theme of urban renewal in nuclear apocalypse narratives.
25. Wylie, *Tomorrow!*, 366–367.
26. May, *Homeward Bound*, 104–105; McEnaney, *Civil Defense Begins at Home*, 110–112.
27. U.S. Federal Civil Defense Administration, *Grandma's Pantry Was Ready*.
28. McEnaney, *Civil Defense Begins at Home*, 38–39.
29. U.S. Federal Civil Defense Administration, *Six Steps to Survival*.
30. Ibid.
31. McEnaney, *Civil Defense Begins at Home*, 49–50.
32. U.S. Federal Civil Defense Administration, *Six Steps to Survival*.
33. U.S. Office of Civil and Defense Mobilization, *Between You and Disaster*.
34. Ibid.
35. Seed, *American Science Fiction*, 23; Seed, "Debate over Nuclear Refuge," 133.
36. Brians, *Nuclear Holocausts*, 260–261.
37. Ketterer, *New Worlds for Old*, 140; Stone, *Literary Aftershocks*, 56.
38. Miller, *A Canticle for Leibowitz*, 158.
39. Ibid., 301.
40. Ibid., 245.
41. Chafe, *Unfinished Journey*, 150–161.
42. Frank, *Alas, Babylon*, 132.
43. Ibid., 175–176.
44. Ibid., 117.
45. Ibid., 188.
46. Ibid., 299.

Conclusion

1. Chafe, *Unfinished Journey*, 161–165.
2. Takei, *To the Stars*, 282–283.
3. Lee and Zia, *My Country vs. Me*, 1.

4. Ibid., 140–141.
5. Ibid., 223–225.
6. Quoted in Lee and Zia, *My Country vs. Me*, 6.
7. Chong, "New Spy Case Prompts Skepticism," B1; Krikorian, "Alleged Spy Offers Defense," B4.
8. Gold, "Mistaken Delivery Reveals Big Trouble in Texas," A17.

Bibliography

"The 36-Hour War." *Life*, 19 November 1945, 27–36.

Adas, Michael. *Machines as the Measure of Men: Science, Technology, and Ideologies of Western Dominance*. Ithaca: Cornell University Press, 1989.

Agassiz, Louis. "Sketch of the Natural Provinces of the Animal World and Their Relation to the Different Types of Man." In *Types of Mankind or Ethnological Researches*, edited by Josiah Clark Nott, George R. Gliddon, Samuel Morton, et al., lvii–lxxviii. Philadelphia: J. B. Lippincott, Grambo and Co., 1854.

Anderson, Poul, and W. N. Waldrop. "Tomorrow's Children." In *Beyond Armageddon: Twenty-One Sermons to the Dead*, edited by Martin H. Greenberg and Walter M. Miller Jr., 146–173. New York: Donald I. Fine, 1985. Originally published in *Astounding Science Fiction* (March 1947).

Andrews, Elaine K. *Civil Defense in the Nuclear Age*. New York: Franklin Watts, 1985.

Appleman, Philip, ed. *Darwin: A Norton Critical Edition*. 2nd ed. New York: W.W. Norton & Company, 1979.

Ashley, Mike. *The Time Machines: The Story of the Science-Fiction Pulp Magazines from the Beginning to 1950*. Liverpool: Liverpool University Press, 2000.

"Atom Bomb Effects." *Life*, 11 March 1946, 91–94.

"Atom-Splitting Test by Science Group Disclosed." *Los Angeles Times*, 7 August 1945, 1:1–2.

"The Atomic Age." *Life*, 20 August 1945, 32.

"Atomic Bomb." *San Francisco Chronicle*, 7 August 1945, 10.

"Atomic Footprint." *Time*, 17 September 1945, 68.

Auchincloss, Louis. *Theodore Roosevelt*. New York: Times Books, 2001.

Augur, Tracy B. "The Dispersal of Cities as a Defense Measure." *Bulletin of the Atomic Scientists* 4 (May 1948): 131–134.

———. "The Dispersal of Cities—A Feasible Program." *Bulletin of the Atomic Scientists* 4 (October 1948): 312–315.

"The Awesome Fireball." *Life*, 19 April 1954, cover photograph.

"Awesome Force of Atom Bomb Loosed to Hasten Jap Surrender." *Newsweek*, 13 August 1945, 30–33.

Badash, Lawrence. *Scientists and the Development of Nuclear Weapons: From Fission to the Limited Test Ban Treaty, 1939–1963*. Atlantic Highlands, N.J.: Humanities Press, 1995.

———, Elizabeth Hodes, and Adoph Tiddens. *Nuclear Fission: Reaction to the Discovery in 1939*. La Jolla, Calif.: University of California, San Diego, Institute on Global Conflict and Cooperation, 1985.

Baker, Lee D. *From Savage to Negro: Anthropology and the Construction of Race, 1896–1954*. Berkeley: University of California Press, 1998.

Bartter, Martha. "Nuclear Holocaust as Urban Renewal." *Science Fiction Studies* 15 (1986): 148–158.

———. *The Way to Ground Zero: The Atomic Bomb in American Science Fiction*. New York: Greenwood, 1988.

Beer, Gillian. *Darwin's Plots: Evolutionary Narrative in Darwin, George Eliot, and Nineteenth-Century Fiction*. 2nd ed. New York: Cambridge University Press, 2000.

Bell, Michael Davitt. "Beginnings of Professionalism." In *The Cambridge History of American Literature*. Vol. 2, *Prose Writing 1820–1865*, edited by Sacvan Bercovitch, 11–73. New York: Cambridge University Press, 1995.

Berkhofer, Robert F. Jr. *The White Man's Indian: Images of the American Indian from Columbus to the Present*. New York: Vintage Books, 1978.

Bernardi, Daniel, ed. *The Birth of Whiteness: Race and the Emergence of U.S. Cinema*. New Brunswick, N.J.: Rutgers University Press, 1996.

The Birth of a Nation. Directed by D. W. Griffith. Griffith Feature Films, 1915. DVD: Image Entertainment, 1992.

Boas, Franz. "The Methods of Ethnology." In *Readings for a History of Anthropological Theory*, edited by Paul A. Erickson and Liam D. Murphy, 121–129. Orchard Park, New York: Broadview Press, 2001. Originally published in *American Anthropologist* 22 (1920): 311–322.

Bogue, Allan G. *Frederick Jackson Turner: Strange Roads Going Down*. Norman: University of Oklahoma Press, 1998.

"Bomb News Withheld but Jap Cabinet Confers." *Los Angeles Times*, 8 August 1945, 1:1–2.

Boyer, Paul. *By the Bomb's Early Light: American Thought and Culture at the Dawn of the Atomic Age*. New York: Pantheon Books, 1985.

———. "'Some Sort of Peace': President Truman, the American People, and the Atomic Bomb." In *The Truman Presidency*, edited by Michael J. Lacey. New York: Cambridge University Press, 1989.

Brackett, Leigh. *The Long Tomorrow*. 1955. Reprint, New York: Ballantine Books, 1974.

Bradbury, Ray. *The Martian Chronicles*. Garden City, N.Y.: Doubleday, 1950.

———. "The Million Year Picnic." In *Invasion from Mars: Interplanetary Stories*, edited by Orson Welles, 181–191. New York: Dell, 1949. Originally published in *Planet Stories* (Summer 1946).

Bradley, David. *No Place to Hide: 1946/1984*. Rev. ed. Hanover, N.H.: New England University Press, 1983.

Brands, H. W. *T. R.: The Last Romantic*. New York: Basic Books, 1997.

Braw, Monica. *The Atomic Bomb Suppressed: American Censorship in Occupied Japan*. Armonk, N.Y.: M. E. Sharpe, 1991.

Brians, Paul. *Nuclear Holocausts: Atomic War in Fiction, 1895–1984*. Kent, Ohio: Kent State University Press, 1987.

Brinkley, Alan. "The Illusion of Unity in Cold War Culture." In *Rethinking Cold War Culture*, edited by Peter J. Kuznick and James Gilbert, 61–73. Washington, D.C.: Smithsonian Institution Press, 2001.

Brown, JoAnne. "'*A* is for *Atom*, *B* is for *Bomb*': Civil Defense in American Public Education, 1948–1963." *Journal of American History* 75 (June 1988): 68–90.

Browne, Janet. *Charles Darwin: Voyaging*. Princeton, N.J.: Princeton University Press, 1995.

Budd, Louis J. "The American Background." In *The Cambridge Companion to American Realism and Naturalism: Howells to London*, edited by Donald Pizer, 21–46. New York: Cambridge University Press, 1995.

Burroughs, Edgar Rice. *A Princess of Mars*. 1912. Reprint, New York: Ballantine Books, 1980.

Burton, David H. "Theodore Roosevelt's Social Darwinism and Views on Imperialism." *Journal of the History of Ideas* 26, no. 1 (January-March 1965): 103–118.

Bush, George W. "State of the Union Address." 29 January 2002. Available online at http://www.whitehouse.gov/news/releases/2002/01/20020129–11.html (accessed 14 September 2005).

Caidin, Martin. *The Long Night*. New York: Dodd, Mead, 1956.

Campbell, John W. Jr. "Atomic Age." *Astounding Science Fiction* (November 1945): 5, 6, 98.

———. "—but Are We?" *Astounding Science Fiction* (January 1946): 5, 6, 117.

———. "Concerning the Atomic War." *Astounding Science Fiction* (April 1946): 5, 6.

———. "Postwar Plans . . ." *Astounding Science Fiction* (February 1946): 5, 6.

Chafe, William H. *The Unfinished Journey: America since World War II*. 4th ed. New York: Oxford University Press, 1999.

Chan, Jachinson. *Chinese American Masculinities: From Fu Manchu to Bruce Lee*. New York: Garland, 2001.

Chen, Edwin. "Bush Urges Unity on Terror." *Los Angeles Times*, 20 March 2004, A1.

Chesney, Sir George Tomkyns. "The Battle of Dorking." In *The Tale of the Next Great War, 1871–1914: Fictions of Future Warfare and of Battles Still-to-Come*, edited by I. F. Clarke, 27–73. Syracuse, NY: Syracuse University Press, 1996. Originally published anonymously in *Blackwood's Edinburgh Magazine* (May 1871): 539–572.

Chong, Jia-Rui. "New Spy Case Prompts Skepticism." *Los Angeles Times*, 17 November 2005, B1.

Clark, Ronald W. *The Survival of Charles Darwin: A Biography of a Man and an Idea*. New York: Random House, 1984.

Clarke, I. F. "Introduction: The Paper Warriors and Their Flights of Fancy." In *The Tale of the Next Great War, 1871–1914: Fictions of Future Warfare and of Battles Still-to-Come*, edited by I. F. Clarke. Syracuse, New York: Syracuse University Press, 1996.

———. *Voices Prophesying War: 1763–1984*. New York: Oxford University Press, 1966.

———. *Voices Prophesying War: Future Wars, 1763–3749*. 2nd ed. New York: Oxford University Press, 1992.

Clarke, I. F., ed. *The Tale of the Next Great War, 1871–1914: Fictions of Future Warfare and of Battles Still-to-Come*. Syracuse, New York: Syracuse University Press, 1996.

Clarkson, Helen. *The Last Day*. New York: Dodd, 1959.

Cloete, Stuart. "The Blast." *Colliers*, 12 April 1947, 11–14, 59–71 and 19 April 1947, 19, 69–87.

Coleman, William. "Science and Symbol in the Turner Frontier Hypothesis." *American Historical Review* 72, no. 1 (October 1966): 22–49.

"Color Photographs Add Vivid Reality to Nation's Concept of H-Bomb." *Life*, 19 April 1954, 21–24.

Cooper, James Fenimore. *The Last of the Mohicans*. 1826. Reprint, New York: Oxford University Press, 1998.

Cottrell, Leonard, and Sylvia Eberhart. *American Opinion on World Affairs in the Atomic Age*. Princeton, N.J.: Princeton University Press, 1948.

Dain, Bruce. *A Hideous Monster of the Mind: American Race Theory in the Early Republic*. Cambridge, Mass.: Harvard University Press, 2002.

Dalton, Kathleen. *Theodore Roosevelt: A Strenuous Life*. New York: Alfred A. Knopf, 2002.

Daniels, Roger. *Asian America: Chinese and Japanese in the United States since 1850*. Seattle: University of Washington Press, 1988.

———. *The Politics of Prejudice: The Anti-Japanese Movement in California and the Struggle for Japanese Exclusion*. Berkeley: University of California Press, 1962.

Darwin, Charles. *The Descent of Man; and Selection in Relation to Sex*. 2nd ed. 1874. Reprint, Amherst, N.Y.: Prometheus Books, 1998.

———. *The Origin of Species*. 1859. Reprint, New York: Gramercy Books, 1979.

———. *The Voyage of the Beagle: Journal of Researches into the Natural History and Geology of the Countries Visited during the Voyage of H. M. S.* Beagle *Round the World*. Rev. ed. 1845. Reprint, New York: Modern Library, 2001.

Davis, Doug. "Future-War Storytelling: American Policy and Popular Film." In *Rethinking Global Security: Media, Popular Culture, and the "War on Ter-*

ror," edited by Patrice Petro and Andrew Martin, 13–44. New Brunswick, N.J.: Rutgers University Press, 2006.

Dawkins, Richard. *The Selfish Gene*. New York: Oxford University Press, 1976.

De Seversky, Alexander. "Atomic Bomb Hysteria." *Reader's Digest*, February 1946, 121–126.

Del Rey, Lester. "The Three Careers of John W. Campbell." In *The Best of John W. Campbell*, edited by Lester Del Rey, 1–6. Garden City, N.Y.: Nelson Doubleday, 1976.

Dempsey, David. "H-Bomb's Aftermath." *New York Times Book Review*, 22 March 1959, 43.

Desmond, Adrian. *Huxley: From Devil's Disciple to Evolution's High Priest*. Reading, Mass.: Perseus Books, 1997.

———, and James Moore. *Darwin: The Life of a Tormented Evolutionist*. New York: Warner Books, 1991.

Dewey, Joseph. *In a Dark Time: The Apocalyptic Temper in the American Novel of the Nuclear Age*. West Lafayette, Ind.: Purdue University Press, 1991.

Dibblin, Jane. *Day of Two Suns: U.S. Nuclear Testing and the Pacific Islanders*. New York: New Amsterdam Books, 1990.

Dick, Philip. "Foster, You're Dead." In *The Collected Stories of Philip K. Dick*, 3:221–238. New York: Carol Publishing Group, 1991. Originally published in Frederik Pohl, ed., *Star Science Fiction Stories No. 3*. New York: Ballantine, 1955.

Dower, John. *War without Mercy: Race and Power in the Pacific War*. New York: Pantheon Books, 1986.

Dowling, David. *Fictions of Nuclear Disaster*. Iowa City: University of Iowa Press, 1987.

Einstein, Albert. Letter to Franklin D. Roosevelt. 2 August 1939. In *The American Atom*, edited by Philip L. Cantelon, Richard G. Hewett, and Robert C. Williams, 9–11. 2nd ed. Philadelphia: University of Pennsylvania Press, 1991.

Eliot, T. S. *The Waste Land*. 1922. Reprint, New York: W.W. Norton & Co., 2001.

Ellingson, Ter. *The Myth of the Noble Savage*. Berkeley: University of California Press, 2001.

Elsbree, Langdon. "Our Pursuit of Loneliness: An Alternative to This Paradigm." In *The Frontier Experience and the American Dream: Essays on American Literature*, edited by David Mogen, Mark Busby, and Paul Bryant, 31–49. College Station: Texas A&M University Press, 1996.

Engel, Leonard, and Emanuel Pillar. *World Aflame: Russo-American War of 1950*. New York: Dial Press, 1947.

"Excerpts from President Eisenhower's Press Conference, March 31, 1954." In *The American Atom*, edited by Philip L. Cantelon, Richard G. Hewett, and Robert C. Williams, 128–129. 2nd ed. Philadelphia: University of Pennsylvania Press, 1991.

"Eyewitness of Nagasaki Bombing: 'Like Looking over the Rim of a Volcano.'" *San Francisco Chronicle,* 11 August 1945, 3.

Fichman, Martin. *Evolutionary Theory and Victorian Culture*. Amherst, N.Y.: Humanity Books, 2002.

"First Target Obscured by Cloud of Dust, Smoke; 'Basic Power of Universe.'" *San Francisco Chronicle*, 7 August 1945, 1.

Flash Gordon. Directed by Frederick Stephani. Universal Pictures, 1936. DVD: *Flash Gordon: Space Soldiers*. Image Entertainment, 1996.

Flash Gordon Conquers the Universe. Directed by Ford Beebe and Roy Taylor. Universal Pictures, 1940. DVD: Image Entertainment, 1996.

Foot, Michael. *H. G.: A History of Mr. Wells*. Washington, D.C.: Counterpoint, 1995.

Frank, Pat. *Alas Babylon*. 1959. Reprint, New York: HarperPerennial, 1993.

Franklin, H. Bruce. "Fatal Fiction: A Weapon to End All Wars." In *The Nightmare Considered: Critical Essays on Nuclear War Literature*, edited by Nancy Anisfield, 5–14. Bowling Green, Ohio: Bowling Green University Popular Press, 1991.

———. *War Stars: The Superweapon and the American Imagination*. New York: Oxford University Press, 1988.

Fredrickson, George M. *Racism: A Short History*. Princeton, N.J.: Princeton University Press, 2002.

Furer, Andrew J. "'Zone Conquerors' and 'White Devils': The Contradictions of Race in the Works of Jack London." In *Rereading Jack London*, edited by Leonard Cassuto and Jeanne Campbell Reesman, 158–171. Stanford, Calif.: Stanford University Press, 1996.

Gallup, George H. *The Gallup Poll: Public Opinion, 1935–71*. Vol. 1, *1935–1948*. New York: Random House, 1972.

Gannon, Charles E. "'One Swift, Conclusive Smashing and an End': Wells, War, and the Collapse of Civilisation." *Foundation* 77 (August 1999): 35–46.

Gernsback, Hugo. "A New Sort of Magazine." *Amazing Stories*, April 1926, 1–4.

Giesy, John Ulrich. *All for His Country*. New York: The Macaulay Company, 1915.

Godzilla. Directed by Inoshiro Honda and Terry O. Morse. Toho Productions, 1956. VHS: Paramount Studios, 1993.

Gold, Scott. "Mistaken Delivery Reveals Big Trouble in Texas." *Seattle Times*, 9 January 2004, A17.

Gould, Stephen Jay. *The Mismeasure of Man*. 2nd ed. New York: W.W. Norton & Co., 1996.

Greene, John C. "The American Debate on the Negro's Place in Nature, 1780–1815." *Journal of the History of Ideas* 15, no. 3 (June 1954): 384–396.

———. *Science, Ideology, and World View: Essays in the History of Evolutionary Ideas*. Berkeley: University of California Press, 1981.

Grossman, Andrew D. *Neither Dead nor Red: Civilian Defense and American Political Development during the Early Cold War*. New York: Routledge, 2001.

———. "Segregationalist Liberalism: The NAACP and Resistance to Civil-Defense Planning in the Early Cold War, 1951–1953." *International Journal of Politics, Culture and Society* 13, no. 3 (2000): 477–497.

Guerrero, Ed. *Framing Blackness: The African American Image in Film*. Philadelphia, Pa.: Temple University Press, 1993.

Haller, John S. Jr. *Outcasts from Evolution: Scientific Attitudes of Racial Inferiority, 1859–1900*. Carbondale: Southern Illinois University Press, 1971.

Haraway, Donna. *Primate Visions: Gender, Race, and Nature in the World of Modern Science*. New York: Routledge, 1989.

Harding, Sandra. *Is Science Multicultural? Postcolonialisms, Feminisms, and Epistemologies*. Bloomington: Indiana University Press, 1998.

Harvey, Robert C. *The Art of the Funnies: An Aesthetic History*. Jackson: University of Mississippi Press, 1994.

Heinlein, Robert. "Solution Unsatisfactory." In *Future Tense*, edited by Richard Curtis, 171–215. New York: Dell, 1968. Originally published in *Astounding Science Fiction* (May 1941).

Hendershot, Cyndy. "Darwin and the Atom: Evolution/Devolution Fantasies in *The Beast from 20,000 Fathoms*, *Them!*, and *The Incredible Shrinking Man*." *Science Fiction Studies* 25, no. 2 (July 1998): 319–335.

Hersey, John. "Hiroshima." *The New Yorker*, 31 August 1946.

———. *Hiroshima*. 1946. New York: Bantam Books, 1948.

"Home Affairs." *Newsweek*, 22 December 1941, 33.

Hopkins, Lisa. "Jack London's Evolutionary Hierarchies: Dogs, Wolves, and Men." In *Evolution and Eugenics in American Literature and Culture, 1880–1940*, edited by Lois A. Cuddy and Claire M. Roche, 89–101. Lewisburg, Pa.: Bucknell University Press, 2003.

Horsman, Reginald. *Race and Manifest Destiny: The Origins of American Racial Anglo-Saxonism*. Cambridge, Mass.: Harvard University Press, 1981.

———. "Scientific Racism and the American Indian in the Mid-Nineteenth Century." *American Quarterly* 27, no. 2 (May 1975): 152–168.

"How to Tell Japs from the Chinese." *Life*, 22 December 1941, 81–82.

"Howls of Jap Anguish Betray Heavy Bomb Damage." *Los Angeles Times*, 8 August 1945, 1:4.

Hudson, Nicholas. "From 'Nation' to 'Race': The Origin of Racial Classification in Eighteenth-Century Thought." *Eighteenth Century Studies* 29, no. 3 (Spring 1996): 247–264.

Hughes, Langston. "Radioactive Red Caps." In *Simple Stakes a Claim*. New York: Rinehart & Co., 1957. Originally published as "Charged with Atoms Simple Takes Charge." *Chicago Defender* (10 July 1954).

Huse, Nancy L. *The Survival Tales of John Hersey*. Troy, N.Y.: Whitston, 1983.

Jackson, Kenneth T. *Crabgrass Frontier: The Suburbanization of the United States*. New York: Oxford University Press, 1985.

Jacobson, Matthew Frye. *Barbarian Virtues: The United States Encounters Foreign Peoples at Home and Abroad, 1876–1917*. New York: Hill and Wang, 2000.

James, Edward. *Science Fiction in the 20th Century*. New York: Oxford University Press, 1994.

Jenkins, Will F. [Murray Leinster]. *The Murder of the U.S.A.* New York: Crown Publishers, 1946.

Kaplan, Gisela, and Lesley J. Rogers. "Race and Gender Fallacies: The Paucity of Biological Determinist Explanations of Difference." In *Challenging Racism and Sexism: Alternatives to Genetic Explanations of Difference*, edited by Ethel Tobach and Betty Rosoff. New York: The Feminist Press, 1994. Reprinted in *The Gender and Science Reader*, edited by Muriel Lederman and Ingrid Bartsch, 323–342. New York: Routledge, 2001.

Kegley, Charles W. Jr., and Eugene R. Wittkopf, eds. *The Nuclear Reader: Strategy, Weapons, War*. New York: St. Martin's Press, 1985.

Kemp, Peter. *H. G. Wells and the Culminating Ape*. 1982. Reprint, London: MacMillan Press Ltd., 1996.

Ketterer, David. *New Worlds for Old: The Apocalyptic Imagination, Science Fiction, and American Literature*. New York: Anchor Press/Doubleday, 1974.

Kinnard, Roy. *Fifty Years of Serial Thrills*. Metuchen, N.J.: Scarecrow Press, 1983.

Klein, Kerwin Lee. *Frontiers of Historical Imagination: Narrating the European Conquest of Native America, 1890–1990*. Berkeley: University of California Press, 1997.

Krikorian, Greg. "Alleged Spy Offers Defense." *Los Angeles Times*, 19 January 2006, B4.

Kuhn, Thomas S. *The Structure of Scientific Revolutions*. 2nd ed. Chicago: University of Chicago Press, 1970.

Labor, Earle, and Jeanne Campbell Reesman. *Jack London*. Rev. ed. New York: Twayne Publishers, 1994.

LaFeber, Walter. *The American Age: United States Foreign Policy at Home and Abroad*. New York: W.W. Norton & Company, 1989.

Lapp, Ralph E. "Civil Defense Faces New Perils." In *The American Atom*, edited by Philip L. Cantelon, Richard G. Hewett, and Robert C. Williams, 161–174. 2nd ed. Philadelphia: University of Pennsylvania Press, 1991. Originally published in *Bulletin of the Atomic Scientists* 10 (November 1954): 349–351.

Laurence, William L. "Nagasaki Was the Climax of the New Mexico Test." *Life*, 24 September 1945, 30.

———. *Dawn over Zero*. 2nd ed. New York: Alfred A. Knopf, 1953.

Lawrence, William H. "Visit to Hiroshima Proves It World's Most Damaged City." *New York Times*, 5 September 1945, 1:4.

Lawlor, Mary. *Recalling the Wild: Naturalism and the Closing of the American West*. New Brunswick, N.J.: Rutgers University Press, 2000.

Lee, Wen Ho, and Helen Zia. *My Country vs. Me: The First-Hand Account by the Los Alamos Scientist Who Was Falsely Accused of Being a Spy*. New York: Hyperion, 2001.

Lewontin, Richard C. *Biology as Ideology*. New York: HarperPerennial, 1992.

———. *The Triple Helix: Gene, Organism, and Environment*. Cambridge, Mass.: Harvard University Press, 2001.

Lifton, Robert Jay, and Greg Mitchell. *Hiroshima in America: A Half-Century of Denial*. New York: Avon Books, 1996.

Lindsey, Hal. *The Late Great Planet Earth*. Grand Rapids, Mich.: Zondervan Publishing House, 1970.

Loewen, James W. *Lies My Teacher Told Me: Everything Your American History Textbook Got Wrong*. New York: Touchstone, 1995.

London, Jack. "The Unparalleled Invasion." In *The Science Fiction Stories of Jack London*, edited by James Bankes, 104–115. New York: Citadel Twilight, 1993. Originally published in *McClure's Magazine* (July 1910).

———. "Give Battle to Retard Enemy." In *Jack London Reports: War Correspondence, Sports Articles, and Miscellaneous Writings*, edited by King Hendricks and Irving Shepard, 99–106. Garden City, N.Y.: Doubleday, 1970.

———. "The Yellow Peril." In *Jack London Reports: War Correspondence, Sports Articles, and Miscellaneous Writings*, edited by King Hendricks and Irving Shepard, 340–350. Garden City, N.Y.: Doubleday, 1970. Originally published in the *San Francisco Examiner*, 25 September 1904.

Long, Frank Belknap. "A Guest in the House." In *Strange Ports of Call*, edited by August Derleth, 259–275. New York: Pellegrini & Cudahy, 1948. Originally published in *Astounding Science Fiction* (March 1946).

Luft, Joseph, and W. M. Wheeler. "Reaction to John Hersey's 'Hiroshima.'" *Journal of Social Psychology* 28 (August 1948): 135–140.

Lurie, Edward. *Louis Agassiz: A Life in Science*. 1960. Reprint, Baltimore, Md.: Johns Hopkins University Press, 1988.

Lutz, Catherine A., and Jane L. Collins. *Reading National Geographic*. Chicago: University of Chicago Press, 1993.

"The Making of the Bomb." *Astounding Science Fiction*, December 1945, 100–124.

Manlove, Colin. "Charles Kingsley, H. G. Wells, and the Machine in Victorian Fiction." *Nineteenth-Century Literature* 48, no. 2 (September 1993): 212–239.

"Man's Most Destructive Force, One Equal to 2000 B-29 Loads, Blasts Nips." *Los Angeles Times*, 7 August 1945, 1:1.

May, Elaine Tyler. *Homeward Bound: American Families in the Cold War Era*. New York: Basic Books, 1988.

McConnell, Frank. *The Science Fiction of H. G. Wells*. New York: Oxford University Press, 1981.

McDonald, Gail. *Learning to be Modern: Pound, Eliot, and the American University*. Oxford: Clarendon Press, 1993.

McEnaney, Laura. *Civil Defense Begins at Home: Militarization and Everyday Life in the Fifties*. Princeton, N.J.: Princeton University Press, 2000.

McWilliams, John. "The Historical Contexts of *The Last of the Mohicans*." In *The Last of the Mohicans*, by James Fenimore Cooper. New York: Oxford University Press, 1998.

Merril, Judith. "That Only a Mother." In *The Science Fiction Hall of Fame*, edited by Robert Silverberg, 344–353. New York: Avon Books, 1971. Originally published in *Astounding Science Fiction* (June 1948).

Miller, Walter M. Jr. *A Canticle for Leibowitz*. 1959. Reprint, New York: Bantam Books, 1997.

Mogen, David, Mark Busby, and Paul Bryant, eds. *The Frontier Experience and the American Dream: Essays on American Literature*. College Station: Texas A&M University Press, 1996.

"Monument to Victory." Photograph and caption. *San Francisco Chronicle*, 12 August 1945, 1.

Morris, Edmund. *The Rise of Theodore Roosevelt*. Rev. ed. New York: Modern Library, 2001.

Morrison, Philip. "Beyond Imagination." *The New Republic*, 11 February 1946, 177–180.

———. "If the Bomb Gets Out of Hand." In *One World or None*, edited by Dexter Masters and Katharine Way, 1–6. New York: McGraw Hill, 1946.

"Nagasaki Plant Life Revives." *New York Times*, 4 September 1945, 7.

Nash, Gerald D. *Creating the West: Historical Interpretations 1890–1990*. Albuquerque: University of New Mexico Press, 1991.

"Nazi Scientists Were on the Trail of Atomic Power." *San Francisco Chronicle*, 7 August 1945, 3.

"New Mexico's Atomic Bomb Crater." *Life*, 24 September 1945, 27.

Norton, Roy. *The Vanishing Fleets*. New York: D. Appleton, 1908.

Nott, Josiah C., and George R. Gliddon. *Types of Mankind*. 1854. Reprint, Miami, Florida: Mnemosyne, 1969.

Nowlan, Philip Francis. "Armageddon 2419 A.D." *Amazing Stories*, August 1928, cover, 422–449.

———. *Armageddon 2419 A.D.* 1928. Reprint, New York: Ace Books, 1962.

———, and Dick Calkins. *The Collected Works of Buck Rogers in the 25th Century*. Edited by Robert C. Dille. New York: Chelsea House, 1969.

Oakes, Guy. *The Imaginary War: Civil Defense and American Cold War Culture*. New York: Oxford University Press, 1994.

Peluso, Robert. "Gazing at Royalty: Jack London's 'The People of the Abyss' and the Emergence of American Imperialism." In *Rereading Jack London*, edited by Leonard Cassuto and Jeanne Campbell Reesman, 55–74. Stanford, Calif.: Stanford University Press, 1996.

Perrine, Toni A. *Film and the Nuclear Age: Representing Cultural Anxiety*. New York: Garland, 1998.

Porter, Jeffrey L. "Narrating the End: Fables of Survival in the Nuclear-Age." *Journal of American Culture* 16, no. 4 (Winter 1993): 41–47.

Proctor, Robert N. *Racial Hygiene: Medicine under the Nazis*. Cambridge, Mass.: Harvard University Press, 1988.

Rainey, Lawrence S. "The Price of Modernism: Reconsidering the Publication of *The Waste Land*." *The Yale Review* 78, no. 2 (Winter 1989): 279–300.

"Results of Experiment—Steel Tower Vaporized, Fire Ball at 40,000 Feet." *San Francisco Chronicle*, 7 August 1945, 1.

Ridge, Martin. "Introduction." In *Frederick Jackson Turner: Wisconsin's Historian of the Frontier*, edited by Martin Ridge, 1–12. Madison: State Historical Society of Wisconsin, 1986.

Roosevelt, Theodore. "The Strenuous Life." In *An American Mind: Selected Writings*, edited by Mario R. DiNunzio, 184–189. New York: Penguin, 1994.

———. *Theodore Roosevelt: An Autobiography*. 1913. Reprint, New York: Da Capo Press, 1985.

———. *The Winning of the West*. Vol. 1, *From the Alleghanies to the Mississippi, 1769–1776*. 1889. Reprint, Lincoln: University of Nebraska Press, 1995.

Rose, Kenneth D. *One Nation Underground: The Fallout Shelter in American Culture*. New York: New York University Press, 2001.

Roshwald, Mordecai. *Level 7*. New York: McGraw Hill, 1959.

"Russian Hints Race for Atomic Power." *New York Times*, 4 September 1945, 1:7.

Sanders, David. *John Hersey*. New York: Twayne, 1967.

Seed, David. *American Science Fiction and the Cold War: Literature and Film*. Edinburgh: Edinburgh University Press, 1999.

———. "The Debate over Nuclear Refuge." *Cold War History* 4, no. 1 (October 2003): 117–142.

Shalett, Sidney. "Arnold Reveals Secret Weapons, Bomber Surpassing All Others." *New York Times*, 18 August 1945, 1:4.

Shute, Nevil. *On The Beach*. 1957. Reprint, New York: Ballantine Books, 1974.

Sinclair, Upton. *The Jungle*. 1905. Reprint, New York: Bantam Books, 1981.

Slotkin, Richard. *The Fatal Environment: The Myth of the Frontier in the Age of Industrialization, 1800–1890*. Middletown, Conn.: Wesleyan University Press, 1986.

———. *Gunfighter Nation: The Myth of the Frontier in Twentieth-Century America*. 1992. Reprint, Norman: University of Oklahoma Press, 1998.

———. *Regeneration through Violence: The Mythology of the American Frontier, 1600–1860*. 1973. Reprint, New York: HarperPerennial, 1996.

Spaatz, Carl, and Charles J. V. Murphy. "General Spaatz on Atomic Warfare." *Life*, 16 August 1948, 90–104.

———. "If We Should Have to Fight Again." *Life*, 5 July 1948, 34–44.

"Speaking of Pictures." *Life*, 22 December 1941, 6–7.

Stanford, Craig. *Upright: The Evolutionary Key to Becoming Human*. New York: Houghton Mifflin, 2003.

Stasz, Clarice. "Social Darwinism, Gender, and Humor in 'Adventure.'" In *Rereading Jack London*, edited by Leonard Cassuto and Jeanne Campbell Reesman, 130–140. Stanford, Calif.: Stanford University Press, 1996.

Stocking, George W. Jr. *The Ethnographer's Magic and Other Essays in the History of Anthropology*. Madison: University of Wisconsin Press, 1992.

———. *Race, Culture, and Evolution: Essays in the History of Anthropology*. 1968. Reprint, Chicago: University of Chicago Press, 1982.

———. *Victorian Anthropology*. New York: The Free Press, 1987.

Stone, Albert E. *Literary Aftershocks: American Writers, Readers, and the Bomb*. New York: Twayne, 1994.

"Superfort Crew Describes Terrific Flash and Blast; 'A Mountain of Smoke.'" *San Francisco Chronicle*, 8 August 1945, 1.

Szilard, Leo. Letter to Lewis Strauss. 25 January 1939. In *The American Atom*, edited by Philip L. Cantelon, Richard G. Hewett, and Robert C. Williams, 8–9. 2nd ed. Philadelphia: University of Pennsylvania Press, 1991.

———. Letter to Sir Hugo Hirst. 17 March 1934. In *The American Atom*, edited by Philip L. Cantelon, Richard G. Hewett, and Robert C. Williams, 7–8. 2nd ed. Philadelphia: University of Pennsylvania Press, 1991.

Takaki, Ronald. *Double Victory: A Multicultural History of America in World War II*. New York: Little, Brown and Company, 2000.

Takei, George. *To the Stars: The Autobiography of Star Trek's Mr. Sulu*. New York: Pocket Books, 1994.

"Targets of Fate." *Newsweek*, 20 August 1945, 22.

Tavernier-Courbin, Jacqueline. "*The Call of the Wild* and *The Jungle*: Jack London's and Upton Sinclair's Animal and Human Jungles." In *The Cambridge Companion to American Realism and Naturalism: Howells to London*, edited by Donald Pizer, 236–262. New York: Cambridge University Press, 1995.

Taylor, Clyde. "The Re-Birth of the Aesthetic in Cinema." In *The Birth of Whiteness: Race and the Emergence of U.S. Cinema*, edited by Daniel Bernardi, 15–37. New Brunswick, N.J.: Rutgers University Press, 1996.

Them! Directed by Gordon Douglas. Warner Brothers, 1954. VHS: Warner Home Video, 1997.

"Three Explosions." *San Francisco Chronicle*, 9 August 1945, 10.

Thomas, David Hurst. *Skull Wars: Kennewick Man, Archeology, and the Battle for Native American Identity*. New York: Basic Books, 2000.

"Truman Tells Warship Crew." *Los Angeles Times*, 7 August 1945, 1:2.

Truman, Harry S. "White House Press Release on Hiroshima, 6 August 1945. " In *The American Atom*, edited by Philip L. Cantelon, Richard G. Hewett, and Robert C. Williams, 64–67. 2nd ed. Philadelphia: University of Pennsylvania Press, 1991.

Tucker, Wilson. *The Long Loud Silence*. Rev. ed. New York: Lancer Books, 1969.

Turner, Frederick Jackson. "The Significance of the Frontier in American History." In Turner, *The Frontier in American History*, 1–38. 1920. Reprint, New York: Dover, 1996.

U.S. Commission on Wartime Relocation and Internment of Civilians. *Personal Justice Denied*. 2 vols. Washington, D.C.: Government Printing Office, 1982 and 1983. Reprint, Seattle: University of Washington Press, 1997.

U.S. Federal Civil Defense Administration. *Duck and Cover*. Short film. Archer Productions, 1951. DVD: *Atomic War Bride/This Is Not a Test*. Something Weird Video, 2002.

———. *Grandma's Pantry Was Ready*. Pamphlet. Washington, D.C.: Government Printing Office, 1955.

———. *Six Steps to Survival*. Pamphlet. Washington, D.C.: Government Printing Office, 1955.

———. *Survival Under Atomic Attack*. Short subject film. Castle Films, 1951. DVD: *Atomic War Bride/This Is Not a Test*. Something Weird Video, 2002.

U.S. National Security Resources Board. Office of Civil Defense Planning. *Civil Defense for National Security*. Washington, D.C.: Government Printing Office, 1948.

———. *Survival under Atomic Attack*. Sacramento: California State Printing Division, October 1950.

U.S. Office of Civil and Defense Mobilization. *Between You and Disaster*. Pamphlet. Washington, D.C.: Government Printing Office, 1958.

———. *The Family Fallout Shelter*. Washington, D.C.: Government Printing Office, 1959.

———. *Handbook for Emergencies*. Washington, D.C.: Government Printing Office, 1960.

———. *Handbook for Radiological Defense Education*. Washington, D.C.: Government Printing Office, 1959.

———. *Individual and Family Preparedness*. Washington, D.C.: Government Printing Office, 1959.

———. *Ten For Survival*. Washington, D.C.: Government Printing Office, 1959.

U.S. Senate. Special Committee on Atomic Energy. *Atomic Energy: Hearings before the Special Committee on Atomic Energy, Pursuant to S.R. 179, a Resolution Creating a Special Committee to Investigate Problems Relating to the Development, Use, and Control of Atomic Energy*. Pts. 1 and 2. 79th Cong., 1st sess., November and December 1945. Washington, D.C.: Government Printing Office, 1945, 1946.

U.S. Strategic Bombing Survey. *The Effects of Atomic Bombs on Hiroshima and Nagasaki*. Washington: Government Printing Office, 1946.

Wagar, W. Warren. *H. G. Wells: Traversing Time*. Middletown, Conn.: Wesleyan University Press, 2004.

———. "The Rebellion of Nature." In *The End of the World*, edited by Eric S. Rabkin, Martin H. Greenberg, and Joseph D. Olander, 139–172. Carbondale: Southern Illinois University Press, 1983.

Walker, J. Samuel. *Prompt and Utter Destruction: Truman and the Use of the Atomic Bombs against Japan*. Chapel Hill: The University of North Carolina Press, 1997.

"The War Ends." *Life*, 20 August 1945, 25–31.

Weart, Spencer. "History of American Attitudes to Civil Defense." In *Civil Defense: A Choice of Disasters*, edited by John Dowling and Evans M. Harrell, 11–32. New York: American Institute of Physics, 1987.

———. *Nuclear Fear: A History*. Cambridge, Mass.: Harvard University Press, 1988.

Weglyn, Michi. *Years of Infamy: The Untold Story of America's Concentration Camps*. New York: Morrow Quill Paperbacks, 1976.

Wells, H. G. *Experiment in Autobiography*. New York: MacMillan, 1934.

———. *The Island of Dr. Moreau*. 1896. Reprint, New York: Tom Doherty Associates, 1996.

———. "The Land Ironclads." In *Wondermakers: An Anthology of Classic Science Fiction*, edited by Robert Hoskins, 58–85. Greenwich, Conn.: Fawcett, 1972.

———. *The Time Machine*. 1895. Reprint, New York: Tom Doherty Associates, Inc., 1992.

———. *The War in the Air*. 1908. Reprint, Lincoln: University of Nebraska Press, 2002.

———. *The War of the Worlds*. 1898. Reprint, New York: Oxford University Press, 1995.

———. *The World Set Free: A Story of Mankind*. New York: E. P. Dutton & Co., 1914.

"Wells Says World Has Choice for Good or Evil." *Los Angeles Times*, 8 August 1945, 1:2.

Westfahl, Gary. "'The Jules Verne, H. G. Wells, and Edgar Allan Poe Type of Story': Hugo Gernsback's History of Science Fiction." *Science Fiction Studies* 19, no. 3 (November 1992): 340–353.

"What Atom Bomb Means to U.S.: Revision of Plans for Defense." *U.S. News and World Report*, 5 July 1946, 16–17.

"What Happened." *Time*, 4 March 1946, 88, 90.

"White Star vs. Red: If Moscow Starts 'Operation America'. . . ." *Newsweek*, 17 May 1948, 30–32.

Will, Thomas E. "The American School of Ethnology: Science and Scripture in the Proslavery Argument." *Southern Historian* 19 (1998): 14–34.

Wilson, Edward O. *Sociobiology: The New Synthesis*. Cambridge, Mass.: Cambridge University Press, 1975.

Winkler, Allan M. "A 40-Year History of Civil Defense." *Bulletin of the Atomic Scientists* 40, no. 6 (June/July 1984): 16–23.

———. *Life under a Cloud: American Anxiety about the Atom*. New York: Oxford University Press, 1993.

Wolfe, Gary K. "The Remaking of Zero: Beginning at the End." In *The End of the World*, edited by Eric S. Rabkin, Martin H. Greenberg, and Joseph D. Olander. 1–19. Carbondale: Southern Illinois University Press, 1983.

"Woman Who Led Way in Atom Research Found." *Los Angeles Times*, 8 August 1945, 1:2.

"Wonder Weapon Developed in Secret Plants Gives Allies Unprecedented Edge in War." *Newsweek*, 13 August 1945, 30–33.

Wrobel, David M. *The End of American Exceptionalism: Frontier Anxiety from the Old West to the New Deal*. Lawrence: University Press of Kansas, 1993.

Wu, William F. *The Yellow Peril: Chinese Americans in American Fiction 1850–1940*. Hamden, Conn.: Shoe String Press, 1982.

Wylie, Philip. *Tomorrow!* New York: Rinehart & Co., 1954.

Yaszek, Lisa. "Unhappy Housewife Heroines, Galactic Suburbia, and Nuclear War: A New History of Midcentury Women's Science Fiction." *Extrapolation* 44, no. 1 (Spring 2003): 97–111.

———. "The Women History Doesn't See: Recovering Midcentury Women's SF as a Literature of Social Critique." *Extrapolation* 45, no. 1 (Spring 2004): 34–51.

Yavenditti, Michael J. "John Hersey and the American Conscience: The Reception of 'Hiroshima.'" *Pacific Historical Review* 43, no. 1 (February 1974): 24–49.

Zinn, Howard. *A People's History of the United States: 1492-Present*. Rev. ed. New York: HarperPerennial Modern Classics, 2005.

Index